10664841

Offending Women

Offending Women

POWER, PUNISHMENT,
AND THE REGULATION OF DESIRE

LYNNE A. HANEY

UNIVERSITY OF CALIFORNIA PRESS
Berkeley   Los Angeles   London

University of California Press, one of the most distinguished university presses in the United States, enriches lives around the world by advancing scholarship in the humanities, social sciences, and natural sciences. Its activities are supported by the UC Press Foundation and by philanthropic contributions from individuals and institutions. For more information, visit www.ucpress.edu.

University of California Press
Berkeley and Los Angeles, California

University of California Press, Ltd.
London, England

© 2010 by The Regents of the University of California

Library of Congress Cataloging-in-Publication Data

Haney, Lynne A. (Lynne Allison), 1967–.
    Offending women : power, punishment, and the regulation of desire / Lynne A. Haney.
        p.   cm.
    Includes bibliographical references and index.
    ISBN 978–0-520–26190–7 (cloth : alk. paper)
    ISBN 978–0-520–26191–4 (pbk. : alk. paper)
    1. Female offenders—California—Case studies.   2. Female offenders—Rehabilitation—California—Case studies.   3. Correctional institutions—California—Case studies.   I. Title.

HV6046.H36   2010
365'.4309794—dc22   2009020586

Manufactured in the United States of America

19 18 17 16 15 14 13 12 11 10
10 9 8 7 6 5 4 3 2 1

This book is printed on Cascades Enviro 100, a 100% post consumer waste, recycled, de-inked fiber. FSC recycled certified and processed chlorine free. It is acid free, Ecologo certified, and manufactured by BioGas energy.

For my guys, András and Tristan

Contents

Acknowledgments

Any project that spans as long a time frame as this one necessarily becomes a collective effort. I began the research for this book in 1992, when I was still a graduate student in the Department of Sociology at UC Berkeley. Were it not for this outstanding department, and the many relationships I formed in it, I would have never pursued the project—and possibly would not have become a sociologist at all. While at Berkeley, I was extremely fortunate to be part of two writing groups, both of which contributed to this book—particularly the analysis in part 1. Among others, I thank Joe Blum, Robert Bulman, Sheba George, Teresa Gowan, Maren Klawiter, Jackie Orr, Arona Ragins, Maria Cecelia Dos Santos, and Millie Thayer. The one thing both of these groups shared was their "fearless leader," Michael Burawoy. From the earliest stages of this project, Michael saw something important in the research and encouraged me to follow through with it despite my other sociological interests. Michael is now well-known for doing many spectacular things for sociology—and the recognition is much deserved. But I will always appreciate him most for his unparalleled commitment to his graduate students. In many ways, this book is a testament to that commitment. There were many other friends, colleagues, and professors at Berkeley who supported and encouraged this work, including Nancy Chodorow, Louise Lamphere, Kristen Luker, Jerome Karabel, Shana Cohen, Sharon Cooley, Laura Lovett, Elizabeth C. Rudd, Lisa Pollard, and Suava Salameh.

Of the many things I learned while a graduate student, perhaps the most important was an appreciation for feminist sociology. In fact, gender studies was such an integral part of my graduate education that it never occurred to me to think of it as anything but a central part of the discipline. It was not until I left Berkeley that I learned just how slow the "feminist revolution" has been in coming to sociology overall. A rude awakening, indeed. Yet it is no overstatement to say that this book is a product of the changes brought about by this revolution. Over the course of the fifteen years I worked on it, I have received an enormous amount of support and encouragement from many feminist scholars. Yet there were two "divine" interventions from gender scholars—one of whom I didn't even know— that came at particularly important junctures and thus led me to develop this project in ways I might not otherwise have pursued.

The first came in 1995 when Paula England, then editor of the *American Sociological Review,* saw promise in a paper based on the first institutional case study in this book and decided to publish it. At that time, *ASR* rarely published the work of graduate students and almost never of ethnographers. Although I would only meet her years later, when the article won an *ASA* award, Paula's encouragement of me as a young sociologist was transformative. It was exactly what I needed to convince me that I had a place within sociology and that the discipline was indeed open to the kind of scholarship I wanted to produce. The second intervention came years later, when I was giving a talk based on that same article in one of Linda Gordon's classes at NYU. Linda had always been an amazing advocate of my work, and after this lecture she pushed me to develop my research further, insisting that there was a book here and that I must already have enough fieldnotes to write it (I did). I'm sure she doesn't even remember that conversation, but it had a lasting impression on me. The seeds of the idea for a follow-up study were planted. The next year, I began my fieldwork at Visions. I mention these acts of intellectual support and generosity because they evidence the real, concrete ways that having feminist scholars in positions of influence can, and have, changed the discipline. And these women provide models for me as I now to try to support a new generation of feminist scholars.

Over the years, countless other encouraging acts have come from folks I am fortunate to call both colleagues and friends. At NYU, Ruth Horowitz, Kathleen Gerson, and Jo Dixon have been my confidants for more than a decade; I thank them for their support and good humor. Were it not for our "women's dinners," which have grown to include Ann Morning, Florencia Torche, Willie Jasso, and Caroline Persell, departmental life would be far less fun and I would be far less sane. Directly and indirectly, I have learned a tremendous amount about the issues discussed in this book from many of my NYU colleagues, including Larry Wu, Tom Ertman, David Garland, Steven Lukes, Neil Brenner, and Dalton Conley. My students are also a constant source of new ideas and inspiration. For their contributions to this book, I thank Allison McKim, Amie Hess, Lienna Gurevich, Miranda March, Dorith Geva, and Sarah Kaufman.

Outside of NYU, many scholars have contributed to this work in immeasurable ways. For listening to me talk endlessly about the research and for writing letters of support for it (often at a moment's notice), I thank Ann Orloff, Nina Eliasoph, Rickie Solinger, Gail Kligman, and Jill McCorkel. Others have provided excellent feedback on papers and talks based on this book, particularly Rachel Roth, Kelly Hannah-Moffat, Julia Adams, Myra Marx Feree, Tom Hilbink, and Eileen Boris. In 2004–05 I was fortunate to serve as a Fulbright New Century Scholar, which not only gave me the time and space to begin writing this book but also connected me to a remarkable group of international feminist scholars. I learned a tremendous amount from our discussions, debates, and travels. For their comments on many of the ideas in this book, I must thank my Fulbright comrades Carolyn Elliott, Christina Ewig, Wendy Chavkin, and Isabella Bakker. I am also extremely fortunate to have found an outstanding editor and champion in Naomi Schneider. Sociology as a whole would be a far less interesting discipline without her.

Ethnographers make a living intruding on people's lives and asking them to make room for us. I did a lot of intruding during this project and I owe an enormous amount to the women who tolerated me day after day. Given how much they taught me over the years, it seems insufficient to thank them anonymously. I hope many of them will recognize themselves in the book. And I hope I did justice to their sense of injustice. I also must apologize to many of them for not using the pseudonyms they asked me to give them in the book: I'm afraid "Nastygirl," "Gangstamama," and "Sweet-thang" just wouldn't have made it through the editing process. Sorry.

While my experiences in the two penal facilities I studied pale in comparison to those of the women residing in them, they did take their toll on my well-being and state of mind. This was especially true of my time at Visions—as I spent my days watching focus seats and competitive confessionals, I frequently left feeling depressed, defeated, and angry. Had I not had a warm and loving family to return home to, I might have become uncomfortably numb myself. On the left coast, the Haney-Hurtado clan often embraced me and corroborated my angst; I thank them all for their insights into the legal system and for their unwavering commitment to social justice. I am especially grateful for my father, whose work reforming the penal system and making the world a better place is awe-inspiring—and has left a deep imprint on both my work and my life. On the other coast, which I now call home, the Yurko clan was always there for me with great meals, big celebrations, and good memories. My mother, stepfather, and sister have sustained me through the good years and the bad: I thank my mom for being a true inspiration as a scholar, a parent, and a feminist; Rudy for being a kind and constant source of support; and Jess for striking the perfect balance between friend and sister.

Finally, without my chosen family I would have been far less happy and sane while conducting this research. My husband, András, was there from the start—from the first day I entered Alliance through my final trip back to Visions. At numerous points, it would have been easy for him to honor my despair by encouraging me to end the project prematurely. Instead, after each and every research hurdle, he helped me dust myself off and head back into the field. In the process, he taught me how to overcome adversity, to value good writing, and to take time to enjoy the ride. Our son, Tristan, gives us more joy and love than we could have ever imagined. He now gets his mommy back—at least until the next book. To you both: *szeretlek.*

Introduction

"This is a very different kind of place," explained the director of Alliance, a group home for incarcerated teen mothers. It was a bright morning in the winter of 1992, and Marlene was taking me on my first tour of the facility. "It's not like the others you've seen," she continued. "Those places don't give women what they need to lead productive lives. They just trap them in the system. We step in to get them out." As Marlene spoke, I looked around and was struck by what I saw. Indeed, it bore little resemblance to other criminal-justice institutions: in place of the small, cold cells of juvenile hall were nicely decorated bedrooms; instead of juvie's large, sterile cafeteria there was an open, well-stocked kitchen; and rather than the hall's barren recreation room there was a living room with sofas, a stereo, and a television set. It almost felt homey.

I

Then I watched as the dozen or so young women, all with their babies in tow, moved around the space, frantically preparing to start their day. Some cleared the half-eaten bowls of cereal from the dining table, while others coaxed their babies to eat one more bite. Still others ran up and down the stairs, from their bedrooms to the laundry room, looking for particular pieces of clothing. Their rapid movements were punctuated by the loud prodding of staff members: "Get going and show some initiative!" and "Let's move and stop this laziness!" Later, I would learn that the young women had nowhere to go that morning since their school, which was located in the basement of the home, was out of session until Alliance could hire a childcare provider. "The point is to teach the importance of routine," the schoolteacher, Rachel, explained when I asked about the drill. She claimed it was a way to get the girls to "take the bull by the horns."

Ten years later, in the winter of 2002, I was similarly greeted while taking my first tour of Visions, a residential facility for incarcerated adult mothers. "This is a special place," insisted Maria Cortes, the house director. "Kind of like a sanctuary. We don't operate like the prisons and jails these women are accustomed to." According to Maria, Visions was a "therapeutic community" that delved into the "real issues" plaguing female prisoners. "We keep it real," she declared. "And the women get better." As Maria spoke, I was once again struck by my surroundings. Far from homey, Visions was still unlike a typical prison. The three-story building housed up to fifty women and their children in twenty dormitory-style rooms furnished with bunk beds and cribs. Except for a large kitchen and small playground in the back, there were few common spaces for gathering. And although it was midmorning, only a couple of women were milling about with their babies. "Most of the women are on the second floor," Maria remarked. "You can go up and meet them."

Alone, I went upstairs and wandered around until I heard voices coming from behind a closed door. I opened the door to find a group of women seated in a large circle, with their heads back on pillows and their feet up on stools. As I got closer, I noticed they had cream all over their faces and feet. "What kind of skin do you have?" asked Collette, a counselor, to Keisha, an African American inmate. Keisha looked perplexed, as if she wanted to reply "black." Collette clarified, "I mean dry, oily or combination skin. I need to know what kind of mask to give you." It was spa day at Visions, and the women had spent the morning getting manicures, pedicures, and facials. Later, Collette explained the "treatment" to me: "We're teaching the women how to care for themselves. They can't care for someone else until they learn how to care for themselves."

My presence in these two institutions almost exactly a decade apart was not a coincidence. I had chosen these sites strategically—or at least as strategically as an ethnographer can ever choose her field sites. Initially, I decided to study these facilities because of what they shared. They were located in the same Northern California city, only a few miles apart. Both were part of the criminal-justice system, albeit ambivalently. Situated in the penal system's "alternative" apparatus, they viewed themselves as correctives to traditional corrections. In part, this meant that their staffs believed they were working against the social isolation of incarceration by locating their programs in community settings. They also insisted that their facilities replaced the criminal-justice system's punitive orientation with a more "empowering" approach: in Marlene Jenkins's words, they set out to teach women to lead "productive lives"; according to Maria Cortes, they dealt with women's "real issues." In a sense, these institutions were part of a feminized arm of the penal system—staffed exclusively by women for women.

The women targeted by these facilities also seemed to be strikingly similar. They were all official wards of the state and had been sent to these institutions to serve out their sentences with their children. They were, quite literally, incarcerated mothers. In the main hierarchies of power and privilege, they were near the bottom: all of them were poor; most had limited formal schooling; and the majority were women of color. Granted, their ages did differ—those at Alliance were juveniles and roughly ten years younger than the inmates at Visions. Because this age gap coincided with the time frame of my research, it turned out to be analytically useful. Among other things, it allowed me to ask what might have become of the Alliance girls had they remained in the penal system, as the group-home staff so clearly feared. What kind of "treatment" would they encounter a decade later? What interpretations of their problems would they confront? What expectations would they be held up to?

In asking such questions, I expected to uncover differences between these institutions. Given the many transformations that occurred in the state arena throughout the 1990s—from specific policies like welfare reform and "three strikes" legislation to broader processes of state devolution and privatization—I was prepared to analyze differences in these agencies' form and focus. Yet I was unprepared for the depth of the differences I encountered: the attributes and relationships that had so troubled the Alliance staff seemed irrelevant to the women in charge of Visions. "Alternative" state institutions that once centered on women's relationship to the state in an attempt to break their public "dependencies" had become fixated on ridding women of their "dangerous desires" and steering them toward "healthy pleasures." And this change affected the inmates in significant and consequential ways.

A brief account of a typical day in these facilities provides a clearer sense of the contours of their differences. At Alliance, days began very much as I described above, except that the mad morning rush usually ended with all of the girls at school in the basement, where they listened to lectures and engaged in GED preparation until early afternoon. After lunch, which they had with their babies, they frequently went on walks to the park or the library. These walks were often quite a scene, with up to a dozen young women, all with babies in strollers, marching down an inner-city street, with staff members at the head and the rear watching over them. Along the way, the group usually made several stops: at a local childcare center to inquire about future placement for the girls' kids, at a nearby community college or beauty school to check on admissions requirements, and at various neighborhood restaurants and shops to ask about job openings and request applications. At each stop, the staff members in the front and back of the group inevitably reminded the women of the importance of becoming "independent" upon release, explaining how securing childcare, employment, and education would make them less reliant on state assistance and more able to "make it on their own." Finally, before teacher Rachel left for the day, she would distribute fake money to those girls who had followed the rules or shown "initiative" that day. The money could then be used at the end of the week to buy cheap goods that Rachel brought in. In Rachel's words, the fake money taught the girls to value the "rewards of independence" and to respond to "economic incentives."

Contrast this to a typical day at Visions in 2002. After breakfast, the women placed their children outside the facility by taking them either to the adjacent day-care center or to the nearby public school. Upon their return, the women went their separate ways depending on the particular "issues" their counselors decided they had. The detailed weekly schedule, which accounted for virtually every minute of the day, laid out all the available groups and classes. At least on paper, these included classes like "Circle of Healing," "Relationships in Recovery," art and drama therapy, and ongoing 12-step instruction. All these classes were run as interactive encounter groups, designed to force women to expose their most serious problems and recount their most painful memories. Interspersed throughout the day were staff-supervised yoga and meditation as well as meetings with individual therapists. Time not spent in groups and meetings could be devoted to "phasing," which meant performing a variety of tasks that, once completed, led to house privileges and freedoms. Before an inmate was eligible for phasing, she had to write a twenty-page autobiography of her past mistakes and future plans to correct them. She also had to construct a personal mantra, or what Visions called a "safe-to-speak," which was an abbreviated form of her autobiography that she had to recite in public to all staff members for a designated period of time. Each day began and ended in the same way—with a "house meeting" in which women connected with the "community," shared their "feelings," and aired grievances about their "sisters."

This book journeys into these two state institutions at two moments in time to analyze their programmatic narratives, practices, and effects. Like individuals, social institutions develop narratives about themselves: they produce scripts to relay their definition of the situation and to explain why they do what they do. For state institutions, these narratives can be produced by national-level politicians or bureaucrats and then sent down to be perfected and enacted by their underlings. Yet more often these scripts get written and rewritten in actual institutional settings, through ongoing negotiation and struggle between state actors and their charges. What is more, these narratives are not only expressed through words; they are also articulated through daily practices and rituals. Institutional narratives thus have quite practical effects and form boundaries around those aspects of clients' lives that state actors attempt to manage and treat.

When seen in this light, the institutional narratives produced at Alliance and Visions can be interpreted as two modes of state regulation: one based on interventions into women's social relationships and one based on incursions into their individual psyches. These narratives were premised on particular definitions of the situation: Alliance's definition problematized the dependency that their young charges had presumably developed on the state and set out to break their reliance on public assistance by making them self-sufficient; Visions's script emphasized the distortions presumably embedded in women's minds and set out to break their addictions by putting them on the road to recovery. And these narratives were propelled by distinct discursive constructions of the other: Alliance used a discourse of need to advance claims about what women needed and how they should meet those needs; Visions relied on a discourse of desire to define what women should want and where they should find pleasure. Understanding why these institutional narratives emerged in the form they did and why they were so consequential for the women they targeted are the central objectives of this book.

GENDERED GOVERNANCE: RIGHTS, NEEDS, AND DESIRES

Few developments in the contemporary U.S. state have been as dramatic and significant as mass imprisonment. The sheer number of U.S. citizens directly affected is astounding: in 2006, over two million were in prison or jail.[1] With these numbers, the United States became the international leader in imprisonment, surpassing Russia and China in the proportion of the population living behind bars.[2] This increase in imprisonment rates is well-known and frequently recited by scholars of crime and punishment.[3] Yet cited far less frequently are data revealing that women's incarceration rates have increased more rapidly than those of men. Since 1980, the number of women imprisoned in the United States has risen by 650 percent, while men's incarceration rates have increased by 300 percent. So while male inmates still outnumber female inmates by more than 9 to 1, the carceral explosion has hit women hard.[4] Moreover, given that over 70 percent of female inmates were responsible for children prior to imprisonment, the effects of mass female imprisonment reverberate throughout family, kin, and community networks.[5]

These shifts in the gendered realities of punishment have not gone unnoticed by social scientists, and there is a burgeoning literature on how mass imprisonment affects women—both as inmates and as the partners of male inmates.[6] While it is unquestionably important to understand how women are faring in this state of hyperincarceration, changes in the U.S. penal system also raise questions about the nature of state power. The policies of mass imprisonment, which systematically remove so many women from their communities, seem to signify a shift in how state regulation is conceptualized and practiced. While poor women have always had their lives regulated by the state indirectly, through social policies, laws, and encounters with caseworkers, more of them are living and raising children quite literally within the state— often for long stretches of time. Moreover, through parole, probation, and "community-based" corrections, the penal system remains in these women's lives for years after release. The state's methods of control also seem to rely more heavily on direct modes of intervention characteristic of total institutions. And these modes of intervention appear to be based on restrictive models of citizenship and forms of claims-making.

Taken together, these shifts prompt us to interrogate contemporary penal policies and practices as examples of the governance of gender. Phrasing the key conceptual issue as a question of governance situates the penal system in broader discussions of state power.[7] Of course, the term *governance* carries with it enormous theoretical baggage. While debates rage on about how to best conceptualize governance, I prefer to employ a relatively broad definition—using it to connote patterns of power and regulation that shape, guide, and manage social conduct.[8]

Similarly, while many scholars have grasped the concept to move away from analyses of centralized state power, I find the framework of governance helpful in illuminating the power relations at work within state systems themselves.[9] I also find that this framework provides a way to conceptualize the linkages that can form across state institutions and to connect the management of conduct in different state spaces.[10] In part, this explanatory power is related to the constructed quality of governance: instead of assuming that some behaviors are inherently problematic, conceptions of governance tend to make such boundary work the object of empirical investigation. They question why certain conducts are subject to intervention; they probe into why some social relations are deemed un/manageable; and they ask why specific strategies are used to carry out such intervention and management.

When put in this way, it is clear that feminist scholars have a great deal to say about how contemporary governance is gendered. Although they may not always use the term itself, feminist scholars have established that decisions about which types of conduct necessitate state management are gendered acts. In a variety of national contexts, they have revealed how state projects to reform welfare policies, regulate marital relations, and re/configure labor markets reflect gender ideologies and anxieties.[11] They have also interpreted the particular strategies used by states to manage social conduct as indicative of their "gender regimes"— that is, of notions of masculinity and femininity and of dominance and difference.[12] These insights about the gendered underpinnings of contemporary governance form the theoretical backdrop of this book, providing one part of the conceptual scaffolding around which my ethnographic analysis is structured.

At the broadest level, feminist scholars have theorized two key strategies deployed in the governance of gender. First, states govern gender relations through the distribution of rights—or the responsibilities, entitlements, duties, and protections that accompany citizenship. Unlike many classical social and political theorists, feminist scholars tend to take an expansive view of rights. For them, rights are not merely a reflection of social differences but are also constitutive of them. By deciding who is entitled to what kind of protection, states can replicate or undermine unequal distributions of resources.[13] Moreover, feminists' notions of the resources that states redistribute are quite broad. Clearly, states allocate material resources: by granting social rights, states determine who has access to what type of employment, protection from discrimination, and public benefits.[14] Feminist scholars also show that social rights shape social reproduction, influencing how the domestic division of labor is structured, who engages in carework, and what conditions caretaking occurs under.[15] And then there is the arena of bodily rights—the ways that states stratify women's reproduction through the differential granting of the right to control one's body; of protection from violence, abuse, and harassment; and of safeguards against incursions into one's private life.[16]

In addition to the state's un/equal codification of rights, feminist scholars have theorized how definitions of need act as a strategy of governance. Here the argument is that the state actively engages in struggles over what different social groups need—struggles that often occur before rights are granted to these groups.[17] As with the codification of rights, constructions of need are reflective and constitutive; they draw on and establish common notions of what is required of certain social roles and positions. To understand how needs become implicated in the governance of gender, some feminist scholars have analyzed state policies as articulations of "needs talk"—showing how, for example, the two-tiered nature of the U.S. welfare state and its distinction between "insurance" and "assistance" was premised on ideas about what women and men needed to survive.[18] Others have examined how state policies produce "subject locations" that require certain behaviors and traits of those who hold them—revealing how, for example, the redistribution of welfare benefits also demarcates the characteristics needed of wage laborers and mothers.[19] Still others have explored how notions of neediness are constructed and transmitted by state actors—exposing how, for instance, caseworkers often link welfare recipients' material neediness to assumptions about their behavioral defects, thus merging a need for resources with a need for character modification.[20]

Throughout this book, I draw on these feminist insights to explicate how state institutions govern women through restrictions on their rights and narrow definitions of their needs. In terms of the former, incarceration clearly involves the suspension of basic rights and freedoms; in the current period it even leads to the denial of public-assistance benefits and infringements on political and voting rights.[21] As in all penal institutions, Alliance and Visions were based on such suspensions. Although the women running these facilities often denied it, their job was to police a variety of restrictions—from restricting inmates' freedom of movement to rescinding their right to privacy.[22] Both facilities restricted women's ability to engage in carework on their own terms and to retain control over their own bodies. These suspensions were so pervasive that they became almost taken for granted. They formed an invisible background around which other institutional practices coalesced; their effects resonated throughout the facilities, yet they were rarely discussed openly. Instead, what was expressed on a daily basis were the blueprints for what women needed to do and who they needed to become before they could reclaim their basic rights. It was here that these institutions diverged—a divergence that raises a series of empirical complexities with important theoretical implications.

On the one hand, as I document in the first half of the book, the institutional relations at Alliance in the early 1990s provide a clear example of how needs talk can be used as a strategy of governance. In this institutional context, state actors used a discourse of need to delimit the resources that the young women under their control should feel entitled to. And they did so in narrow and restrictive ways. In effect, the Alliance staff tried to undermine the girls' arguments that they "needed" government assistance and to convince them that they "needed" to become independent and self-sufficient. The staff also mobilized a discourse of need to give meaning to the young women's caretaking, defining good mothers as those who no longer relied on state support and who could make it on their own. Ultimately, the goal was to define what young, unwed mothers needed as well as what was needed of them.

These definitions of need were closely linked to the allocation of rights. In the immediate sense, they formed the criteria used to evaluate the young women. Those girls who adhered to the staff's expectations were allowed to reclaim some freedoms and rights—from seemingly mundane acts like making phone calls or wearing certain kinds of clothing to more consequential activities like caretaking and mothering. What is more, Alliance's needs talk ended up encompassing positive, albeit unintended, statements about women's general entitlements and protections. As the staff lectured the young women about the joys of independence through wages, they implicitly suggested that women should have access to well-paid employment; as they stressed the importance of schooling, they subtly indicated that women should be given a quality education; and as they distributed fake money for good behavior, they implied that women should be remunerated for fulfilling their responsibilities. The young women at the receiving end of such messages often picked up on these implications, using them as a collective platform upon which to demand a broader understanding of their actual inability to cash in on such promises—that is, of impediments to their working for decent wages, obtaining a decent education, engaging in carework, and carving out a bit of control over their own bodies. So in addition to serving as a strategy of governance, Alliance's needs talk became a channel through which claims to justice and fairness could be voiced.

In this way, by tracing how needs talk operates in a concrete institutional setting, the Alliance case study adds to our understandings of gendered strategies of governance. Too often, feminist scholars have treated rights and needs as abstractions, as analytical tools with which to evaluate entire state systems and policy structures. And too often such abstraction has led to a view of rights and needs as opposing forces: states can privilege one over the other, while polities that emphasize rights are considered more "women-friendly." Thus, the opposition itself becomes gendered: states are said to discriminate by responding to men's claims as rights and women's claims as needs. In the process, rights become masculine and needs feminine. But when we move to the practices of concrete state institutions, such oppositions break down. At Alliance, rights and needs did not operate as rivals but rather stood in complex relation to one another. Instead of divorcing itself from rights, Alliance's discourse of need was replete with cracks and fissures from which an expansive notion of substantive rights could seep out. The result was a set of institutional conflicts over women's social relationships—over what they needed from those relationships and what kind of support they were entitled to.

Yet this is only one part of the story I tell in this book. In the second part, another key strategy of governance emerges—a strategy that feminist scholars have yet to theorize fully. Rather than centering on what women need, this technique highlighted what women should want through the regulation of their desires. Here I am not simply referring to the control of sexual practices and reproduction, which has been heavily theorized in feminist accounts of the "patriarchal" state.[23] Instead, I use the regulation of desire to connote a general patterning of emotional attachments and passions. It is an arena similar to what R. W. Connell calls the structure of cathexis.[24] Drawing on Freudian conceptions of the psychological charge and energy assigned to certain objects, Connell gives the notion of cathexis a distinctly sociological bent. He uses it to describe how we form emotional attachments to particular social relations and objects and how those attachments end up shaping what we experience as pleasurable and painful.

So while the regulation of desire does include physical pleasures, they are not merely sexual. They encompass a variety of sensory pleasures of taste, smell, sight, and touch—from what we eat and drink to how we change our appearance to what we clothe ourselves in. Moreover, the regulation of desire impinges on emotional pleasures and feelings of joy, fulfillment, and comfort—from what we use to feel "high" to where we turn to feel attachment to where we look to feel safe. The regulation of desire is thus a way to satisfy physical urges, experience emotion, and conform to a lifestyle.

As with the structure of cathexis, a range of public and private actors engage in the regulation of desire. At least in the contemporary United States, they often try to tap into people's "real" desires by getting them to profess and confess their "true" selves.[25] Once exposed, desires can be reworked and regulated; those pleasures considered acceptable can be differentiated from those deemed dangerous, addictive, or pathological. Then, once separated, good and bad desires can be constituted as enticing and/or prohibitive through a variety of techniques, from public policies to religious mandates to social norms. Of course, these dividing lines are never so easily demarcated—particularly since we often end up wanting what is forbidden and rejecting what is socially sanctioned.[26]

It might seem far-fetched, and even a bit paranoid, to view the state as engaged in the realm of physical and emotional pleasure. Yet this is precisely what I document in the second part of this book, devoted to the institutional relations at Visions. In this context, state actors developed a discourse of desire to delimit the physical and emotional pleasures women should experience. In part, this involved defining a series of substances as completely out-of-bounds because of their artificial sensory effects and highs. Such substances included drugs and alcohol, even in moderation, as well as caffeine and tobacco. At the emotional level, certain attributes were also prohibited. For example, women who exhibited an attitude of toughness or detachment were considered in denial of their addictive selves. To rid them of such distortions of the mind and body, Visions had women engage in some quite tortuous practices: from public self-disclosure to emotional exposure to communal confrontation. Visions also tried to steer its charges to other kinds of desires. Yoga, meditation, and physical closeness with a child were all said to produce natural, authentic highs—and were thus positioned as key to the emotional transformation Visions claimed to facilitate. Ultimately, the goal was to rehabilitate the "self" by cleansing and ridding it of all dangerous desires. This resulted in institutional exchanges and conflicts fought on the terrain of women's psychologies and psyches.

Feminist scholars know very little about discourses of desire as a strategy of governance. Clearly, such strategies are on the rise in a variety of state arenas, with therapeutic models surfacing in welfare-to-work programs and with therapeutic communities sprouting up in correctional institutions across the United States.[27] Yet, unlike discourses of need, it remains unclear how therapeutic discourses of desire actually operate. How do some desires become prohibited while others remain acceptable? Why do some pleasures get positioned as enticing while others become pathological? How do those articulating this discourse come to make sense of it? Why do they set its parameters in the ways they do? At an even more general level, how does the regulation of desire relate to social conceptions of needs and rights? In the late 1980s, Nancy Fraser suggested that needs talk emerged as a counter to rights discourse—as a way of undermining arguments about equitable resource redistribution and legal protection.[28] Decades later, has a discourse of desire surfaced as an alternative to needs talk? Has it become a way to counteract even the notion of socially recognized needs? Is it a way to replace broad statements about women's entitlements with individualizing gestures to their emotional states and psychological compositions?

These questions are not only relevant for feminist theories of governance—they are also consequential for the women caught in these state institutions. It matters that the women in Visions confronted a discourse of desire as opposed to a discourse of need. First and foremost, it matters because of the institutional practices that accompanied this discourse: the women at Visions received counseling not education, group therapy not job training, and treatment for personal addiction not preparation for social integration. While not all women accepted these practices, few could disrupt them in a consistent or collective way. Unlike the young women at Alliance, who used the prevailing needs talk as they challenged it, the women at Visions turned on themselves and one another. Although some Visions inmates tried, few were able to move the emphasis from personal to societal failings. At Visions, the discourse of desire seemed like a channel through which claims to social justice and fairness were silenced; the women subjected to this discourse seemed one step closer to a state of disentitlement. It was precisely this state of disentitlement that prompted me to broaden my analysis to encompass not only *how* women were governed in state institutions but also *why* strategies of governance took these particular forms at this historical moment.

HYBRID STATES AND GOVERNMENT FROM A DISTANCE

Analyses of mass imprisonment usually point to the total number of U.S. citizens in prison as a benchmark for the scale and scope of the carceral revolution. Yet there is another equally revealing statistic that is cited far less frequently: in 2006, over seven million citizens were under some form of correctional supervision.[29] Of these, roughly five million were regulated by the penal system outside the confines of prison or jail, either in community-based programs or in parole and probation departments.[30] These numbers are even more pronounced for female offenders. In the semicarceral arena, the gender gap narrows: while women make up only 10 percent of all prison inmates, over 25 percent of those in noncustodial settings are women. Put another way, there are close to five times as many women in semicarceral institutions as there are in prison—while roughly 200,000 female inmates reside in U.S. jails and prisons, over a million women live under other forms of correctional supervision.

These numbers are indicative of a critical, yet largely unexplored, aspect of the carceral revolution: much of it has taken place outside the walls of traditional prisons. Gone are the days when "doing time" necessarily meant going away to the "big house" situated in some far-off location. For many, time is now served by attending mandatory counseling sessions, submitting to ongoing drug tests, and doing stints in halfway houses, group homes, or community-based programs. The big house has changed form and shrunk in size. It is quite likely to be a smaller, more discrete building, located in a major city or suburban neighborhood—as both Alliance and Visions were. So while social scientists continue to try and break into prisons to learn what goes on "behind bars," many of the critical changes in the penal system have occurred beyond these bars.[31] And while these same scholars often bemoan the end of rehabilitative ideals and programs, some rehabilitative models have simply migrated from the traditional prison system to semicarceral settings. Although these other settings may be less conducive to "macho" prison studies, their emergence raises questions about shifts in the structure of the state and in the discourses circulating through its institutions.

In this way, changes in the penal system need to be seen in light of broader patterns of state restructuring. Political theorist Nikolas Rose has characterized these patterns as "government from a distance," arguing that—with the dismantling of the centralized social state under advanced liberalism—the arena of government has devolved, decentralized, and diversified.[32] At one level, there has been a vertical distancing: since the Reagan era, ongoing processes of state devolution have meant that decisions about the nature of public programs are increasingly handled at the state and local levels.[33] This not only affects the allocation of public funding but also the delivery of social services and the administration of state policy. At the same time, there has been a horizontal distancing. Accompanying state devolution has been heightened decentralization at the local level.[34] Through "partnerships" with a variety of nongovernmental entities, from nonprofit organizations to neighborhood alliances to "faith-based" groups, the site of state policy has become more diffuse. The scope of state authority has also dispersed and diversified, thus becoming more difficult to set boundaries around. Further complicating this picture is the acceleration and broadening of state privatization: as more public provisions and services are outsourced to for-profit agencies and private companies, the logics of the market and of public-private joint ventures have infiltrated the state arena in new, more encompassing ways.[35]

Although it is tempting to equate these processes with state retrenchment, this would be a misrepresentation and simplification. Too often, social scientists confuse the changing face of the state with its withdrawal. Rather than signifying a state in retreat, government from a distance has created an environment of state hybridity. Public partnerships with nonprofits and private companies have led to a multiplication of actors now playing the role of the state. Quite often, these actors are disguised as community members, therapists, businessmen, or NGO activists. Their organizations may have clever names that do not even mention government or the state. And they may appear to operate according to different logics, claiming to prioritize business models over bureaucratic norms or faith-based initiatives over government directives. But they remain part of the state arena through their budgets, contracts, staffing, and legal mandates. In many ways, these agencies are akin to satellite states—they circle and hover around the centralized "mother ship," relying on her for material survival, legitimacy, and authority. Yet, on a day-to-day level, they claim autonomy from her and the ability to set their own agendas.

Evidence of this kind of institutional hybridity abounds in the contemporary U.S. state. In the welfare arena, the 1996 Personal Responsibility and Work Opportunity Reconciliation Act (PRWORA) shifted control over public assistance to states and locales. This then gave rise to a full public-private hybrid as policies related to job retraining, education, and workfare were contracted out to nonprofit organizations, for-profit companies, and religious groups.[36] The trend toward hybridity is equally pronounced in the penal system. Community-policing programs, non-profit treatment facilities, and for-profit prisons have all brought different groups into the field of corrections. The result is a layering of penal institutions that often define themselves in opposition to each other: those working in the penal system frequently represent it as bifurcated between a coercive arm, characterized by punishment, and an alternative arm, characterized by rehabilitation.[37] Yet even this distinction fails to capture the complexity of the terrain because different organizational logics merge and conflict across and within penal institutions. The most traditional of prisons also rely on nonprofits and private companies to provide services to inmates. This often leads to a collision of approaches within facilities—collisions that are even more pronounced in those "alternative" institutions struggling to carve out niches for themselves in such a crowded arena.

In this state of hybridity, the relationship between satellite and centralized institutions is complex and varied. Occasionally, their relationship is one of direct oversight, as when a religious NGO sets up shop in a state welfare department to hold self-esteem training or when a traditional prison allows for a "therapeutic community" to function in a special ward of its facility.[38] But more often, satellite institutions are located outside the confines of central state structures or departments. This geographical distance has not led to increased institutional or interpretive flexibility; rather, these satellites are simply governed through new checks and balances. In some cases, this governance operates through general mandates about the treatment of entire social groups—such as PRWORA's rules against felons, teen mothers, or immigrants receiving public assistance; or three-strikes sentencing laws for certain categories of felons. In other cases, governance is expressed through management practices—such as program evaluations, performance measures, and accountability scales that focus on "outputs" and force competition among agencies. In still other cases, it is articulated through the operation of budgets and funding—such as the granting of coveted state contracts through competitive requests for proposals (RFPs) that pit agencies against each other.

So while satellites may claim programmatic autonomy, their conduct remains managed and directed.

Just as government from a distance is frequently mistaken for state retrenchment, state hybridity is often thought to defy systematic analysis. Granted, such hybridity can appear to breed chaos and contradiction—as distinctions between public/private and non/state institutions blur or break down. But there remains a method to what may seem like institutional madness. And many of our theories of state governance are ill-equipped to make sense of the method behind the madness. For instance, in this era of state hybridity it no longer makes sense to trace the form and content of specific state programs solely to national-level political actors.[39] While these figures certainly shape the overall landscape of the state, their agendas undergo too many levels of translation to exert a direct or consistent influence on actual institutional programs. Nor is it analytically useful to reduce these projects to the "needs" of broad economic and political systems—such as capitalism, patriarchy, or, more recently, the "prison-industrial complex." Such reductionism not only seems conspiratorial, but it leaves unspecified precisely what needs to be explained—how larger ideological or material imperatives operate through concrete institutions.[40] In this way, it misses the most interesting empirical and conceptual challenges of state hybridity. What we need are new ways to analyze hybrid state structures and to account for the factors shaping their practices.

If many of these ideas seem overly abstract and disconnected from social reality, this is because they often are. While theorizations of state hybridity are quite compelling, its theorizers rarely venture out into the messy world of actually existing institutions to reveal how and why they govern as they do.[41] So while we know a great deal about broad shifts in governmental power, we know far less about their institutional reverberations. I take up this issue by analyzing why satellite states target certain areas of conduct and mobilize certain strategies to manage their charges. Here I argue that the structures of state hybridity have unusually malleable boundaries that open them up to a variety of discursive influences. To return to the metaphor used earlier, if we think of satellite states as hovering around a more centralized apparatus, it makes sense that they would be more apt to pick up different interpretive frameworks along their journeys. It also makes sense that, with the inclusion of all sorts of new actors playing the role of the state, their institutional practices and agendas would diversify; the tools they use to interpret and respond to their institutional worlds would multiply. As a form, hybrid states are less bounded institutionally and more permeable discursively.

The case studies of Alliance and Visions document precisely how this permeability operates and thus offer insights into the processes and effects of state hybridity. Both Alliance and Visions were state satellites—they emerged from reforms to decentralize the penal system and formed connections to a variety of public and private organizations. While these connections helped sustain them, they also transformed their structure by opening them up to diverse influences and imperatives. At the material level, like other hybrid institutions, Alliance and Visions relied on resources from different places: in addition to their contracts with the California Youth Authority and the California Department of Corrections, they depended on grants from public foundations and charity from private agencies. They also relied on support from other state agencies, which created ties among state arenas once considered separate. For instance, while traditional prisons operate with clear budget allocations, these community-based facilities tap into public assistance programs; Alliance and Visions used Aid to Families with Dependent Children/Temporary Assistance to Needy Families (AFDC/TANF) benefits, food stamps, Medicaid, and Section 8 to run their programs. Thus, welfare reforms had a domino effect in these facilities, making their institutional boundaries more malleable. In fact, bridge agencies have emerged recently to ensure such malleability and to coordinate the practices of the welfare and penal systems in quite explicit ways.[42]

These material exchanges then opened the door to new discursive engagements across state institutions. Along with the blurring of institutional boundaries, there are striking similarities in state actors' strategies of governance. These overlaps are perhaps clearest in my case study of Alliance. The discourse of need so central to Alliance's institutional narrative echoed key tenets of the welfare-reform debate of the 1990s, particularly its more conservative voices. Both discourses fixated on women's state dependency as the root of their problems. Just as dependency discourse served as the main interpretive framework used to administer and assess PRWORA, it surfaced in penal institutions like Alliance. Moreover, from this common definition of the problem arose a similar solution: if the obstacle was women's dependency, then the solution must be to make them independent. Even their routes to independence converged to lead to wage labor. PRWORA's mandatory work requirements were presented as the pill to cure all kinds of social ills; its job retraining programs became promises of self-sufficiency and transformation. This parallels Alliance's programmatic focus, which tried to teach young women to develop a work ethic, take the "bull by the horns," and respond to economic incentives—all the while promising self-sufficiency, dignity, and transformation. Far from coincidental, these discursive parallels were facilitated and enhanced by institutional hybridity.[43]

A similar form of migration characterized Visions's discourse of desire. While traces of this discourse can be found in welfare-reform debates and policies, it emanated most directly from the substance-abuse models used in other state facilities. By the early 1990s, these models had even surfaced in the U.S. court system through the drug-court movement. Operating like big group therapy sessions, drug courts linked defendants' willingness to deal with their emotions to their ability to conquer their desires for drugs and alcohol—a linkage that then shaped treatment and sentencing.[44] A similar connection occurred in the therapeutic communities that have sprouted up in traditional prisons since the early 1990s: here, too, an Alcoholics Anonymous–inspired treatment model targeted inmates' psychologies in order to teach them to behave in acceptable ways and to rid them of destructive urges.[45] These were the precise linkages at the center of Visions's discourse of desire and its attempts to rid women of distortions in their minds and bodies. So just as dependency discourse moved across institutions, therapeutic constructions of desire traveled through different state spaces—and, through this traveling, they combined and coordinated institutional strategies of governance.

Of course, anyone even remotely familiar with U.S. popular culture will also notice its imprint on these strategies. Since the 1990s, fears of dependency, particularly of women's dependency, have reached a fever pitch; everyone from politicians to policymakers to media pundits has warned of its dangers.[46] Although dependency discourse has a long history in the United States, it has certainly been amplified—leading to what Richard Sennett calls a cultural "panic of dependency."[47] The public preoccupation with cathexis and the regulation of desire have also reached new heights. A vocabulary of therapeutics now resounds throughout public life: media machines work on overdrive to create and control desires for sensory pleasures. Some advertisers have even begun marketing drugs to target the "pleasure center" of the brain in an attempt to end addictive impulses.[48] Politicians of all persuasions have become well-versed in therapy talk—from Bill Clinton's confessional exposés to public tell-alls of political victory through personal redemption. Even the popular feminist movement has taken to Oprah-like, confessional methods en route to self-esteem, self-transformation, and Gloria Steinem's "revolution from within."[49]

Such cultural preoccupations clearly found expression in state institutions. At one level, this should not be surprising. As political scientist James Scott has shown, state institutions are vehicles for the transmission of cultural rules and conduct.[50] And as sociologists Julia Adams and Tasleem Padamsee remind us, when states manage conduct, they tend to draw on socially recognized signs and symbols to mobilize powerful feelings and desires.[51] Although the U.S. state has always absorbed and articulated larger cultural scripts, this influence does seem to be taken to a new level. From state institutions' forms of governance to the content of their messages, the cultural imprint on these institutions seems deeper than ever before. There are organizational reasons for this: with their porous borders and linkages across subsystems, hybrid state institutions are more clearly connected to surrounding communities, cultures, and contexts.

I take these connections as the object of empirical investigation—they are key parts of my ethnographic story. Like others, I am concerned with the ways in which larger material and cultural imperatives make their way into state institutions. But instead of assuming this to be a straightforward route—from the "macro" needs of neoliberal governance regimes to "micro" state spaces—I investigate the concrete exchanges through which such imperatives emerge. I also link the content of these exchanges to the form of the institutions they emerge through, suggesting that state actors adhere to particular governance strategies in response to the organizational possibilities and constraints of state hybridity. To argue that contemporary governance reflects the broader economic and political culture is not saying very much. But to show why specific dependency discourses and therapeutic vocabularies were institutionalized in specific state agencies at specific moments—and why they resonated so strongly with those institutionalizing them—is far more challenging and rewarding. Not only does such an analysis uncover the "nuts and bolts" of state governance, it exposes how these systems become lived realities for those they target. In the process, it can also point to tangible arenas for change and alternatives to existing strategies of governance.

JOURNEYING ACROSS STATES

The ethnographic analysis that follows is divided into two parts, corresponding to two institutional case studies—with part 1 documenting the dynamics of Alliance's state of dependency and part 2 examining the contours of Visions's state of recovery. However tempting it may be to see the differences between these institutions as reflective of a vast regime change, or as symptomatic of shifting epochs of governance, this is not the point of the ethnographic account. Instead, my goal is to juxtapose these penal institutions and to compare their strategies of governance. Thus, the ethnographic analyses in both parts are structured around common nodes of comparison—I analyze each facility's institutional narrative, practices, and effects. Through these comparisons, I grapple with the larger questions of how gendered strategies of governance operate, why they take particular forms, and what they imply for the women they target.

The research this comparative analysis is based on was conducted in two phases, roughly a decade apart. The first fieldwork phase ran for six months in 1992, during which time I became part of everyday life at Alliance. I began by serving as a tutor for the girls, sitting in on their classes and assisting them with their schoolwork. With time, I branched out beyond the confines of the classroom to gain access to additional aspects of the group home: I went on afternoon outings; I "hung out" with the staff and the girls in the home; and I attended staff meetings, house gatherings, and planning sessions.[52]

My findings and observations from this work are documented in part 1. Chapter 1 goes inside everyday life at Alliance to explicate its program of dependency and corresponding discourse of need. In this chapter, I examine different aspects of this discourse—from its preoccupation with promoting self-sufficiency to its focus on freeing girls from destructive social relationships to its practices designed to instill initiative and self-reliance. I also explain the appeal of dependency discourse for the staff, linking it not only to the larger cultural panic of dependency but also to the staff's own institutional dependency and need to carve out organizational space for their facility. This analysis is followed by a discussion of the effects of Alliance's discourse of need in chapter 2. Here the focus shifts from those institutionalizing dependency discourse to those it targeted. This chapter documents how the girls contested and reinvented dependency discourse to serve their own needs. It also shows how Alliance's program of dependency gave rise to battles over social justice and entitlement—battles that eventually undermined the institution's ability to regulate and govern its girls.

Chapter 3 extends beyond the everyday struggles at Alliance to expose the structural shifts in the state arena underway throughout the 1990s. While the women at Alliance were locked in their battles over dependency, major changes were occurring around them. Often out of focus at the local level, the structure of the state reconfigured in ways that had profound effects on institutions like Alliance. These include everything from "get-tough" criminal-justice policies to the reform of AFDC and creation of TANF to the privatization of social services. In chapter 3, I outline these shifts and discuss the state hybridity they gave rise to—that is, how the arena of government devolved, decentralized, and diversified. In this way, the chapter serves as a bridge between the two case studies. By providing a structural backdrop for the transition between these cases, the chapter also sets the stage for the second phase of ethnographic research.

Conducted over a three-year period, from 2002 to 2005, my fieldwork in Visions occurred in a different organizational context. By then, "alternative" justice institutions for women no longer seemed as exceptional as in the early 1990s. In fact, this state sphere had become a crowded arena, with a variety of "alternative-to-incarceration" programs vying for public funding and clients. This shaped the kind of research I ended up doing. Just as Visions exemplified government from a distance, my study of it was a kind of ethnography from a distance. Instead of working in the facility on an uninterrupted basis, I remained connected to it over several years—in between long research stints, I made short visits to the facility and remained in e-mail contact with the staff and inmates. Over three years, I spent roughly eight months in the actual field, observing and participating in the facility's trials and tribulations. My research stays were often spread out in time; they usually occurred over two- to three-month intervals. Despite my varied and even rhapsodic presence in the field, my access to Visions was even greater than it had been at Alliance. I had complete access to all parts of the facility. The staff also included me in the summer curriculum by allowing me to teach writing classes to the inmates—which ended up enabling me to form unmediated relationships with the women and to gain insight into their lives and institutional survival strategies.

Part 2 analyzes the complex layers of control and contestation that characterized Visions's program of recovery. Chapter 4 centers on the therapeutic discourse of desire articulated and practiced by the Visions staff. It deconstructs the different dimensions of this discourse: from its preoccupation with uncovering women's "dangerous desires" to its focus on training women what to want to its practices of self-discovery and public exposure. This chapter also explains the power of state therapeutics for those institutionalizing it—arguing that the staff's discourse of desire allowed them to grapple with the internal conflicts rooted in Visions's hybrid structure, while also securing a place for their program in this crowded arena of the penal system.

Chapters 5 and 6 move on to explore Visions's program of recovery from the perspectives of the inmates. Chapter 5 critically analyzes Visions's claim to empower women through community-based therapeutics. It reveals how Visions's therapeutic practices left the inmates feeling exposed, surveyed, and ultimately out of control. It also demonstrates how these experiences were rooted in the context and content of Visions's program of recovery. Here I argue that Visions's version of state therapeutics emotionalized injustice and transformed social vulnerability into personal pathology. This analysis is then extended in chapter 7 through a discussion of how the inmates responded to their sense of disempowerment. These pages document the real underside of Visions's program of recovery—exposing how the individualization and pathologization the women experienced led them to turn on themselves and one another in quite painful and destructive ways. I also explicate how this program left the women in a state of disentitlement, effectively silencing them from speaking of social injustice or envisioning societal change. In the conclusion, I return to this state of disentitlement to theorize its causes and consequences and to contemplate how penal institutions could be reformed to pose real alternatives to it.

PART ONE   In a State of Dependence

ONE

Limited Government

TRAINING WOMEN WHAT TO NEED

"Who can tell me what 'limited government' means?" Rachel Brennan asked the group of teen mothers gathered in her small, makeshift classroom. The question was met with blank, uninterested stares, so she followed up: "Well, you should know what it means since it's the basis of our system of government. I'll give you a hint." Rachel walked to the board and wrote two words, *dictatorship* and *anarchy*, with a space in between them. She explained that the former was a system of too much government, the latter of no government. But there was an alternative. "Democracy is in the middle," she noted as she wrote it in the empty space. "It's when the government doesn't have too much power, like under dictatorship, but isn't without power, like under anarchy." Then she reached the idea of limited government, describing it as a series of checks and balances designed to minimize the control the government wields over its citizens.

Sensing that this might be a bit too abstract for her students, Rachel launched into a lecture about the importance of limited government for "girls like you." She explained how tired she was of young women claiming that the government "owed" them something and complaining that their "rights" had been violated. It was as if they turned their reliance on others into a virtue. In doing so, they forgot how important it was to keep the government out of their lives. After all, she reminded them, limits on the power of government were hard-fought American "rights." So the next time they got angry about being denied something or waiting for a late welfare check, they should remember this lesson. "The government doesn't owe you very much," she proclaimed. "And that's good, sometimes."

Without a context for this lecture, one might assume it occurred in one of the countless welfare-to-work programs that sprouted up in the late-1990s era of welfare reform. Indeed, similar speeches have taken place in welfare offices across the United States since the enactment of the Personal Responsibility and Work Opportunity Reconciliation Act in 1996.[1] But this particular rendition was delivered in early 1992, years before the official onset of reform. Moreover, it was not delivered to an audience of Temporary Assistance to Needy Families recipients; it was presented to a group of incarcerated teen mothers residing in Alliance, a state-sponsored group home. And it was not given by a politically conservative ideologue or an administratively challenged welfare worker; it was delivered by a self-proclaimed "radical feminist" so committed to helping "disadvantaged women lead productive lives" that she left a lucrative job in business to become Alliance's underpaid schoolteacher.

Yet the first time I heard Rachel's limited-government lecture, neither its timing nor its context struck me as particularly noteworthy. Instead, like many of the arguments advanced by the Alliance staff, I was most surprised by how its content seemed at odds with notions of the "patriarchal state" at the center of so much feminist theorizing.[2] For decades, feminist scholars asserted that state policies and institutions controlled women by fostering their dependence.[3] But here were state actors arguing that such dependence was wholly destructive to women's well-being. At the time, there were few clues that such arguments would soon become discursively dominant—or that, in the decade to follow, they would congeal into a dependency discourse and become ubiquitous in national policy debates, especially among conservative politicians.[4] Nor was it apparent that this dependency discourse would filter down to the institutional level to revamp the structure of state agencies. Yet, in retrospect, Alliance's fixation with dependency was a sign of what was to come on a larger scale. Its institutional narrative encompassed key elements of an emergent panic of dependency: it positioned women's use of state assistance as the source of their social problems; it pathologized poor women's public and domestic relations; and it presented women's reliance on others as a devalued social condition to be overcome before they could reach the promised land of self-sufficiency.[5]

But, again, in the penal system of the early 1990s these arguments had yet to become dominant.[6] In fact, according to the Alliance staff, they constituted an altogether alternative approach. In their view, the penal system ignored the needs of those it served, while institutions like juvenile hall and the California Youth Authority (CYA) trapped kids in a "destructive system."[7] Thus, the Alliance staff considered their focus on the "real needs" of young offenders to be different and even subversive. What is more, the Alliance staff claimed that the penal system had particularly damaging effects on women—by putting them on a "cycle of welfare and dependency," the system used and abused them. But the Alliance staff set out to understand girls' distinctive needs. They showed these girls what kind of resources and relationships they needed to survive. They taught them how to meet their needs and secure their well-being. In short, the Alliance staff insisted on fighting the system on behalf of women; they formulated a discourse of need in opposition to what they perceived to be the system's control of young women.

Given what happened to this kind of needs talk the following decade, it would be easy to dismiss these on-the-ground state actors as politically naïve. In fact, this is often how they are portrayed in social-scientific analyses of welfare reform—as blindly following the "party line" or as mouthpieces for dependency discourse.[8] But this portrayal misses important insights into the power that dependency discourse had over those articulating it. As a result, it leaves us without an understanding of the institutional appeal of dependency discourse or the intensity with which many local actors latched onto it. When the Alliance staff articulated this discourse in the early 1990s, they did so for their own reasons: it allowed them to carve out new state spaces and differentiate these spaces from those of their predecessors. Dependency discourse was not simply forced or coerced—it was rooted in state actors' specific political and institutional needs.

This chapter begins by outlining these institutional needs and the way they drew the Alliance staff to focus on their charges' social dependency. Here I reveal how dependency discourse enabled Alliance to justify its existence and to secure itself vis-à-vis the more powerful institutions it was reliant on. In this way, I argue that the staff's institutional dependency led them to fixate on the dangers of dependency for their young clients. I then analyze the concrete ways Alliance transmitted this construction of need to the women under its control: from staff lectures on initiative and independence to the organization of everyday life, the goal was to break women's public dependencies and to convince them they no longer needed state support. I also describe how the regulation of women's social relationships formed the centerpiece of Alliance's program of independence—as the staff set out to redefine women's roles as workers, mothers, and citizens in ways they insisted would make their girls autonomous, self-sufficient, and self-reliant.

INSTITUTIONAL DEPENDENCE

When Alliance opened its doors in 1989, it considered itself a new kind of state institution. It was considerably smaller than traditional criminal-justice facilities: housed on a residential street in a rough, crime-ridden neighborhood, Alliance looked more like a big, dilapidated mansion than a facility for convicted felons. The house held up to thirty residents, although it never got that full. In part because the inmates had (or were expecting) babies, the staff rarely allowed the house to reach more than half its capacity. This meant the staff/inmate ratio remained high. Alliance employed eight staff members, including the director, house manager, schoolteacher, counselors, and day/night staff. All staff members were women; approximately half were African American, half Anglo. These women insisted that Alliance be as unprison-like as possible. So there were no bars on the windows, no heavy steel doors, no security cameras, and no surveillance technology in the house. From the street, there was no indication that Alliance was a CYA facility for official wards of the state of California.

Perhaps even more than its size or staff composition, Alliance's funding structure marked it as unique for the period. Alliance relied on three funding sources. First, it had a contract with CYA whereby any girl who entered the prison system pregnant or with an infant had the option to come to Alliance to serve her sentence. CYA then provided funds for the inmates' upkeep and maintenance.[9] Second, once admitted to the program, each girl was put on Aid to Families with Dependent Children. According to the house director, AFDC funds were pooled to help purchase food for the entire house; a small percentage of this money was also given to the girls to buy personal items. Finally, Alliance received funding from Fellowship for Change, the large nonprofit organization from which it had been born.[10] Created in the 1950s, the Fellowship had a reputation in the community as the main NGO assisting ex-cons. In fact, the Fellowship leadership considered Alliance an experiment: after decades of working with men, it decided to widen its scope to include young female offenders. So it donated the house Alliance was located in and funds to cover the salaries of the facility director and house manager.

In this way, Alliance combined funds from different public programs, thus situating itself in a space between the state and nonstate sectors. While this hybrid space would expand dramatically in the following decade, in 1989 it was a relatively uncrowded arena. In fact, when it came to community-based facilities for incarcerated teen mothers, Alliance was the only game in town.[11] This meant Alliance did not face many of the dilemmas that would come to haunt other state hybrids—for instance, Alliance did not have to compete with other facilities for residents or resources. But Alliance had other dilemmas to contend with: it struggled to convince other institutions of the need for its services and to carve out some legitimacy. This was particularly challenging since Alliance was sandwiched between two larger, more powerful institutions. On the state side was CYA, with its harsh, punitive orientation. On the NGO side was the Fellowship, with its focus on male offenders. The Alliance staff knew their fate rested on the cooperation and support of those in charge of these other entities. This awareness gave the Alliance staff a mission—a gendered mission that enabled them to develop a common institutional narrative of what their young charges needed.

Us versus Them . . . and Them

Alliance's institutional narrative became apparent in my initial interactions with its staff. With most state institutions it can take years for ethnographers to piece together a picture of shared assumptions and meanings. Not so with Alliance, which presented me with a clear, unified mantra that replayed itself constantly over the course of my fieldwork. At times, the message seemed to have been collectively crafted and recited to the point of perfection. The mantra also seemed to be the glue that held Alliance together, bonding a group of otherwise diverse and potentially divided women. After all, there were critical differences among the Alliance staff—not only were they racially divided, but they differed in their educational level, class background, and job assignments.[12] Yet none of these differences proved decisive or divisive. Or, more precisely, none of them trumped the dividing lines Alliance established between itself and the larger institutions hovering over it. In effect, Alliance's institutional mantra emphasized how and why it differed from other penal facilities; the staff's narrative was based on their common opposition to those surrounding them.

Because I had been referred to Alliance from its parent institution, my first meetings with the staff focused on how they differed from their Fellowship colleagues. "I bet they tried to get you to work in one of their other programs," Dwan, Alliance's house manager, speculated when she first met me. Indeed, the staff at the Fellowship not only suggested I work in their male halfway house but actually tried to dissuade me from working at Alliance. Warning me that working at Alliance would be a negative experience, the Fellowship director claimed that "they throw

temper tantrums all the time." He insisted that they "manipulated everyone around them" and were "out of touch with reality." As he noted
at one point, "The program over there is our newest one. It's just three
years old and I'm telling you they act like it—like toddlers with all the
tantrums and fits." It was unclear whether the "they" he referred to were
the inmates or the staff; in fact, he seemed to have been purposefully
vague. While I never mentioned his comments to the Alliance staff, I did
not have to. They knew the line the Fellowship had about them.

For their part, the Alliance staff also had a line about the Fellowship.
Whenever Alliance director Marlene asked for funds from the Fellowship, she spoke about going to "big daddy" to beg for her "allowance."
Other staff members often described the "scolding" and "reprimands"
they received from the Fellowship guys, which they attributed to sex-
ism and chauvinism. Yet the staff did not appear fearful of such reprisals.
Instead, they portrayed the Fellowship as enamored with the image of
the "tough guy criminal." The men who ran the Fellowship liked the idea
of hanging around with the bad guys; they got off on the idea that they
could "tame the beast." But the Alliance staff insisted they were different.
As women, they did not approach their work with the same "macho" attitude. Some of them were from the surrounding community, while others
had spent years in the NGO world. So their motivations were different.
Their goal was to help young women instead of satisfying their own egos;
they taught the girls life lessons instead of getting off on their criminality.
They represented themselves as truly committed, as the "real deal."

In addition to differentiating their motivations, the Alliance staff
emphasized how their diagnoses of their charges' problems diverged
from those of the Fellowship. Because the Fellowship men had backgrounds in substance-abuse counseling, they saw drugs and alcohol as
the main threat to their clients' well-being. They connected substance
abuse to criminal behavior—and then linked criminal behavior to men's
inability to integrate socially.[13] According to the Fellowship formula,
chemical dependency led to social dependency. But the Alliance staff
insisted that it worked in the reverse for their charges. For their girls, the
biggest threat was social dependency—it motivated them to act criminally. Moreover, state dependency was the most insidious of all; once

hooked on the state, the girls' futures were sealed. So Alliance had to work differently from the Fellowship. And this difference then became the rationale for Alliance's institutional existence, unifying its staff and solidifying one part of their "us versus them" stance.[14]

The second part of this stance was the staff's opposition to CYA. To a large extent, CYA was the bread and butter of the facility—it supplied Alliance with residents as well as the bulk of its funding. This made Alliance quite dependent on CYA; the staff relied on CYA sending girls to them.[15] Without the CYA contract, Alliance would not exist. So this was where the real institutional struggles lay. Alliance did everything it could to secure a steady stream of residents from CYA. This involved making sure CYA officials knew about their program—what director Marlene called their "advertising" and "marketing" work. It also meant exerting pressure on CYA to release more girls than it wanted to. "If left alone, they would never send us anyone," Dwan once noted. "So we have to bully them." Sometimes the staff used their connections for this bullying. For instance, they had a few sympathetic probation officers whom they could count on to transfer their pregnant clients from CYA to Alliance. There were also a few judges who would use their authority to get eligible girls released to Alliance. Yet, overall, it was up to the Alliance staff to keep pressure on CYA, thus ensuring the future of their program.

The Alliance staff spoke about this work as if they were on a rescue mission. They viewed CYA as a destructive place, and it was their calling to wrestle as many girls as possible from CYA's grip. Here, too, the Alliance staff motivated themselves to continue the struggle by accentuating their difference from the youth prison. Or, more specifically, they developed a rhetoric of need to legitimize their approach. Over and over again, the Alliance staff differentiated their program from CYA through the prism of need: CYA was not attentive to what girls needed, but they were; CYA was not able to fulfill the prenatal needs of pregnant teens, but they could; and CYA did not equip girls with the life skills they needed, but they did. To substantiate their claims, all staff members could recite reincarceration rates on the spot, data they used to indicate just how poorly the system addressed girls' "needs." In effect, they used the notion of need as a platform from which to oppose CYA. "They just trap girls in the system," counselor Olivia explained to me. "But we step in to get them out." Or, as schoolteacher Rachel once put it, "They get nervous that we help girls make it on their own." In this way, the Alliance staff resembled nineteenth-century child savers, representing themselves as on a mission to serve the needs of neglected young people. They also resembled those female reformers from the same period who tried to save women from male prisons—both their arguments about women's distinctive needs and their claims that women were unduly exposed to the harshness of the penal system echoed the ideas of earlier reformers.[16]

At the same time, Alliance's conception of need enabled the staff to strengthen their own institutional bonds and connections to each other. One of their favorite bonding rituals was to tell stories about the horrors of CYA. Over the years, they had collected an archive of stories to draw on. They recounted cases in which CYA officials forced young women to have abortions. They described instances when girls had their babies in their cells, without proper medical care. They listed all the complications these mothers had due to the lack of prenatal care at CYA. And they talked incessantly about a CYA policy that forbade girls who became pregnant in CYA from requesting a transfer to Alliance. "They actually think our existence will encourage girls to get pregnant [while in prison]," Marlene exclaimed in a staff discussion. "It's a perfect example how just how out of touch they are with what girls need." These conversations served to remind the staff of what they were up against and the importance of their work. They also reminded these women of what they shared—how, despite their racial, educational, and class differences, they were bonded by a commitment to saving girls from a destructive system.

There was yet another way Alliance used CYA to its own advantage: in interactions with the girls, the staff often deployed the threat of CYA. The staff frequently told their CYA horror stories in front of the girls— as if to remind the girls of what awaited them if they got kicked out of the program. At times, such reminders became explicit: when the girls broke house rules, the staff would raise the possibility of returning them to CYA. This happened to Maria who, after being caught smoking out of her bedroom window, was reminded of what she would have to do for cigarettes if sent back to CYA.[17] It also happened to Tonya who, after failing to awake before noon for several days, was told no one would notice her sleeping patterns at CYA since she would be confined to her cell all day. While the staff rarely followed through with such threats, they remained a tool of behavior modification. The CYA threat could convince the girls how indebted they were to the staff. "If CYA had it their way, you would be stuck in little cells and your babies would be mothered by the government," Dwan declared to the girls. "We are doing this for you, so you won't be in jail or on welfare all your life."

In this way, it would be far too simplistic to view Alliance's discourse of need as coerced or manipulated. This discourse was more of a strategic response to Alliance's institutional environment. The uncertainty produced by this environment could have provoked internal strife; it could have led this diverse group of women to turn on one another as they struggled to legitimize their place in the system. Instead, the Alliance staff insisted on internal programmatic consistency. And this stance was made possible precisely because the dividing lines between Alliance and CYA seemed so clear. In this early form of state hybridity, it was possible to demarcate who the "us" and the "them" were—the Alliance staff believed they could discern how and why women's needs were ignored by "them."[18] This enabled the staff to coalesce around an alternative approach to those needs. Interestingly, the approach that emerged ended up reproducing the terms of the struggle itself: from a position of institutional dependency, the staff advanced a discourse of need that warned their charges of the dangers of state reliance.

Breaking the Dependency

To say that the staff's experience of institutional dependency informed their approach to clients is not to minimize their commitment to these young women. In fact, they were quite dedicated to their work and to saving "their girls" from the system.[19] They spent an enormous amount of time trying to figure out how to protect the girls from the many threats to their well-being. They saw girls as young as fourteen years old who had already made their way through the juvenile-justice system to land in the worst place of all, the state youth prison.[20] They saw girls who had very little education and no work experience. They saw girls who had spent years on AFDC and appeared to take this support for granted. They saw girls who had babies at very young ages, only to become sole mothers after their babies' fathers left them. They saw girls who had been cast out of their own homes, often by families that were themselves unstable and volatile. In effect, the Alliance staff saw a group of girls with a slew of problems and very few reliable safety nets to catch them when they fell.

Of course, there are many ways to interpret these experiences and the complicated lives they represent. The Alliance staff did so through a prism of dependency that highlighted the girls' reliance on others. Like other forms of dependency discourse, Alliance's version was multilayered. It did not center on the girls' personal or familial relations, or what might be called their "private dependencies." Because these girls were essentially manless and familyless teen mothers, the staff did not view their personal relationships as particularly threatening. Instead, Alliance fixated on what it perceived to be the girls' public dependencies and reliance on state support. In effect, dependency discourse became a way to read the girls' histories: it encompassed abstract arguments about how the girls' reliance on the state had to be broken so that they could mend the past, improve the present, and thrive in the future.

In terms of the past, the staff repeatedly presented the girls with explanatory arguments for why they had ended up as incarcerated mothers so early in their lives. At the center of this explanation was their dependency on others—a dependency that propelled them onto two equally destructive paths. First, there was the path that led to distorted social relationships. In daily interactions, the Alliance staff frequently suggested that their girls had become malformed by their state dependency. They had become lazy and indifferent; they had become content to wait passively for state officials to tell them what to do; and they had become accustomed to relying on everyone from social workers to prison guards to decide how to live.

These traits then made the girls incapable of forming mature relationships with others—or, as counselor Charlene put it in a house meeting, they were "parasites" who relied on others for everything. "They lack the most basic life skills," schoolteacher Rachel once explained to me. "They don't know what it means to give and take; they only know how to take." Without these skills, the staff insisted that the girls would never lead productive lives. Instead, they would remain entangled in the system's web, which would only exacerbate their problems with dependency. These arguments implied a clear causal sequence: rather than attributing the girls' reliance on state support to social marginalization, the staff reversed the order. For them, dependency caused marginalization and left the girls unable to form strong relationships.

In addition to distorting their relationships, the girls' dependent pasts were said to have put them on the path to incarceration. Here the Alliance staff insisted that the girls' imprisonment was an outgrowth of their dependent ways—but not because it led them to crime. Unlike state actors working in other parts of the welfare and penal systems, the Alliance staff did not conflate criminal behavior and state reliance.[21] In fact, there was almost no talk of the actual crimes their girls committed; many staff members did not even know what the girls were in for. Instead, they linked dependency to the act of incarceration itself, claiming that the girls' CYA sentences were evidence of the risks involved in relying on others for survival. For instance, whenever the girls complained about how they had been wronged by someone in the system—from a heartless judge to an incompetent public defender to a ruthless probation officer—they received little sympathy. Instead, the staff reminded them of the lesson to be learned from these experiences: no one could count on the system to protect them. Perhaps they thought they could trust the system to defend their interests. But that was the myth of the dependent, a lie dependents told themselves to justify their dependency. In effect, the staff tried to convince their girls of the real risks involved in relying on faceless others for survival. Having taken the risk, the girls were now suffering the consequences.

Of course, Alliance's dependency discourse was not only about the mistakes of the past—it also had clear prescriptions for how to improve life in the present. The staff constantly told the girls they had reached the end of the line; director Marlene often described their incarceration as a "wake-up call." What is more, they were mothers, which changed everything. Maybe they could get by with their dependent ways before, but now they *had* dependents. Counselor Charlene put this succinctly in a house meeting: "You are women. You have babies. Babies must be cared for. Women care for others. Until you learn this, you'll be doin' a lot of crying in your lives." So motherhood was the first way the girls could break their dependency: by accepting their roles as caretakers, they would stop looking to others for support. The reverse was also true: as they became more independent and less reliant on state support, they would become better mothers.

Yet motherhood was only one of several possible avenues away from dependence. Day in and day out, the staff presented the girls with arguments for how the most mundane activity could help end their dependency. Rachel had a phrase she constantly repeated to her class—she insisted the girls "take the bull by the horns" as a way of prompting initiative. "Why does she [Rachel] always say that?" Janice, a new inmate, asked the others one afternoon. Smiling, Jamika responded that it meant Rachel wanted them to "get off our butts." Perhaps the best definition came from Mildred, who referred to the staff's "talk of bein' self-full." And this talk could surface at any moment: simple activities like getting up in the morning, washing the dishes, and feeding a child became opportunities for a lecture on initiative. The same was true of the girls' failure to do these activities—the staff responded to such refusals with lectures on the perils of passivity. "We won't let them rely on us," counselor Colorado explained after I watched her lecture a girl who forgot to do laundry and had no clean clothes for her son. "This is their chance to learn to start doing things for themselves and to stop asking for help all the time."

In fact, Alliance's dependency discourse was so powerful that it often overrode all other ways of explaining the girls' behavior. This became apparent one afternoon during a special meeting called to deal with a problematic girl. The week before, the staff had sent Nikita to juvenile hall for a "cool out period" and now had to decide whether to make her removal permanent. Dwan began the meeting by discussing how "tough" and "pissed off" Nikita was—she had started several fights with the girls and constantly argued with the staff. The others agreed but noted that Nikita's real problem was her laziness and "self-defeated attitude." Nikita's counselor described her as "too passive about what was going down around her" and as taking "no role in changing her own life." As they talked about her passivity, the phone rang—it was Nikita calling from juvie. She heard there would be a meeting to discuss her and wanted to put in a few words on her own behalf. On speaker phone, Nikita promised to change if they took her back. But she also remained defiant, disagreeing with much of the staff's representation of her behavior and attitude. Nevertheless, the staff's tone changed after the call. Impressed, they began to wonder if Nikita's tough demeanor was not a sign of her independent mind and thus potential for self-sufficiency. "Maybe she is capable of taking the bull by the horns," Rachel suggested. Within minutes, they decided to take her back.

Ultimately, Alliance's dependency discourse encompassed a template for change in the future. It offered the girls a vision of what their lives could become if they broke their dependencies. The staff often discussed how the girls would feel fulfilled once they were self-sufficient and self-reliant. They spoke of the girls' future independence as if it were the promised land: it was a time when the girls would have their GEDs or high-school diplomas; when they would have secured their own jobs; when they would have found their own housing; and when they would care for their own children. References to these ideals occurred on a daily basis. While watching television or walking down the street, the staff would begin to fantasize about the new lives awaiting the girls upon release. One morning, while walking from Alliance to the library, I listened as Rachel imagined the life awaiting Janice upon release: she could put her son in the childcare center we passed by, enroll in a beauty school on the next block, work part-time in a salon on the next block, and get an apartment on the following block. By the end of the walk, Rachel had constructed an entirely new life for Janice—all within a three-block radius.

Moreover, when the girls wanted to do something that was not permitted, the staff would tell them they had to wait until they were free of their dependencies. Here, too, something as simple as doing laundry or eating lunch could lead to a lecture about the future. For instance, one afternoon Debra's attempt to feed her son prompted just such a lecture. As she took out a can of baby food, Dwan stopped her. "You know the rule. At Alliance we grind table food for the babies." Debra rolled her eyes, annoyed at having to spend the extra time preparing the food while holding a hungry, crying infant. Dwan continued, "When you become independent and care for yourself, you can decide these things." Now even more annoyed, Debra responded that she was paying for herself with her AFDC check. Dwan immediately countered that AFDC was not her money—and when the government pays, it got to decide. The message was clear: feeding her child bottled food was something Debra could do once she reached the goal of independence.

In this way, Alliance's discourse of dependency categorized the girls' social relationships and reliance on the state as problematic. This implied rereading past dependencies as dangerous, presenting current dependencies as subject to change, and envisioning the girls' futures as free of dependency and full of independent possibilities. This dependency discourse was not only a collection of words and images—it also became a concrete model around which the staff organized everyday life in the facility.

PRACTICING INDEPENDENCE

Alliance's dependency discourse was an unusually tight institutional narrative. Because it served to bond the staff and to differentiate them from those in other penal facilities, it had to be consistent and coherent. Yet, almost ironically, the tightness of this discourse created dilemmas for its institutionalization. The staff's dependency discourse encouraged the girls to "take the bull by the horns" and become "self-full." Yet the staff still had an institution to run—and dozens of young women insisting on their initiative and independence could pose real problems for the facility's stability.

The Alliance staff were not alone in facing this dilemma. As dependency discourse became dominant later in the 1990s, other state institutions began to grapple with a similar conflict. For instance, in her work on post-TANF welfare offices, sociologist Sharon Hays shows how caseworkers' mandate against client dependency and the call for self-sufficiency butted up against the practicalities of running a welfare office—practicalities that often led welfare workers to undermine their own mandates by fostering client obedience and subservience.[22] The potential for such contradictions was even more pronounced in penal institutions—where enforcing conformity and discipline in their subjects tends to be the modus operandi. But what happens when this disciplining purports to be about making subjects independent, autonomous, and self-reliant?

At Alliance, the staff addressed this dilemma by conceptualizing independence as a process. It was something that had to be taught and learned over time. It was something that required training and rehearsal. This then became Alliance's work: to set up a facility in which the girls could practice and perfect independence. But it would not happen overnight; the girls could not be expected to give up their dependent ways immediately. So while they learned new ways of being, they were not ready to be self-reliant or autonomous. As they remained en route to independence, the girls were expected to continue to exhibit conformity and obedience. To help them along, Alliance structured its practices around two related goals: teaching the girls about the limitations of government and giving them the survival strategies needed in a system of limited government.

A Government of Limits

As soon as a girl was transferred from CYA to Alliance, the staff put her on AFDC. Most Alliance girls had been on AFDC before—their eligibility had simply lapsed during their time in CYA. So all the staff had to do was help them reapply for assistance. There were only a few girls who had never received public assistance. Helping them took longer because it involved a lengthy application process, interviews, and home visits. Yet in both cases, the act of putting the girls on a much-maligned state program like AFDC created a looming disjuncture between the ideology and reality of Alliance. After all, here was a facility that prided itself on breaking women's state dependencies and teaching self-sufficiency. Yet one of its first acts was to put its girls on public assistance. The potential contradiction was obvious.

As they so often did, the Alliance staff turned this potential liability into an asset. They did so by making the girls' receipt of AFDC the first of many lessons about the limitations of government. Over the course of applying for assistance, whenever the girls mentioned "their money" or "their checks," the staff quickly corrected them. No, AFDC was not their money; it was the state's money. They were applying to use state funds. This instruction continued once the girls' checks began to arrive. At the start of every month, the girls had to sign over the AFDC checks to the facility. During these transfers, the staff would remind the girls yet again that these were not their funds: not only did they have no control over when the money would arrive, but they had no say over how it would be used. In effect, they had no real claim to these funds. Of course, these lectures were also a way for the staff to hide the facility's own dependence on AFDC funds. Without AFDC, Alliance could not maintain itself. Yet this could be swept under the rug in lectures about the girls' lack of entitlement to and control over public money.

Once the girls signed over the AFDC checks, the funds seemed to disappear into an institutional abyss. This was also part of the lesson: the staff purposefully refused to tell the girls were the money went. Except for a small amount of money they put into a house account for each girl, the staff never revealed what the money was spent on. Food shopping for the house was done by the staff alone; most of the inmates' toiletries were purchased for them. What is more, this shopping seemed to happen magically—there was never any discussion of who did the shopping, when they did it, or where they did it. "We don't want them [the girls] to get accustomed to being taken care of by the government," Dwan explained to me when I asked why she never told the girls how she used the AFDC money. "It's not their money and we shouldn't treat it like it was."

Not surprisingly, this lesson did not go over very well with the girls. Instead, the use of AFDC checks was one of the most contentious issues in the facility. It was the source of countless fights between the staff and inmates. These fights were played out in the same way every month, like a broken record. At the beginning of every month, the girls demanded to know when "their checks" had arrived. The staff refused to tell them, reminding the girls that AFDC was not their money. Eventually, the staff gave in and informed them of the checks' arrival so the girls could sign them over to Alliance. This was always a moment of conflict, as the girls often refused to turn the checks over until they were told where "their money" would go. The staff remained steadfast in their refusal to tell, and eventually the girls gave up their demands. Then, toward the end of the month, when household supplies became scarce and the money in the girls' individual accounts dried up, they would revive their demand for an accounting of how "their funds" had been spent. Another series of staff refusals would follow, leading the girls to accuse the staff of stealing "their money." The accusations would continue to fly until the cycle began anew at the start of the next month. While these conflicts exhausted the staff, they comforted themselves with the idea that such fights were all part of the girls' learning process—pit stops on their rocky road to independence.

In addition to refusing to tell the girls where the AFDC money went, the staff denied the girls' requests to influence what was purchased with the money. They refused to give the girls a say in the kinds of food and goods bought for the house. This was part of the same lesson: to teach the girls that when state funds were used, the state decided what was needed. Until the girls reached a state of independence, they were not allowed to make decisions about their consumption patterns. Debra was not alone in her desire to feed her son bottled baby food—almost all the girls preferred prepared food to ground table food. They insisted that grinding table food was just too time consuming. The staff countered that bottle food was too expensive to use on a daily basis and encouraged indolence. "They'll just take the easy way out," counselor Charlene noted in a staff discussion about baby food. She claimed that forcing the girls to grind food for their children taught them to be resourceful and budget conscious. Similar issues surfaced with other household goods, from diapers to laundry detergent to shampoo to soap. The girls continually tried to get Alliance to buy name-brand items, but the response was always the same: when the state pays, the state decides.

Consumer constraint was not the only string attached to state dependence. When the staff placed limits on the girls' movements, they justified it by referring to the physical surveillance that accompanies state reliance. Just as the welfare office could invade the girls' private lives, the government could control their comings and goings. Unlike other community-based facilities, Alliance did not allow its charges to enter or exit the facility as they pleased.[23] Instead, whenever they left the facility, they had to be escorted by an Alliance employee. As a result, the girls were always trying to get staff members to take them places, which in turn led to constant negotiations over where the girls needed to go. In these negotiations, the girls' lack of power was attributed to their dependencies. "Why do I need to tell you why I need to go to a drugstore?" Jamika exclaimed to counselor Colorado. "I need to get some personal items." Colorado insisted on knowing what these personal items were—after all, Jamika was a prisoner and had no "right" to freedom of movement. This infuriated Jamika, who countered that she was planning to "use her own money" at the store; Colorado deemed this irrelevant. Eventually, Jamika refused to tell Colorado why she needed to go the store, and Colorado refused to take her. Later, Colorado explained her refusal, claiming that Jamika needed to "take responsibility" for her actions. "It's just simple," Colorado lectured. "She needs to live with the consequences of what she says and does and what she's willing to say and do."

While most of Alliance's lessons about the limits of government were transmitted through such reprimands, one program tried to teach the girls the same lesson through incentives. Named after schoolteacher Rachel, the "Brennan Bucks" program distributed fake money to the girls when they showed initiative or independence. Initially, the girls were supposed to get the bucks only when they did something noteworthy. But, with time, Rachel began distributing bucks whenever a girl did what she was asked to do. So waking up on time got a buck; turning in an assignment by the deadline yielded two bucks; and helping another girl with schoolwork earned several bucks. These amounts were subject to negotiation. If a girl was the only one to return to school after lunch, she could negotiate more bucks than if the entire class was in attendance. Then, every Friday, the girls used their bucks to purchase cheap goods Rachel brought in for them. As Rachel proudly described it to me, the program promoted initiative and taught the girls to respond to "material incentives just like the rest of us in the normal world."

Indeed, Brennan Bucks did connect behavior modification to market incentives. The program's goal was to convince girls that there were financial payoffs to acting in institutionally acceptable ways. This message was only enhanced when juxtaposed to Alliance's control of state funds. Unlike AFDC money, the girls spent their bucks as they wished. Rachel always reminded them that there would be no control over their bucks spending. Never mind that Rachel implicitly set limits on these purchases by deciding what goods to bring in each week. It was the semblance of consumer choice that mattered. So no one stopped Janice from buying only lip gloss, even though she did not "need" it; no one questioned Maria's decision to buy only body cream, even though she had stocked up countless bottles during her time at Alliance. The bucks were theirs to spend.

This point was brought home most forcefully on those rare Fridays when Rachel forgot to bring in her goods and took the girls to a local drugstore to spend their bucks. These were glorious times for the girls: they ran up and down the aisles, pointing out possible purchases along the way. Thrilled with their newly acquired consumer freedom, they spent hours looking over hundreds of items as they decided how to spend their few bucks. In the end, they usually bought things available to them at Alliance, like toys for their babies or toiletries, makeup, and hair products for themselves. Yet they celebrated their purchases as victories, insisting that they reflected their own personal style. Again, the message was so clear that Rachel never had to state it explicitly: there were real benefits to "earning" money. Even if it was earned it by conforming to others' rules, this money came with freedoms denied to those reliant on state support.

In this way, Alliances' practices focused on the girls' social relationships—on changing the girls' roles as potential workers, mothers, and consumers. At Alliance, there was almost no discussion of the girls' psychological or emotional composition. The staff never questioned if the girls were emotionally prepared for independence. Nor did they doubt the girls' psychological ability to break their dependent ways. Instead, the staff assumed their girls just needed lessons about the limitations of government. When presented with the rewards of independence, from unfettered consumption to physical freedom, the girls would want to limit the role of government in their lives. "Where there's a will, there's a way," Rachel always told the girls, demonstrating her uncanny ability to use the perfect cliché to describe key aspects of the Alliance program. Finding this way then became the second component of Alliance's program of independence.

Controlled Chaos

It was one thing for Alliance to teach their girls the limits of government. But it was quite another to try and teach them how to survive in a system of limited government. Despite evidence to the contrary, the Alliance staff did know they were working with extremely disadvantaged young women. Their girls lacked formal education, came from extremely impoverished backgrounds, resided in the most troubled of areas, and were bound by few family ties. The staff were also aware of what all of this meant for the girls' lives. A glimpse at the girls' school records indicated that most of them had moved around constantly—from city to city and from foster home to foster home. A look at their guardianship records revealed constant changes in who was legally responsible for them—from biological parents to grandparents to aunts to other state appointees. And even a short conversation with them revealed long histories of neglect and abandonment—from relatives to lovers to foster parents. Their lives tended to lack even the semblance of stability and consistency. Needless to say, these were hardly the life conditions under which the staff's version of "independence" would likely flourish.

Alliance could have responded to these realities in a variety of ways. Like other state institutions dealing with a similar population, it could have tried to stabilize the girls' life conditions in the hopes of enabling changes in their behavior. But Alliance took a different approach. Instead of altering the conditions of the girls' lives, the staff seemed to replicate them, particularly in the instability and uncertainty of their daily lives. To an outsider, life at Alliance seemed quite chaotic and unpredictable. Nobody ever seemed to be in charge; the daily schedule was always in flux; and the girls' in-house activities remained more or less unsupervised. The staff claimed this was all part of their master plan—by re-creating a life of uncertainty, they would force the girls to figure out what they should do on their own. Yet it was always unclear how much of the staff's laissez-faire approach was intentional. In reality, the staff were quite disorganized, which led to constant changes in the facility's activities and plans. They also preferred to work in the back office, which left the impression that no one was in charge and the girls had the run of the house. So, as with the home's reliance on AFDC, it is possible that the staff simply transformed a liability into a virtue—insisting that the lack of centralized control was part of their agenda to teach the girls what life would be like in a state of limited government.

Whether or not it was planned, chaos often prevailed at Alliance. As long as the girls remained in the facility, they could do more or less what they wanted. In all my time at Alliance, I never saw a staff member force a girl to wake up on time, attend school, or participate in house meetings and functions. Walking into Alliance in the morning, it was hard to tell if there were collective activities underway, since a few girls always seemed to be milling about the house, seemingly clueless as to what others were doing. The house's unpredictability was exacerbated by the staff's continual revision of the daily schedule. Although Rachel insisted on school time every morning, her lessons constantly changed, often on a whim. Plans for special, week-long lessons were often abandoned midway for no apparent reason. When the girls arrived to class on any given day, they usually had no idea what they would be studying. While they were supposed to alternate among math, social studies, and English, this never happened. In fact, the bulk of their school time was devoted to art projects, which were not even part of Alliance's standard curriculum.[24]

After school, it was anyone's guess as to what would occur. The official schedule bore little resemblance to actual life. In the afternoon, the girls usually went on some sort of outing with their children. But the exact destinations remained unclear; the staff routinely cancelled outings and added new ones at the spur of the moment. For instance, every Tuesday, the girls were to go to the local high school to turn in their time sheets and record their attendance. Yet I never saw them make the trip. The staff always came up with something else that had to be done. Quite often, an idea would come to Rachel during the morning lesson and then

become the afternoon outing. For instance, during a math lesson on frac-
tions, Janice mentioned how she calculated how much hair dye to use
on her long hair. After other girls mentioned their own dye formulas,
Rachel changed the afternoon plan: suddenly, the scheduled walk to the
park was replaced by a trip to a local beauty school to check on admissions procedures. Then there was the time our outing to the library was
abruptly switched to a trip to fast-food restaurants for an exercise in
filling out employment applications. Rachel insisted that these changes
made Alliance life "fresh." But they also made it impossible for the girls
to plan anything. Debra put the situation best during one of Rachel's
lectures on limited government. Rachel was looking for an example of a
dictatorship and suggested Alliance. Debra jumped in to disagree: "We
got all these people saying different stuff and telling us to decide. There
ain't no one in control here. It's no dictatorship. It's anarchy."

This lack of centralized control extended to the girls' experiences outside the facility. The staff rarely monitored or supervised the girls' movements on the outside. After watching over the girls as they journeyed
to their destination, the staff's control would cease once they reached
it. Initially, this lack of supervision shocked me. On my first house outing to a nearby park, I was stunned by the complete lack of oversight of
the girls. For over two hours, the girls came and went as they pleased,
wandering around and talking to strangers. None of this prompted staff
concern; when I asked where a particular girl was, the staff members
simply shrugged their shoulders. With time, I learned that this was the
norm—wherever we went, the girls had freedom of movement. Never
mind that this left them free to engage in all sort of possible rule violations. While in the library, they could use pay phones to make unauthorized calls; while in stores, they could purchase all sorts of off-limits items.
This was all part of the laissez-faire approach. By refusing to watch over
the girls, the staff claimed to be facilitating their independence; by not
telling them what to do, the girls had to choose to do the right thing, of
their own volition.

Here, too, rewards awaited those who ended up doing the right thing.
In addition to Rachel's Brennan Bucks, Alliance's overall program was
designed to reward those who exhibited initiative, independence, and

self-control amid chaos. The program was comprised of a series of "steps" the girls moved up when they did anything the staff considered evidence of their budding independence. In my time at Alliance, I watched girls move up the steps when they did everything from take the GED exam to enroll in courses at a nearby beauty school to go on job interviews to secure postrelease childcare and housing. The girls got more credit for these activities if they did them on their own, without staff help or prodding. As the girls ascended up the step system, they had access to more freedom and privileges. Some incentives were built into the formal program. Once a girl reached a certain step level, the staff notified the court and probation department of her progress; they also placed official program evaluations in the girl's court files. Other incentives were more informal. For instance, the staff regularly allowed girls at the higher steps to ignore house rules: they could use the phone after hours, make more than the allotted number of phone calls, dye their hair, and wear revealing clothing while on outings. In effect, the staff gave these girls even more leeway in daily life since, as counselor Colorado once put it, "they're gonna make it cause they're doin' things for themselves . . . not just asking others for help all the time."

In addition, the staff celebrated these girls as the "stars" of the house. Alliance had a few girls they considered models of self-reliance and self-sufficiency. Maria, a seventeen-year-old former drug dealer, was one such girl. Over and over again, the staff applauded Maria for getting her act together and moving up the house steps quickly. In preparation for her release, Maria began to look for a job and submitted applications to neighboring fast-food chains. She found childcare for her son at a local center. She made arrangements to take her GED. She even went back on the birth-control pill, which, according to Charlene, was evidence that she had "taken control of her own body." For all these reasons, Maria became the superstar of the program and was held out as an example for the other girls. "Why can't Nikita be more like her?" Dwan asked in a staff discussion about whether to take Nikita back after a "time out" in juvenile hall. In this way, girls who became the real success stories demonstrated more than rhetorical competency in Alliance's discourse of need; they did more than recite the perils of state dependence and public assistance. They also demonstrated new life practices—and proved they could survive in a state of limited government, without having their hands held or being told what to do.

Of all the rewards given to those who demonstrated these changes, the most coveted was motherhood. At Alliance, the girls had to earn motherhood. They did so by exhibiting the initiative the staff tried to instill in them. Those girls who showed signs of breaking their dependencies were given more access to their children and more freedom to raise them. For instance, "stars" like Maria had the flexibility to decide what to feed their kids, how to dress them, and where to take them on weekend outings. The reverse was also true: the staff frequently punished recalcitrant girls by restricting the availability of their children. It was quite common for the staff to take away the children of those who refused to "take the bull by the horns."[25] Usually, such restrictions were followed by speeches about how impossible it was to be a good mother while remaining passive and indifferent. Moreover, whenever a girl acted out, the first thing the staff did was to remove her child from the area, claiming that the girl might harm the child in anger. Yet such removals also served as a key form of punishment—a way to deny the caretaker role to those who failed to conform to Alliance's standards of independence.

Perhaps the best example of this denial was Alliance's battle over childcare. When I began working at Alliance, the staff allowed the girls to keep their kids with them in the classroom during the school day. With time, Rachel began to disapprove of the arrangement, sensing that the girls used their children to avoid schoolwork. "Instead of pushing themselves, they just started playing with them [the kids] when they don't understand something," she once explained to me. When her Brennan Bucks program failed to alter this, she demanded that the children be removed from the classroom. The girls interpreted this as a punishment and refused to work altogether. "If my baby can't be here with me, I ain't doin' shit," Janice proclaimed. Then Rachel went on strike, arguing that it was impossible to teach girls who placed "motherhood" before "education." Finally, director Marlene gave in and provided childcare. This concession to Rachel was clearly a reprimand for the girls—retribution for the girls' refusal to alter their priorities.

So although the girls' status as mothers is what got them to Alliance, motherhood quickly became a reward for those who could rid themselves of state reliance and exhibit independence. Only after they demonstrated their ability to "do the right thing" amid chaos could the girls enjoy unfettered access to their children. In this way, the staff's use of motherhood was symptomatic of Alliance's program of independence. At its core, this program was designed to revamp the girls' social roles and reorder their priorities. The goal was to convince them that state dependency was destructive and to create an institutional environment that prompted them to live differently. At the center of this environment was an incentive structure that remunerated all signs of initiative and independence. And at the center of this incentive structure were enticements to lead girls in the right direction—from economic freedom to consumer choice to maternal control. So by the time the girls made their way down the rocky road to independence, the cultural rewards awaiting them could not have been grander: as workers they would earn material autonomy, as citizens they would be free from state surveillance, and as mothers they would determine their own caretaking practices. The possibilities were endless.

TRAINING WOMEN WHAT TO NEED

From the perspective of the early 1990s, it is easy to see why the Alliance staff viewed their facility as an alternative to traditional corrections. Structurally, Alliance was at the forefront of changes that would sweep through different state spaces in the following decade. Their facility was a smaller, more "homelike" version of the big, anonymous juvenile-justice institutions of the period. It was one step removed from the coercive, punitive "core" of the justice system—subjected to the system's rules and regulations, but operating separate from it on a daily basis. Its organization was more decentralized and diverse than that of conventional penal facilities. Its institutional logic combined that of a state facility like CYA and of a local NGO. Its funding structure was a complicated mixture of funds from different public programs. And its staff were comprised of a new breed of state actor—guided less by bureaucratic imperatives and norms and more by political commitments and feminist ideals.

Even the staff's discourse of need seemed somewhat distinctive. Their discourse made definitive claims about what women needed and how they should meet those needs. Of course, there is nothing distinctive about Alliance's claim to superior knowledge of what its female charges needed. Since the nineteenth century, female reformers have staked claims to the state on the basis of their unique insight into poor women's needs. And, for decades, female state actors construed women's needs as related to their dependency—often by deeming their familial relationships as undependable and by tightening their ties to public institutions. Yet this was what made Alliance's discourse more distinctive: its approach to female dependency diverged from that of generations of state reformers before it. Instead of normalizing female dependence, it tried to convince young women they "needed" to end their reliance on others. Rather than pushing them to replace male support with state assistance, it tried to get women to become self-sufficient. Alliance's was a dependency discourse with a twist, an early attempt to change the meaning of women's attachments to others and of their social relationships.

Alliance's dependency discourse did not emanate magically from some abstract cultural condition, nor was it imposed on the facility through mandates attached to state funds and resources. Instead, it was a culturally available script that captured the imaginations and interests of this diverse group of state actors. In part, its resonance came from the struggle between Alliance staff members—all women—and their own institutional dependence. It also came from their assessments of what allied and divided them from one another and from their charges. Dependency discourse thus served multiple needs for those institutionalizing it. So the Alliance staff set out to transform it into concrete institutional practices—through everything from the house's step system to its Brennan Bucks to its controlled chaos to its restrictions on girls' mothering.

Through these institutional practices it became clear that Alliance's needs talk served as a form of governance. It was intended to guide and manage social conduct. The staff strove to make the girls conversant in this needs talk and prepared to explain why dependency was so damaging for them. They also set out to shape the girls' behavior and push them to act in ways consistent with Alliance ideals. Needless to say, if all went as planned, the end result would have aligned the girls' behavior with the needs of government. Alliance's practices would have taught the girls just how little they were entitled to—and how turning to public support was a mark of their troubles and criminality. The girls would have been left believing that state assistance came with restrictions on their freedom of movement and choice—and that such restrictions were entirely legitimate and acceptable.

But was this what the girls actually took from Alliance's practices? Did they become governable subjects? How did they respond to this state of independence?

TWO

Deconstructing Dependency

NEEDS, RIGHTS, AND THE STRUGGLE
FOR ENTITLEMENT

"Who's in charge here?" Jamika asked as she barged into a closed-door staff meeting. Stunned by her flagrant violation of a key house rule, everyone fell silent. "I said I want to know who is in charge," Jamika continued. "I hate this place and I want to talk to the head." Director Marlene reminded Jamika that there was not one person in charge at Alliance and instructed her to go to her room to cool off. "I need someone to help me," Jamika pleaded, with tears streaming down her face. If no one would help her, she wanted to leave—even if it meant returning to the California Youth Authority. The staff agreed that maybe this was best, again telling Jamika to go to her room as they made the necessary arrangements. After Jamika left, Marlene rolled her eyes and ordered the meeting to continue. Everyone then returned to the discussion about what kind of lunch meat to buy the house that week.

A few minutes later, Jamika interrupted the meeting again—this time to apologize for her earlier behavior. "Well, we can't just accept your apology," counselor Colorado proclaimed. "You need to live with the consequences of your actions." Hysterical, Jamika ran out of the staff office. The sound of the front door slamming prompted the staff to rush outside. By the time they exited the facility, Jamika had made it down the block, stopping only after her eight-month pregnant body gave in. When Colorado reached her, Jamika was lying on the sidewalk, crying. "So now you want to help me, but before no one cared." As Colorado approached, Jamika spit at her to warn her off. "Get up girl, don't let them keep you down," Janice yelled from an open window, prompting other Alliance girls to shout their own words of encouragement to Jamika from the porch. By the time Jamika was coaxed back to the house, the police had arrived. She was immediately handcuffed and returned to CYA to complete her sentence.

Whenever I recount scenes like this, I am usually asked similar questions: So what happened to her baby? Did she give birth in CYA? Where did the baby go afterward? In fact, in most discussions of my work at Alliance, it is usually the experiences of the Alliance children that prompt particular interest. This is quite understandable: indeed, it is hard to fathom that the United States now imprisons families and incarcerates infants. And, indeed, the image of small children being raised in penal institutions should alarm and unnerve. Among other things, it throws into bold relief how mass imprisonment reverberates through kin networks to reshape the conditions of caretaking.[1] Yet of the many ways that life at Alliance surprised me, here was one of the most unexpected: the story of the inmates' children turned out to be the less interesting one. Perhaps it was because the children were so small that it was difficult to see Alliance's effects on them. Perhaps it was because many were too young to respond to what went on around them. Perhaps it was because the kids' alternatives, from foster care to unstable relatives, were so unappealing that life at Alliance did not seem so bad after all. Or perhaps it was because the children appeared to be doing alright at Alliance—at least they had three meals a day, a warm place to sleep, and a lot of caregivers surrounding them.

What is more, the children were not the main target of the Alliance regime. They were tools, or a means to an end, for the Alliance staff. The inmates were the objects of intervention. They were the ones the staff wanted to mould and, ultimately, to empower. Yet the inmates were also the ones who had the most to say about this empowerment agenda. It turned out that they disagreed with almost everything about it, from its representation of their past to its plan for the present to its recipe for the future. Over and over again they opposed Alliance's dependency discourse and its ideal of limited government.[2] In response, they engaged in continual battles with the staff over what they needed and felt entitled to—interpretive battles that made this part of the Alliance story particularly explosive and revealing. This chapter begins by describing these battles and examining why the girls felt so threatened by Alliance's needs talk.

As the Alliance girls waged these institutional wars, something quite interesting happened: cracks and fissures began to surface in the staff's narrative. Although the staff were probably unaware of it, their needs talk could be reinterpreted as encompassing expansive notions of women's entitlements. Their arguments about the joys of independence through wage labor implied that women should have access to well-paid employment; their use of market incentives to mark good behavior implied that women should be remunerated for fulfilling their responsibilities; and their insistence on "taking the bull by the horns" implied that women should have the ability to act on their own behalf. The Alliance girls picked up on these implications and used them as a platform from which to demand a broader understanding of the realities of their lives. They pointed out how difficult it was for young women like them to secure employment, obtain a decent education, engage in effective carework, and control their own bodies. This is another reason why their side of the story is so intriguing and revealing: the Alliance girls ended up reinventing dependency discourse and turning it into a channel through which claims to justice and fairness could be voiced and acted on.

And act on these claims they did. As I reveal in the second part of the chapter, Alliance's institutional battles did not remain at the discursive level. Once they opened up gaps in the program, the girls acted to defend what they perceived to be their interests. On the one hand, they embarked on individual acts of rebellion—by fighting with the staff, manipulating their babies, and escaping from the facility. The girls also engaged in a variety of collective actions designed to protest the facility's needs talk and institutional practices—by going on strike, creating their so-called Welfare Club, and using other state actors as protective shields. As I argue in this chapter, these individual and collective acts of protest not only helped deconstruct Alliance's program of dependency but also undermined the facility's ability to regulate and govern its girls.

THE POLITICS OF DEPENDENCY

Although the Alliance staff often exaggerated their role as rescuers of "their girls," many of these young women had endured long and difficult journeys to reach the group home. It was unquestionably difficult to get CYA to release girls to Alliance's care. Simply informing CYA inmates of their eligibility for the program was a challenge; unlike women in adult prisons, who share information about different community-based programs, girls in the juvenile system are frequently unaware of the options available to them.[3] Thus, most Alliance girls found out about the facility through a judge or probation officer. What is more, it was usually these sympathetic justice officials who took the lead in getting them to the facility, either by notifying the Alliance staff of their eligibility or by forcing CYA officials to approve their transfer to the group home. Yet even with such legal assistance, most girls told stories of having to struggle to get to Alliance: some were given false information about their eligibility; others were told the facility was full or no longer accepting new inmates; still others were made to wait so long that their pregnancies had advanced so far that transferring them to a facility in another part of the state no longer seemed feasible.[4]

In addition to viewing these obstacles as evidence of CYA's opposition to their work, the Alliance staff claimed that such practices affected the kind of girls who made it to their facility. On the one hand, some staff members claimed that CYA only let go of the most troubled young women, those with problems so severe that the CYA staff were not equipped to deal with them. On the other hand, some staff insisted that CYA officials' paternalism prompted them to "protect" certain girls from incarceration. In this scenario, Alliance got those girls who did not seem to belong in prison, girls with less serious problems and/or who conformed to gender norms.[5]

Alliance did not collect data on the girls' backgrounds, so it is impossible to determine which interpretation was correct. But the Alliance girls were such a diverse group that both assessments were probably accurate. The girls came from across California, from urban and suburban environments. They had committed an array of crimes, from drug possession to assault with a deadly weapon to armed robbery to gang-related offenses. They were also racially and ethnically diverse, comprised equally of African Americans, Anglos, and Latinas.[6] While these differences could have become a recipe for institutional disaster, they did not. Instead of turning on one another, the Alliance girls turned their differences into a site of allegiance from which to oppose the staff's program of dependency.

The Danger of Dependency Discourse

When the girls arrived at Alliance, few of them anticipated that they would form such a contentious relationship with the facility. Quite the opposite: at least initially, most of them shared the staff's sense that they had been successfully rescued. Having been released from the confines of CYA, most girls enjoyed their first few days at Alliance as if they were on a honeymoon. They reveled in the homelike environment, walking around the facility in awe of its amenities and décor. "Shit, I ain't ever lived in such a nice place," Gloria exclaimed while on a tour of the house. "Damn, we even have one of those VCRs!" They marveled at the well-stocked kitchen and the idea that they could prepare many of their own meals. They celebrated bedrooms they shared with only one other girl, seemingly unfazed by the rooms' excessively feminine furnishings and accoutrements.[7] Most of all, they relished their newfound access to their children. Those who were pregnant talked incessantly about what a relief it was to plan a life with their kids; they no longer had to come to terms with being separated from their babies after birth. Those who already had children were delighted to be reunited with them; they had spent much of their time in CYA depressed about their inability to be a part of their kids' lives. In those first few days at Alliance, the future seemed bright.

As with many honeymoons, the Alliance one rarely lasted more than a week. What began as optimism quickly morphed into an "us versus them" stance toward those in charge of the facility. I encountered this on my first day in the facility. Having spent much of the day impressed by the homey surroundings and the staff's talk of empowerment, I was surprised to overhear a group of girls whispering in the classroom. "I don't know about the new one," Nikita noted, clearly referring to me. "They have us outnumbered now and I don't like it." Then Maria hypothesized that my presence would allow "them" to control "us" more effectively. Initially, I interpreted their comments as a natural reaction to confinement and the realities of their incarceration. But with time, I realized these remarks as my first clue to how oppressed the girls felt in Alliance—and how their us versus them attitude emerged from the program's two main pillars.

First, there was the staff's resounding dependency discourse. It is impossible to exaggerate the girls' opposition to this needs talk. You could see it on their faces—whenever the staff launched into lectures on the dangers of dependence and virtues of independence, the girls would roll their eyes and tune out. At times they also seemed disturbed and even scared by the discourse. They were troubled by the way it pathologized them for seeking assistance. They hated the implication that they were failures if they looked to others for support—or, in Mildred's words, if they refused to be "self-full." In a poignant outburst, Jamika made these implications explicit one afternoon, after a long, contentious house meeting in which the girls were accused of being too needy and passive. After remaining silent for most of the meeting, Jamika proclaimed that the staff's "talk of dependence" sounded like Ronald Reagan. Those were fighting words, and Jamika knew it: as soon as she voiced them, she stood up as if to signal her readiness for battle. This prompted schoolteacher Rachel to turn red with anger and counselor Charlene to send Jamika a warning: "Just stop. Stop and think, girl, before you go any further." When Jamika continued with the Reagan analogy, she was sent to her room and the meeting came to an end.

In many ways, it was not surprising that the girls found dependency discourse so threatening. Despite their differences, the girls did have one important thing in common: they had few private, familial resources at their disposal. Many of them could be considered "familyless." Some came from severely troubled and unstable familial environments; others came from families that had broken apart due to imprisonment, substance abuse, or violence; still others had never experienced family life per se, having been shuffled among foster homes and state institutions for most of their lives. These familial realities became painfully obvious on Alliance's designated visiting days, when the girls sat alone and waited in vain for visitors; or when the girls earned weekend home visit passes—only to discover that they could not use the passes because their families were not interested in seeing them.[8] Moreover, the girls had trouble forming their own familial ties. Many told stories of being left by their boyfriends and lovers once they became pregnant. While they still dreamed of these men, and fantasized about futures with them, they were basically without men. This reality also became apparent at tragic moments, like the week before Valentines Day, when the girls spent hours making cards for "their men," decorating them with romantic poems and proclamations of their undying love. When the big day came, disappointment inevitably set in after the girls failed to receive anything from their men in return.

Almost ironically, these kinds of experiences forced the girls to develop their own survival skills of "independence." They had certainly learned to rely on themselves quite a bit in their lives. Since most of them had grown up without any sort of familial support system, they were forced to figure out where else to look for nurturing and care. Since most of them were raised without the stable, consistent presence of parents or family members, they were forced to discover their own ways to anchor themselves. And since most of them had experienced abandonment and betrayal by men they thought they could depend on, they were forced to struggle to preserve themselves and their babies on their own. So the Alliance staff's proclamations that they rely on themselves even more must have made them wary and exasperated. Given the realities of their personal lives, it is no wonder Alliance's diagnosis of their dependency was met with suspicion and opposition.

These same realities also made the girls suspicious of Alliance's agenda to break their reliance on the state. The Alliance girls had few survival networks and yet an urgent need for support. After all, they were teen mothers—young women with small children dependent on them. So it is not surprising that they rejected the call to rid themselves of the one safety net available to them, or that they contested the staff's reading of their past, present, and future through the lens of dependency. Instead of viewing their past as distorted by state dependency, they often recalled how state programs and institutions had been the safety nets that caught them when they fell—whether a much-needed Aid to Families with Dependent Children check or an urgent foster-care placement. They were thus troubled by the staff's insistence that they deny themselves this fallback position. Because the girls' ability to "free" themselves from state assistance was limited at best, Alliance's continual proclamations that they should do just that sounded threatening; its insistence that they break their institutional dependency did not appear viable or desirable.

The same was true of the second key aspect of Alliance's program—its emphasis on doing the right thing amid chaos and uncertainty. Nothing provoked more anger and panic in the girls than the instability of everyday life in the facility. They despised that no one seemed to be in charge and in control. They pleaded for consistency and coherence in their schedule—frequently arguing that such stability would help them plan their lives more effectively. When the staff did not comply with their requests, the girls pleaded some more. It got to the point when even the most seemingly insignificant change in their routine prompted pushback from the girls: they demanded a justification for each and every shift in schedule or alteration in agenda. "This is my class and I get to decide what we'll learn when," Rachel declared after an hour-long argument about why she had changed the morning lesson from English to social studies.

Of all the explosions that erupted between the girls and the staff, the most intense were those that involved sudden or unexpected changes in the girls' routines. In fact, this was what set off Jamika in the incident described at the beginning of this chapter—that morning, without consulting her, Jamika's counselor changed her schedule so she could meet with her psychologist instead of going to school. This enraged Jamika, prompting her to barge into the staff meeting and flee the facility altogether. Only a week earlier, Janice, another Alliance girl, responded similarly to a change in the daily program. It was an unusually warm March day, so Rachel decided to take advantage of the weather. Instead of going to the high school to turn in their attendance records as planned, she decided to take the girls on an unplanned trip to a nearby pool. But Rachel was stunned by the girls' response: as soon as they heard about the change in plans, they went crazy. How dare she "mess with" their schedule? Who did she think she was to unilaterally change their day? Janice insisted that she was not going. When Rachel told her she had to go, Janice lost her temper. "Fucking bitch, fucking bitch," she repeated as she stormed out of the classroom and upstairs to the living room where her son, Shane, was sleeping.

Rachel followed her and a fight ensued. With every curse that came out of Janice's mouth, Rachel threw a warning note at her—each note carried with it a "point" that would be counted against any requests Janice made for special house privileges or home visits. This continued for a few minutes until Janice announced that she had enough and was taking Shane up to her room. In response, Rachel put a warning note on Shane's head and instructed Janice not to touch him. That was the last straw. Janice started throwing things around the living room and gesturing as if she was going to hit Rachel. "How dare you touch my son!" she yelled. "How dare you tell me that I can't touch my son. He's mine, not yours." More toys were thrown; one of them narrowly missed Rachel's head. When there was nothing left to throw, Janice glared at Rachel as she grabbed Shane and left the room: "Don't ever touch my baby again or tell me when I can touch him. He's not yours to touch. Take this as your warning."[9]

The intensity of Janice's response suggests that she was reacting to more than a simple change in her daily routine. The pervasive uncertainty at Alliance seemed to overwhelm the girls emotionally and to conjure up intense feelings of rage and anxiety. Perhaps the instability took them back to the unpredictability of their childhoods—when they moved from home to home, or city to city, with little warning. Perhaps it harkened back to the many times others had abandoned them and ignored their desires. Perhaps it reminded them of just how little control they had over their lives. Or perhaps it prompted them to recognize just how little their opinions mattered. Whatever the source, Alliance's institutional instability destabilized the girls. The rage Janice exhibited when Rachel pulled Shane into their fight was also typical: many girls went ballistic when their status as mothers was called into question. It was as if Alliance tried to claim the one relationship they had some control over and the one social role they found security in.

Care versus Dependence

The girls' sense of destabilization then led to intense verbal confrontations with the staff. Arguments between "us" and "them" occurred so frequently and loudly that they often drowned out what was actually said. But had the staff been able to listen to what the girls were saying, they might have found some merit in their arguments. They might even have found them to be quite ingenious. Irrespective of the specific issue at hand, the girls advanced two arguments with striking consistency: they questioned the staff's conflation of their need for help with state dependence and they accused the staff of ignoring key realities of their lives. What is more, they did so in ways that drew on central elements of Alliance's dependency discourse—thus mobilizing Alliance's needs talk at the same time that they challenged it.

To understand how the girls did this, it is important to recall that Alliance differentiated itself from the "system" by claiming it was responsive to girls' needs. Yet the girls saw things differently—they continually questioned just how well Alliance understood what they needed. This divergence then evolved into an ongoing battle over who knew what the girls needed: the staff stressed the need to "take the bull by the horns," while the girls contended that they needed to be helped and cared for. The girls asked for guidance and direction all the time—even when they did things they were entirely competent at. Whenever Rachel gave the girls an assignment to do on their own, revolt ensued. "Excuse me, but

I need some help over here," was Yolanda's constant refrain, which she repeated whenever she had a task to complete. The girls even demanded assistance when they did art projects; they asked for help cutting paper, gluing images, or drawing designs. In fact, they always seemed to be seeking attention and help. For them, getting help was a sign that others cared for them—not of a dangerous dependence they had developed on others. It was a sign they were worthy of the nurturing and guidance that most young people crave, even if only implicitly and indirectly.

On occasion, the girls made the distinction between care and dependence explicitly. Tired by the girls' constant demands that she help them, Rachel began leaving the classroom after she gave the girls assignments to complete. She claimed this was the only way to get them to do the work "on their own." The girls knew these were tests, moments when they were to demonstrate initiative. So as soon as Rachel left the room, they would stop working altogether and begin talking about how they were not getting the support they needed. The girls spent hours detailing how their educational needs were being ignored and how Rachel's absence was proof of this. While Rachel interpreted this behavior as laziness, the girls insisted on the opposite—for them, being left alone in the classroom was evidence that no one cared and they had been abandoned yet again. "She must think that I can pass this [GED exam] all by myself," Janice declared during one complaint session. "Like it will happen magically . . . even if she don't help us or nothing."

Thus, imagine the girls' reaction when Rachel really did decide to leave them: toward the end of my fieldwork, Rachel concluded she had had enough and needed to find another teaching job. Not surprisingly, the meeting to announce her departure was very emotional and tense. Even though the girls had a contentious relationship with Rachel, they valued the time she devoted to them. Hence, they immediately interpreted the news of Rachel's resignation as proof of their neglect. Or, as Nikita put it, that "no one in the world cares about us and that's why we are so fucked up." So the girls used the occasion to educate the staff about how their needs had been misinterpreted. "Maybe if someone really cared for us and showed concern, we could improve our lives," Mildred suggested. Janice followed up by arguing that they could not do everything on their own; even when they made an effort, no one seemed to care or acknowledge their endeavors.

As the girls spoke, the staff shook their heads, insisting that the girls had demonstrated just how "needy" they were. "This is exactly the problem," Rachel proclaimed. "You blame others, you never blame yourself . . . that's what got you in trouble and it's what's gonna be trouble in the future." In response, the girls protested that, once again, the staff made them feel guilty for needing help. Isn't the role of the teacher to help students? How could they be expected to change without guidance and direction? Wasn't this the Alliance promise? As they went back and forth for over an hour, the girls' questions went unanswered. But the girls raised some important points: indeed, there was a difference between care and dependence. And, indeed, the staff's discourse often confused and conflated them.

The longer these debates went on, the less likely the girls were to have their informal pleas for care and nurturing met. So the more likely they were to transform their pleas into formal demands—thereby expressing a sense of entitlement to assistance and care. After months of listening to staff accusations of how weak and helpless she was, Tonya launched into a speech about how Alliance made it a "crime" to ask for help and that was "all messed up." It was all messed up because it was the staff's *job* to help them; it was their *responsibility* to show them guidance. Maria, the house superstar, was the girls' most articulate spokeswoman here: she frequently reminded the staff that they had come to Alliance to get help. "We're not here for our health," she always said. Maria was also quick to note that even CYA recognized its obligation to help inmates "get our shit together." After all, that's why they were incarcerated in the first place. In one particularly heated fight with the staff, Maria demanded to see Alliance's CYA contract—she was sure it said something about how the staff had to help the inmates. In this way, girls like Maria turned the staff's dependency discourse against them. The girls also advanced a fairly damning critique of this discourse, suggesting that the staff's calls to independence hardly made their approach "alternative." Instead, perhaps these calls were excuses for neglect and the shirking of responsibility. Perhaps Alliance was not so different from CYA after all.

In addition, the girls questioned the applicability of Alliance's dependency discourse for young women like them. In doing so, they suggested that the staff develop a better understanding of the social constraints the girls faced in becoming "independent." For example, one of the staff's favorite ways to convince the girls of the virtues of independence was to draw on their own life experiences—staff members discussed being forced into dependent relationships, their feelings of disempowerment, and their struggle to break free.[10] Clearly, the goal was to get the girls to envision concrete ways to follow suit. But instead of prompting the girls to see the light, the staff's stories served to highlight their differences from the girls. After listening to these accounts, the girls often asked some pointed questions: How old were they when they faced these struggles? Were they teenagers? Did they have family to fall back on and help them out? Did they have criminal records following them around and limiting their employment options? Did they have small children to worry about and take care of?

Here, too, a latent critique developed through the girls' questions. By pointing to the specific limitations they faced as familyless teen mothers with felony convictions, the girls questioned the viability and desirability of the staff's needs talk. Embedded in their questions was also the suggestion that the staff look beyond the confines of Alliance and their own experiences to acknowledge the social realities the girls would confront upon release. "It's like they [the staff] don't know what's up," Lakisha explained to me. "The talk is OK for them but not for us. They aren't with us." The girls' sense that the staff was out of touch was one reason why they kept their distance when the staff tried to plan their postrelease lives. On house outings around the neighborhood, staff members like Rachel, Colorado, and Dwan often tried to plot the girls' futures, noting where they could work, live, and secure childcare. As they did this, the girls always seemed a bit detached—as if they knew the talk of their new lives was little more than fantasy. "Ya know, it's easy for Rachel to say we can do it on our own," Janice once put it succinctly. "She gots all her degrees. She don't need no help and says we don't either."

One of the most common ways the girls got this message across was through the idiom of "fairness." Fights about what was un/fair and who was un/fair repeated themselves like broken records at Alliance. Interestingly, these fairness fights surfaced most often in regard to Rachel's Brennan Bucks program. Like the larger consumer market it was modeled after, few formal rules guided the bucks market. Rachel wanted it this way; she claimed it forced the girls to figure out how to exhibit initiative on their own. Instead, it ended up leading to continual battles over what behavior or action should count as bucks-worthy. Initially, bucks were to be given only when a girl did something exceptional. With time, the girls insisted on getting bucks when they adhered to the norms of everyday life—they expected bucks for waking up in the morning, feeding their babies, getting to school on time, and so on. If Rachel questioned their demands, the girls responded with arguments about how "unfair" it would be if they were treated any differently from her: since she got paid when she did what was expected of her, it was only "fair" that they get bucks for fulfilling their responsibilities. Unable to counter their logic or concede that the "market" did not treat all women equally, Rachel eventually gave in to their expansive notion of bucks worthiness.

Yet the bucks battles did not end there. The girls pushed it further with new fights over how many bucks should be given for a particular behavior. Was it really fair that waking up on time got one buck while coming down to school on time could yield three or four? Why did feeding your baby get only one buck while helping another girl with schoolwork got three? It often seemed like the bulk of Rachel's time was spent bartering with the girls over bucks. In these exchanges, the girls remembered everything: they recalled exactly how many bucks other girls received for an activity weeks earlier. They recited the rationales Rachel gave for her allocation of bucks months earlier. And they advanced quite sophisticated arguments about why certain allocative criteria should be used over others—like Janice's argument that a behavior should be worth more if it was done by only one girl since this meant she had more initiative than others. When confronted with such arguments, Rachel usually gave in. "The squeaky wheel always gets the grease," she once explained to me. Yet these battles indicated something more significant. In a sense, the girls reminded Rachel that, in the real world, economic incentives were not distributed evenly and markets did not operate fairly—both were subject to barter and manipulation, which not all women could engage in equally.

As the girls argued and tussled with the staff, they often acted like "typical" teenagers. Indeed, as I watched the daily skirmishes, I was frequently struck by how much the girls' protests resembled normal teenage behavior. Even the issues they struggled over seemed reminiscent of teenage rebellion: from their desire to gain some control over their everyday lives to their claims that others did not understand them to their obsession with defining what was un/fair. And it might have been possible to dismiss their protests simply as teenage angst—had it not been for the context. The girls were official wards of the state of California, convicted felons serving serious sentences in the state penal system. Unlike other teenagers, their rebellions did not occur within familial relationships of trust, care, or even longevity; their relationships at Alliance were far less intimate, trusting, and steady than those of other teenagers. Unlike real parental relationships, their connections with the staff were extremely conditional; the girls were subjected to constant judgment and assessment, often of an official nature. So, in the course of their rebellion, if the girls overstepped a line, misjudged a boundary, or had an explosive reaction to something—all things that teenagers are known for—the consequences of their actions were far more serious. If they got overly emotional and broke a few rules, as Jamika had done on that fateful spring day, the police would be brought in to end their rebellion.

In fact, it was Alliance's structure of power and control that ended up heightening the significance of the girls' contestation. The penal context effectively upped the ante of the girls' rebellion, transforming what could have been individual teenage angst into an incisive social critique. Through their battles, the girls developed broad arguments to oppose Alliance's dependency discourse. And their arguments emphasized issues of justice: the girls pushed the staff to differentiate between care and dependence, to acknowledge their claim to social assistance, and to recognize the social realities of their lives. In doing so, the girls extended dependency discourse to encompass an expansive notion of their needs and to speak in a language of rights. So while the staff used dependency discourse to get the girls to take individual responsibility and appreciate the limits of government, the effect was very different—the discourse morphed into a social critique and a defense of collective responsibility and rights.

To be sure, the Alliance staff found it easy to dismiss this critique. After all, it was voiced by teenage girls in not always the most articulate ways. But while the staff could dismiss the girls' words, they found it more difficult to ignore the individual and collective actions that emerged from these words.

FIGHTING THE POWER, STRUGGLING FOR ENTITLEMENT

Political sociology is full of examples of the yawning gaps that separate analyses of power from responses to it. If it were easy to turn a sense of injustice into collective action, large-scale protest would be less an exception and more the rule. The rarity of such revolts is one reason why social scientists often find themselves researching everyday acts of resistance.[11] It is also why many such analyses end up documenting how everyday battles miss their intended targets—as when welfare recipients see only the power wielded over them by welfare workers and fail to acknowledge the systemic roots of their dislocation.[12] As a result, feelings of discontent can end up spewing out in all directions to become self-destructive— as when prison inmates turn on one another as they grapple with the humiliation and dehumanization of incarceration.[13]

One of the most intriguing aspects of the Alliance girls' opposition to the facility's dependency discourse was how the girls avoided this depoliticizing path. There was a striking consistency between the girls' analysis of the power structure and their protests against it. In their everyday battles, the girls rarely became distracted from their common targets; they rarely turned on one another through infighting or backbiting. The possibility for such internal strife was clearly present given the girls' diverse backgrounds. Yet, even as they engaged in individual acts of rebellion, the girls retained an us versus them stance. This attitude not only served to ally them but also motivated the collective actions they planned and executed. While it is tempting to attribute the girls' ability to sustain collective resistance to their strategic brilliance, it had more to do with the institutional tools at their disposal. It turns out that there were numerous practical and discursive resources available to the girls, many of which they mobilized to disrupt Alliance's program of dependency.

Singing the Praises of Welfare

On an everyday level, there were three primary groups at Alliance: the girls, their babies, and the state.[14] This made Alliance a relatively closed environment. It was also a confining environment in which the girls were monitored physically and spatially. In such a setting, the sites of both control and contestation multiplied. Since the staff tried to have a say in everything the girls did—even if the intent was to get them to feel like they were doing things on their own—all sorts of daily acts took on strategic significance and disruptive potential. What is more, because the staff and the girls were in constant contact, the number of outlets for disruption increased. At any moment, the most seemingly mundane activity could transform into an arena of confrontation and conflict.

At Alliance, the potential for conflict seemed to be in the air all the time, permeating every floor and every room of the facility. In fact, the girls seemed to do everything they could to keep the staff off balance and on guard. One way they did this was by singing, or, more precisely, by rapping: these were the early days of rap music, before its full commercialization, when many inner-city kids dreamed of becoming rap stars. The Alliance girls were no different—they were obsessed with rap music and spent hours perfecting their rhyming skills and rhythmic style. They spent evenings adding their own words to existing rap songs. The idea was to replace the lyrics with ones they could relate to. But this musical exercise also became a way to express their opposition to Alliance's program and to communicate secretly with one another.[15]

The Alliance girls walked around the facility singing to themselves and each other in rap. When one listened carefully, it was possible to discern some of their lyrics—and to realize that they often made fun of the staff and their needs talk. The girls rapped about being confined by women who did not know the "score." They sang about the anarchy of the facility and how they were told different things by different people and then instructed to "do the right thing" on their own. And they harmonized about the contradiction implied by the staff's imperative that they be self-full and compliant at the same time. Tonya always sang "I'm on welfare and it's gonna take care of me forever" to the tune of a popular rap song. She did this just loud enough so the staff could decipher what she was saying. The goal was to annoy and frustrate—and to remind the staff, through the constant humming, that the girls opposed what was required of them. So the girls seemed most gratified when the staff unwittingly began singing their catchy raps themselves. Indeed, it was funny when Rachel would walk by humming the rhythm of Tonya's "I'm on welfare" song, seemingly unaware of where the tune came from.

If resistant rap provided the soundtrack for everyday life at Alliance, additional props of protest filled the home. Throughout the facility, one could find small signs of the girls' battles; they left evidence of their defiance strewn throughout the facility. After breakfast and lunch, empty cans of forbidden baby food mysteriously remained on the counter or dining table. On occasion, I even watched the girls intentionally leave out empty food bottles—as if to indicate that they refused to abide by the no-bottle-food rule. The girls left behind phone numbers scribbled on scraps of paper after making calls on the office phone, which was officially off-limits to all inmates. They "forgot" to throw away receipts for forbidden items like cigarettes, fast food, or expensive beauty products. Then there were the times when Rachel would return to the classroom after having left the girls to do an assignment on their own, only to find a pile of blank assignment sheets nicely stacked on her desk. These were all physical reminders of the girls' refusal to live according to Alliance's dictates. The girls littered the facility with them on purpose, in anticipation of the angry responses of whichever staff member discovered them.

Of all the props the girls used to transmit their message of defiance, their babies were one of the most effective. In part, this was because the messages thus sent were more pointed: specific statements about how Alliance ordered the girls' priorities. Recall that the staff organized everyday life to get the girls to put "independence" and "initiative" above all else. So the girls used their babies to reassert a definition of themselves as mothers above all else. In doing so, they inverted the staff's ordering of their priorities. "I can't do that, my baby needs me" was the most common line I heard the girls tell the staff. No matter what they were engaged in, they would stop as soon as they heard their babies crying. The girls dropped anything and everything if they thought their babies needed them. Not surprisingly, this provoked countless arguments with the staff, who maintained that the girls were coddling their children and needed to toughen them up. But the girls refused to alter their behavior, claiming "everyone knows" that good mothers put their children "above everything else."

This game of priorities played itself out most often in the classroom. Or, more precisely, it surfaced during the tests of independence Rachel so frequently administered during class time. As soon as she gave the girls their assignments and left the classroom, the girls stopped working and turned to their babies. Even if their babies were sleeping quietly, they found reasons to attend to them instead of their schoolwork. Perhaps their blankets needed to be rearranged or their clothing changed; perhaps they needed a bottle or a diaper change. Then, upon Rachel's return, the girls were quick to explain that they had not worked because of their obligations as mothers. While Rachel usually interpreted this as a sign of the girls' laziness, the message was a bit deeper: yet again, the girls expressed their contempt for Alliance's regulation of their responsibilities. They proclaimed that the staff's demands were secondary to those of their babies. And they questioned just how viable it was for them to always be "self-full" when they had small children reliant on them.

While these individual acts of rebellion were constant reminders of the girls' opposition, their resistance could escalate to a higher level. During my time at Alliance, I observed several girls try to escape from the facility. By the end of my fieldwork, it seemed like there was an escape attempt every few weeks. This was a more extreme form of contestation for several reasons. First, the girls knew that trying to escape would effectively end their stay at Alliance. Those who managed to escape were always turned over to CYA once caught by the police; those intercepted while trying to escape were immediately banished from the home and not allowed to return.[16] Inmate escapes were treated so harshly because they struck a real blow to the facility; they were public statements about the girls' discontent. They also exposed the staff's inability to control and contain their charges. Thus, CYA did not look favorably on Alliance's high escape rate and frequently ordered the staff to get a handle on it. The stakes were particularly high when it came to escapes; while the staff could overlook the girls' small acts of protest, the big acts of flight could not be ignored.

Although it was not hard to escape from Alliance given the open-door policy, the decision to do so was not one the girls made lightly. Instead, most of them crossed this line when they saw no other alternative. Those who resorted to escapes had become so ensnarled in Alliance's contradictions that they felt they had no other way out. They felt wronged by the facility and had exhausted all other channels of discontent open to them. Perhaps the best example of this was Maria, the one-time house superstar.[17] After months of applauding her "initiative" and "potential for independence," the week before her parole hearing the staff called her into a meeting. They then confronted her with evidence that she had made unauthorized phone calls from the front office, thus officially breaking the phone rule. Although everyone knew this rule was flexible, the staff decided to enforce it with Maria. They gave her two options: she could spend six more months at Alliance or take her chances before the parole board with this new violation on her record. Maria said very little in the days following the meeting, while everyone in the house quietly debated which of the two options Maria would take. In the end, she took neither: the night before her original release date, she escaped with her baby through a basement window. She was never found.[18]

The girls' reaction to Maria's escape was telling. They immediately saw the incident as poetic justice and used it to relay a message to the staff about the underside of the program. The morning after the escape, Rachel devoted some class time to a discussion of Maria's escape; her goal was to let the girls "air their feelings" about Maria's actions. But the girls remained tight lipped. Although they knew a lot about Maria's plans, they were unwilling to discuss them for fear of unwittingly revealing details to the staff. When they did speak, they used the occasion to criticize the house theme of initiative. "Look at that," Tonya remarked to Rachel.

"Maria really took the bull by the horns last night." Later in the day, as Liz was reprimanding Debra for idly sitting around and doing nothing, Debra deployed Maria's actions as a warning: "Well, there was no laziness last night at Alliance! She sure did learn good from Alliance."

Of course, it was not only Maria who had learned from the Alliance example: through their acts of defiance, the girls showed considerable insight into the central tenets of the program. Although these acts were often carried out individually, they were patterned. And although they seemed random and unruly, these acts transmitted pointed statements about the source of the girls' opposition. Most importantly, the girls' actions targeted the precise sites of institutional power. As the girls recited their rap music, they twisted the staff's dependency discourse to relay very different messages. As they used forbidden consumer products, they undermined the staff's myth of consumer freedom. As they turned to their babies in the classroom, they questioned the staff's ranking of their identities and priorities. And as they jumped out of basement windows, they exposed the politics of confinement upon which Alliance was premised. In effect, the sites of institutional power became sites of institutional struggle. This connection between control and contestation was even clearer in the girls' collective actions.

Men in Suits

Since the girls' individual acts of defiance occurred on a constant, daily basis, the staff seemed most preoccupied with them. In fact, during my first months at Alliance, these actions also preoccupied me: my early fieldnotes were full of stories of the girls' resistance, which struck me as rich with humor and insight. With time, I noticed that their protests were not only consistent but actually seemed to be coordinated. The girls' actions exhibited striking uniformity; individual girls often used the same words and metaphors in their critiques of the program and frequently waged these critiques to the same staff members around the same time. In effect, the girls' actions seemed to evidence an awareness of their common positions and interests—as well as a desire to turn their us versus them talk into sustained collective action.

The first outward sign of this awareness was the formation of the "Welfare Club." The club emerged out of a house meeting in which the staff accused the girls of being too dependent and needy. In response, Jamika and Maria started to discuss how the staff were not preparing them to take their GED exams—and how this meant that they would be on welfare for the rest of their lives. Then Tonya began singing her welfare song: "I'm on welfare and it's gonna take care of me forever," rang out. Debra interjected that they were all in the same predicament and hence should form a club, the Welfare Club. Laughing, the others nodded in agreement. At first, the club seemed like a joke. But a few days later, it actually materialized: the girls held secret meetings at secret times in secret places. It is unlikely that they talked about welfare at the meetings, but the name was symbolic. It signaled their opposition to Alliance's program of dependency—and the extent to which their resistance was scripted by the form of control exerted over them.

The Welfare Club also allowed the girls to plan and synchronize their actions. For instance, the week after the group's formation, the girls organized a strike to protest Alliance's hiring of a childcare provider during school hours. Unlike Rachel, who had herself gone on strike to get Alliance to hire the childcare worker, the girls wanted their babies to remain in the classroom so they could care for them while they did schoolwork. This resulted in a face-off: collectively, the girls refused to attend class for a week and camped out in the living room with their babies. While their protest ended when director Marlene decided to keep the childcare worker and ordered the girls back to school, it emboldened the girls. After the strike, they stepped up their actions. Their tactics also became less random and more targeted. Instead of using whatever weapons they happened to have at their disposal, the girls began to mobilize the one weapon they shared: the state. In doing so, the girls advanced their most damning critique of Alliance's program. Despite the staff's talk of the perils of state dependency, the girls revealed how the state could be used to their advantage. In the process, they began to see how the state accorded them valuable rights and to defend these forms of public protection.

In particular, the girls drew on three institutions in their battles with the staff. First, there was the city welfare administration. Here it is important to recall that the girls' AFDC checks were a constant source of tension and strife: the staff refused to tell the girls where the money went for fear that doing so would further the girls' sense of entitlement to state assistance. For similar reasons, the girls demanded to know how "their checks" were spent. After months of fighting about this, the girls decided to try another approach. Their strategy emerged after Tonya, the creator of the welfare song, asked to use part of her check to purchase a new baby blanket. Unconvinced that she needed another blanket, the staff rejected her request. This infuriated Tonya and prompted her to submit several written appeals, all of which the staff rejected based on their determination of her "needs."

So one afternoon, Tonya called the local social services office to report a stolen AFDC check. She even insisted that a caseworker come to Alliance and investigate the charge, noting that she had a "right" to such an investigation. Apparently, a caseworker did pay Alliance a visit later in the week, taking the staff completely by surprise. Tonya then demanded that the caseworker receive a full accounting of her AFDC checks, again emphasizing her "right" to such an accounting. To the embarrassment and outrage of the staff, the caseworker uncomfortably agreed to Tonya's demands—while the girls watched from the sidelines, with delight and enjoyment. After this incident, whenever Tonya got annoyed with the staff, other girls would encourage her to call the caseworker again. Although Tonya never did, the threat put the staff on alert. It also sent an important message about how useful the state could be and how the rights it accorded the girls could be used to trump Alliance's assessments of the girls' needs.

The girls sent a similar message when they mobilized another arm of the state—the county's rules and regulation department. This state body was responsible for licensing and overseeing publicly funded residential programs, including mental-health facilities, alternative-to-incarceration programs, and group homes. Its mandate was to monitor these institutions' practices to ensure compliance with state law and county rules. Even though the department was not well-known outside of local bureaucratic circles, somehow the Alliance girls found out about it. And they figured out how to get in touch with its officials and to get them to come to the rescue. So director Marlene was shocked when she got a call one afternoon from an official in the department. Someone in the facility had called in an anonymous complaint about a series of rule violations in the group home. By law, the department had to send an investigator to check the facility and evaluate the complaints. The official anticipated that the investigation would take an entire day, an indication that the list of rule violations was long and extensive.

As soon as Marlene hung up the phone, panic set it. The day's activities were canceled and all available staff members were called back to work. A cleaning frenzy ensued as the staff worked well into the night to prepare the facility for the morning examination. While this was going on, Mildred secretly admitted to me that she had called the department: seven months pregnant, she found it unfair that the staff forced her to do so many household chores. "They say all this shit about being self-full," she explained. "Forget it, it's slave labor."

When the investigator arrived the next day, she spent the morning touring the facility with the girls and listening to their complaints. As they walked around the home, the investigator carried a large binder full of checklists, which she used to interrogate the girls about life at Alliance. The tour ended with a closed-door meeting with the girls in the living room, which lasted for over an hour. During this time, the staff paced around the home, occasionally peeking through living room's glass doors to see what was going on inside. What they saw made them all the more anxious: the girls sat in a large circle, talking with their arms flailing in outrage, as the department investigator furiously scribbled comments in her enormous binder.

Before leaving, the investigator called a late-afternoon meeting with the staff and the girls in the dining room of the home. She began by scolding the staff publicly for making minors, especially pregnant minors, do household labor. This, she argued, was illegal. She also cited a county rule stipulating that public institutions needed to hire outside workers to carry out the kind of facility maintenance that Alliance had the girls doing. She then presented the staff with a long list of regulatory and code violations: from inoperative fire alarms to broken children's furniture to unsafe infrastructures to unfair house practices. As she made her way down the list, she stopped periodically to point out which violation had been revealed by the girls themselves and to thank them for the "care" with which they assisted her investigation.

The investigator concluded by handing the staff several pages of required changes. The staff sat in utter disbelief, looking angry and betrayed—as if they only then realized the extent of "their girls'" opposition to them. They then started to plead with the official, saying they did not have the funds to make all the changes or the support to revamp the program so completely. As the staff begged the department official to acknowledge the social context of their work, the girls looked on with victorious smiles. Mildred in particular sat tall in her chair, with a huge grin on her face, rubbing her protruding pregnant belly. After the meeting, Nikita whispered to me, "We done told Alliance today, didn't we?" Indeed, they had. Not only did the girls turn the tables on Alliance to reveal the staff's own inability to "take the bull by the horns," but they demonstrated their ability to use their "state dependency" in their defense.

The girls' use of the welfare administration and county rules and regulations department were one-time occurrences. But the girls drew on a third official body in a more recurrent, ongoing way: CYA became a constant reference point for the girls in their struggles with the staff. Whenever the staff required the girls to do something they did not like, they threatened to call CYA; whenever the staff denied the girls something they wanted, they threatened to report Alliance to CYA. To bolster their claims, the girls would ask for a copy of Alliance's contract with CYA— they wanted to know exactly what they were entitled to and could thus legitimately claim. Since the staff never showed them the contract, they used their collective memory of what they had access to while in CYA. So if the staff cancelled a house outing, the girls accused them of violating their "right" to time outside the facility guaranteed by CYA. If the staff refused to purchase certain food or consumer goods that had been available at the CYA canteen, the girls insisted on their "right" to the products. If the staff changed the girls' daily routine without advanced warning, the girls would claim a collective "right" to a consistent schedule posted for all. Of course, they threatened to report these violations to CYA.

For the most part, the girls' warnings remained empty threats. But there was one girl who followed through. After she escaped from Alliance, Maria did call CYA to report a series of rule violations. Perhaps influenced by Mildred's successful use of the rules and regulations department, she relayed a long list programmatic infringements and infrastructural problems. Alliance got the call from CYA the night before the agency representatives' scheduled arrival, so the staff had little time to prepare the house for the visit. Thus, the morning of the visit, the staff was all the more frantic. When the officials arrived, everyone was a bit surprised: all four of the officials were men dressed in suits. The dynamics of the visit were therefore a bit different than the previous two, as the girls led a group of men in suits around the house, instructing them on what life was like at Alliance and pointing out all the regulatory violations. The CYA men seemed less concerned about physical problems with the home and more interested in possible program violations. The staff could hear the men asking the girls all sorts of pointed questions: Was there really no fixed schedule? Where were their school lesson plans? When was the last time they had done their required visits to the local high school? Why were pregnant girls doing physical labor?

After the CYA men left, the girls refused to reveal to the nervous staff what they had told the men. Since the visit did not conclude with a collective meeting, the staff was left hanging for months—until the men's confidential report was issued and staff members were called up for meetings with high-ranking CYA officials. And since the staff also kept the content of these reports and meetings confidential, it was not apparent if the girls' action led to any concrete changes. But one thing was clear: the legacy of the Men in Suits lived on at Alliance. When the girls got angry, they'd say "I'll call the Men in Suits if you don't watch it," or "Those Men in Suits liked us, I'm gonna ask them to come back." The girls knew how much comments like these irked the staff. At the practical level, such taunts prompted fear because CYA had the power to withdraw Alliance's contract and close down the group home. At the symbolic level, the girls' reliance on the Men in Suits struck at the core of the staff's institutional narrative by exposing its mythical qualities. It was as if the girls were working according to the old dictum that your enemies' enemy is your friend. In the process, the girls demonstrated that sometimes Men in Suits can be of help; they showed that sometimes state "dependency" could be reworked and used for their own ends.

Of course, this was not a lesson the Alliance staff wanted to be teaching. In fact, demonstrating the practical benefits of state reliance could not have been further from the staff's intentions. Instead, the girls learned this lesson after months of using the institutional tools at their disposal. Many of these tools were tied to the state—they were rights and entitlements accorded to the girls as official wards of the state and as recipients of state assistance. Their battles with the Alliance staff thus led the girls to become even more reliant, indeed "dependent," on public forms of protection. In the end, the girls became invested in the exact social relations that Alliance sought to undermine.

The girls' renewed reliance on the state was made clear in my last interaction with them on the day of my departure. As we went on our afternoon walk, with the girls pushing their baby strollers single file down a busy street, I asked what they planned to do after their release. Tonya, Lakisha, and Mildred said they wanted to have more babies immediately. Mildred claimed that babies made her feel "somethin' special." Tonya added that she also planned to continue the Welfare Club on the outside. "I'm on welfare and it's gonna take care of me forever," she rapped, checking to see if Rachel was listening. The others laughed in agreement. They had learned their lesson well.

THE POSSIBILITIES AND LIMITATIONS
OF DEPENDENCY DISCOURSE

Around the same time as girls like Tonya rapped their way to a critique of Alliance's dependency discourse, feminist theorist Nancy Fraser was contemplating the political implications of the state's emphasis on defining women needs.[19] Like many scholars, Fraser noted a shift from state policies premised on social rights to those based on need. She also expressed concern over the politics of needs interpretation, worrying that it could drown out women's claims to social protection.[20] Unlike a discourse of rights, which tends to be premised on common entitlement claims, needs talk can individualize and depoliticize. Yet Fraser also held open the possibility that the politics of need could be transformed in unexpected ways. While the intention of needs talk may be to depoliticize, opposition can form from it—as women assert their own definitions of what they need and as social movements bring women together to advance collective interpretations of their needs. In the process, needs interpretation can become a site of discursive struggle; at times, it can even evolve into a struggle for social rights. So while Fraser remained aware of the dangers inherent in the politics of need, she also acknowledged the difference between political intentions and effects.

In many ways, the everyday battles among the women at Alliance exemplify the possibilities and limitations of needs talk. As I pointed out in the previous chapter, dependency discourse held numerous possibilities for the staff: it allowed them to differentiate themselves from those with power over them, ally with each other, and claim collective authority over their young charges. Interestingly, the possibilities that this needs talk offered the Alliance girls were not all that different. The staff's insistence that they knew what the girls needed prompted a great deal of resistance. The result was to embolden the Alliance girls to stand up for themselves; to enhance their defiance and solidify an alternative construction of their needs; and to push them to join forces, drawing together a diverse, spirited, and unruly group of young women who could have easily become rivals. What is more, for the Alliance girls this needs talk became a stepping stone to rights talk: they used it to expose the inconsistencies in the Alliance program, develop a social critique of the staff's panic over dependency, and argue for a more expansive notion of justice and fairness. And eventually their talk of rights became a route to collective action—prompting the girls to rap in unison, protest together, and draw Men in Suits into their battles. In Fraser's terms, they kept their struggle in the realm of the social and used it to unite rather than divide.

Lest we idealize the girls' struggle over needs, we need only examine the results of the battle to see its downside. While this struggle may have emboldened these young women, it rarely produced tangible results. The girls could spend their time coming up with ingenious responses to the staff's institutional narrative, but the practical outcomes were limited. The girls could develop funny and pointed ways to annoy the staff and make their lives difficult, but these efforts were also easily ignored when it came to programmatic reform. In part, the girls' limited success was related to the defensive posture they were often forced into—they spent so much energy reacting to the staff's definition of their needs that they never figured out how to turn their definitions into concrete institutional practices. As a result, their ideas were not translated into any rules or regulations that could have shaped life at Alliance in sustainable, long-lasting ways. Nor were the girls' protests codified in any legal protections or entitlements that could have made serving time at Alliance a bit more productive for the next batch of girls from CYA.

This leads to the final limitation of the Alliance girls' politics of need—a limitation that becomes clear when viewed with some historical distance. Over a decade later, it is possible to see how the girls' struggle may actually have backfired. The state actors these girls found so immediately useful turned out to have their own agenda, and they used all the evidence that the girls handed over to advance that agenda: the continual stream of complaints coming out of the group home became evidence of its ineffectiveness; the repeated visits to and scrutiny of Alliance exposed each and every instance of staff incompetence. Eventually, those Men in Suits shut down the facility.

What is more, beyond the walls of Alliance, the state began to change in broader, more encompassing ways; it devolved, diversified, and decentralized to a greater degree than ever before. As I describe in the next chapter, these structural changes altered the terrain upon which "alternative" penal institutions operated. This terrain became much more crowded, expanding to include state institutions with very different programmatic narratives and modes of governance—all of which would require different survival strategies from the women living in them.

THREE Hybrid States and Government from a Distance

Throughout the early 1990s, as the women at Alliance remained locked in battles over dependency, the foundations upon which the institution rested began to shift. While the corresponding tremors reverberated through the facility, the staff seemed unaware of the depth of the quakes they were experiencing—they never spoke of them in meetings or strategy sessions. With so much time spent on crisis management, they had little opportunity to reflect on the big picture. Even if they had had time to reflect, it is unclear whether the cracks and fissures surrounding them would have been visible from where they stood. Yet, over a decade later, they are quite visible: in retrospect, this was a moment of profound change in the theory and practice of government.

Indeed, there is no shortage of social-scientific analyses of this era of state restructuring. The conceptualizations go by different names and deploy different imagery, depending on the state arena theorized and on the theoretical orientation reflected. Some scholars focus on the "scale" of the state, arguing that the spatial terrain states operate on has become simultaneously more global and more local.[1] Others center on who carries out the work of the state, claiming that outsourcing has made state boundaries increasingly malleable and porous.[2] Others are interested in emergent forms of public funding, suggesting that new allocative procedures link states, nonprofits, and community groups in unexpected ways.[3] And still others are preoccupied with the interlocking channels of power flowing through state institutions, revealing that they circulate in more spherical and less linear ways than previously imagined.[4]

Of all these portrayals, one of the most compelling is the characterization of the neoliberal state as governing "from a distance."[5] This representation captures how, as the centralized social state was dismantled, the arena of government devolved, decentralized, and diversified. In this new governmental arena, decisions about the allocation of public funding and the delivery of services have been handed over to local officials. At the local level, partnerships with nongovernmental and private entities then made the boundaries around state policies even more diffuse. Making matters all the more complex, these processes migrated across state spheres with striking speed—reshaping everything from welfare provisions to social-service delivery to educational policy to urban renewal programs. Even the criminal-justice system shows signs of such diversification and decentralization: recall that three times as many citizens live under correctional supervision in the semicustodial arena than in the centralized prison system.[6]

Amid these broad shifts in government, institutions like Alliance struggled to survive. As the world around them changed, they were forced to reinvent their form and focus. Themselves governed from a distance, facilities like Alliance confronted new external and internal dilemmas. With decentralization, many of them moved outside the formal arena of government; some began to use clever names that made no mention of the state and thus masked their reliance on public resources. Their distance from a political center required these institutions to discover new ways of sustaining themselves—for instance, through competitive funding processes like government grants and renewable contracts, or through assistance from private foundations and businesses. It also forced them to grapple with the mass of new regulatory checks and balances that linked them back to central governmental structures. This all heightened the competition among institutions as they had to package and market themselves to vie successfully for limited funds—and to gain legitimacy and authority in this crowded arena.

Then there were the internal institutional dilemmas. Their hybrid structures opened these institutions to enormous diversity in their staff and clientele; their porous borders exposed them to various cultural and community influences. All of this bred conflict in the everyday life of such institutions. In this context, some thrived but most did not: staff turnover rates were shockingly high, while organizational reshufflings ran rampant. Hence, much of what we once thought we knew about public institutions—from their bureaucratic procedures to their organizational longevity to their programmatic consistency—no longer holds in this era of spatially scattered, hybrid states.[7]

This chapter describes what we do know about these satellite state institutions. I begin by analyzing the broader structural context in which the practice of government changed—exploring how devolution, decentralization, and diversification created new forms of state hybridity. Like these restructuring processes, my account operates at different levels; I examine restructuring overall and in particular state arenas. I then turn to the implications of this hybridity for concrete state institutions, arguing that newly emergent satellite states confront external and internal challenges that, if mismanaged, can make them ungovernable. Finally, I conclude by tracing the rise of one network of state satellites—penal facilities for incarcerated mothers.

RESTRUCTURING ACROSS STATE ARENAS

Social change always seems more coherent and consistent when viewed from afar. One of the biggest dangers of analyses of large-scale social transformation is thus the tendency to smooth over its rough edges and to represent change as a linear progression. This danger is particularly acute in accounts of state restructuring, which often come across as grand narratives of clear, unidirectional change. Yet the state is such a complex, multilayered entity that shifts in its policies and institutions are usually far more jagged and inconsistent. There are countless contemporary examples of such unevenness: welfarist policies that persist despite the overall push toward workfarism, interventionist "family values" programs funded by state actors promising to scale back the state, or welfare offices that cling to a social-work perspective amid the larger movement toward punitive bureaucratism. Despite these contradictory developments, most social-scientific research continues to represent welfare reform as following a straightforward, linear trajectory.

Of course, it is possible to acknowledge the contradictory nature of state restructuring while insisting that, overall, the state arena has changed. This is the difference between focusing on the forest or the trees. And social-scientific portrayals of the contemporary forest tend to share a few key features. Instead of depicting the state as an encased, bounded entity, they represent it as "multiscalar" and even fragmented. Rather than imagining the state as having a clear, centralized "core," they view it as a series of "polycentric" and even scattered spaces.[8] Perhaps most importantly, instead of attributing change to one causal force, such accounts tend to highlight a combination of causal processes, which usually include devolution, decentralization, and diversification.

The Holy Trinity of State Reform

One of the most striking aspects of recent retheorizations of the state is their heavy reliance on spatial imagery. To some extent, this is due to these scholars' disciplinary background; much of this conceptual work has been done by geographers and anthropologists. Yet there are other reasons for the strong scalar imagery; unlike other social institutions, it is impossible to "see" a state.[9] Because the state is not simply an abstract concept, like inequality or punishment, we often think it can be seen while studied. Of course, the state is both an abstraction and a concrete entity, which is precisely why our images of it remain so important. Spatial metaphors and scalar representations provide a much-needed way to orient ourselves to studying the state and to envisioning changes to it.

As anthropologists James Ferguson and Akhil Gupta argue, the old spatial images of the state simply do not work anymore.[10] The top-down imagery in which the "state" hovers above "society" obscures far more than it illuminates. The same is true of bottom-up imagery in which "society" struggles to wrestle power back from the "state." Both images fail to capture how power connects through state and social institutions in a more circular fashion—and how power relations get rearranged and reconfigured in the process. This is one reason why the idea of government from a distance is so appealing: the notion of distancing does not imply a particular track or pathway. It is possible to gain distance in different ways and from different directions. Distancing can occur along several dimensions and can be both vertical and horizontal.

This is precisely what has occurred in the contemporary state. On the one hand, in the 1990s, government underwent a vertical distancing through which all kinds of decisions about all kinds of public programs moved from the national to the state level.[11] To return to the old top-down metaphor, the national government has downloaded many of its responsibilities to state and local entities. Of course, U.S. state governments have always had significant power. But since the Reagan era, this downloading has reached a rapid rate. It has also extended to new areas—involving everything from program management to program design to program expenditures to program eligibility/entitlement. What is more, once responsibility moves to the state level, there can be further vertical distancing. Particular locales, whether cities, counties, or municipalities, become key sites for the control of public programs. For instance, the allocation of public funding is now more localized than ever: it often follows a chain-of-command through which agencies compete for state funds that are then allocated by networks of local officials.[12] Similar processes determine who manages the programs created by these funds. Together, these processes fall under the rubric of devolution, the first part of the holy trinity of state reform.

Much of the empirical work on state devolution has focused on the welfare arena. Although they do not always call it devolution, welfare scholars use different words to denote similar phenomena: *policy pilots, federal waivers, program experimentation.* In fact, one of the main sources of welfare devolution was legislation granting federal waivers for states to experiment with pilot programs. As sociologist Robin Rogers-Dillon has shown, these waivers had become the policy norm in the mid-1990s, pushed by the Clinton administration as a way to introduce "innovation" and "experimentation" at the state level.[13] And experiment they did. State pilot programs revamped everything from the Aid to Families with Dependent Children eligibility criteria to sanctioning procedures. The effects of state piloting were also more far-reaching than is often assumed. Not only did such programs alter how policies were created and conceived, but they moved much of the control over AFDC from the national to the state level. In this way, the culmination of welfare devolution was not the introduction of the Personal Responsibility and Work Opportunity Reconciliation Act in 1996, but the "superwaiver" provision included in its 2002 reauthorization—a policy that allowed states to opt out of virtually all federal guidelines for assistance programs, thus bypassing the national legislative process altogether.[14]

This downloading of responsibility not only applied to policy formulation: it also reshaped the delivery of social services and supports. As geographer Jamie Peck has revealed, the "fast policy transfers" of the devolved welfare state led to massive variation in local-level assistance.[15] Here, too, the U.S. state has always been characterized by grave variation in local administration.[16] Yet devolution deepened this trend and extended it to new areas. Now everything from access to essential services to the quality of those services to the types of available support to basic eligibility criteria all vary by states and locales. Localization therefore seems to have exacerbated the uneven developments and structural inequities of the U.S. welfare state. It has also led to inconsistent definitions of basic citizen rights and their unequal application across locales. For example, in one state a mother with a felony conviction might be provided social assistance, but not in a neighboring state; in one locale, an immigrant family might receive income support, but not in the adjoining county.

The political effects of such inconsistencies have been significant. With the downloading of assistance has come the downloading of conflict and political struggle. So when resistance to reform does occur, it tends to be localized both in its political base and political targets.[17] While local political struggles are unquestionably important, particularly when they occur in urban environments and take aim at entrenched urban bureaucracies, they can also miss the mark. As Peck points out, national actors have retained their role as regulators and rule makers—through new checks, balances, and regulatory schemes, they remain key orchestrators of this downloaded system.[18] Yet, in the devolved state, this orchestration is less explicit and more directive, which can mask the control that national actors continue to wield, keeping them out of the political fire.

At the same time as this downloading of responsibility led to a vertical distancing in the contemporary state, there was also a horizontal distancing. Accompanying devolution were new forms of decentralization at the local level. Throughout the 1990s, there was an explosion in the number and variety of actors playing the role of the state. Of the many actors now involved in this role-playing, one of the most common are state-funded NGOs and community groups. As government moved to a distance, it started to work through "community."[19] Instead of opposing the community, or competing with it for citizens' hearts and minds, a co-optation began to form. States forged financial "partnerships" with nongovernmental entities, funding NGOs in exchange for control over their budgetary priorities, staffing decisions, and approaches to clients. In return, the state appears softer and less threatening when it governs through community; it claims to be adopting a kinder, gentler mode of governance. Or such is the promise.

Often referred to as the "NGO-ization" of the state, this form of decentralization transformed the terrain of government. Sociologist Nicole Marwell has revealed the breadth and depth of this transformation.[20] In terms of resource allocation, federal support to nonprofits has increased by 400 percent since the mid-1970s—jumping from $23 billion in 1973 to $175 billion in 1995. Similar trends characterize employment: in 1995, the nonprofit sector employed 8.6 million full-time workers, which is roughly half the size of public-sector employment overall. What is more, community-based organizations and nonprofits have taken over public responsibilities in nearly every arena of government—from welfare programs to social-service delivery to urban development to health care to crime control. With such decentralization, the scope of state authority has dispersed and diversified, thus becoming more difficult to set boundaries around.

While publicly financed NGOs may be the most common form of state decentralization, the most controversial form is probably state-funded "faith-based" groups. Here, too, their increase in power has been stunning: while religious organizations have a long history in social-service provision in the United States, throughout the 1990s they have become more deeply involved in policy implementation in more arenas of government.[21] From welfare-to-work programs to "responsible fatherhood" policies to Head Start programs, faith-based groups have emerged as major players in the decentralized U.S. state. Nowhere is their presence felt more strongly than in the arena of abstinence-only education and programming.[22] Yet, as sociologist Amie Hess has shown, enormous disjunctions have surfaced between what abstinence-only groups say to secure government resources and what they ultimately practice.[23] In fact, there is so much discretion in this field that "faith" does not end up shaping organizational practices in a consistent way. But this is precisely the point: decentralization has led to a diversification of institutions playing the role of the state and to a differentiation in their practices.

Similar changes have emanated from another controversial form of decentralization: the outsourcing of public provisions and services to for-profit and private companies. Perhaps because of its stronger political connotations, state privatization has garnered far more criticism than government through community.[24] Yet their effects are comparable; public-private joint ventures have also bred diversification in institutional approach and practice. Of course, they have done so by extending the logic of the market into the state arena. Since the profit motive is arguably even less compatible with public services than the logic of community or of "faith," there have been more calls to subject these joint ventures to public oversight. However, even these calls for regulation seem to mimic the logic of government from a distance: like state-funded NGOs, these public-private undertakings are less likely to be regulated through fixed bureaucratic rules and more likely through indirect orchestration.

Here it is important to recall Peck's argument about the distinct modes of regulation at work in hybrid states. Devolved and decentralized states do not operate without regulation. Rather, new checks and balances allow the federal government to forge a unique regulatory relationship with these satellite states. Only occasionally is this relationship one of direct oversight—as when a national policy includes clear mandates for the treatment of specific social groups, like PRWORA's denial of assistance to drug felons, teen mothers, and immigrants; or the 1998 Higher Education Act's denial of Pell Grants and federal student loans to all students with drug-related convictions.[25] More often the relationship is expressed through new management practices—from program evaluations to performance measures to accountability scales to ranking systems, all of which focus on "outputs" and force competition among agencies. Oversight can also be articulated through budgetary and funding procedures—for instance, by withdrawing coveted state contracts or "encouraging" participation in competitive RFPs. So while institutions may appear to be unencumbered in this era of state hybridity, or even to have dissolved into a morass of random, loosely coupled organizations, their conduct remains coordinated, managed, and directed.

Punishment from a Distance?

Most analyses of state hybridity draw empirical material from welfare reform, urban development, or poverty programs. This focus can leave the impression that similar reforms have not occurred in other state arenas, which would be a faulty conclusion. One distinctive aspect of contemporary state restructuring is the rapid linkages such restructuring forms across state subsystems. So while many state scholars try to stay clear of the penal state, the patterns they describe do apply to many recent developments in the criminal-justice system.

But the fit is not always perfect. Take, for example, the first part of the holy trinity of state reform: devolution. In many ways, this is the trickiest of the three to draw systemic parallels to. On the one hand, the U.S. penal system has always been devolved and localized. From its inception, it has been characterized by profound variation in state-level penal policies and institutions, the organization of parole, and judicial due process. Since the 1980s, there have been many attempts to reduce this local discretion or, more precisely, to curtail judicial decision-making power. These include several mandatory sentencing policies legislated by the federal and state government—the most notorious of which are "three-strikes" laws and other forms of fixed sentences for particular crimes and/or repeat offenders. The 1987 federal sentencing guidelines and the 2003 Feeney Amendment are further examples, both of which fixed sentences to offense type and left little room for judicial consideration of offenders' histories or life circumstances. In doing so, these laws invested more power over sentencing in the hands of national-level political actors who operate at a distance from the details of actual cases.[26] Taken together, these developments seem to butt the devolutionary trend toward the downloading of state responsibility and control.

If only it were so simple. For the most part, attempts to control local discretion have targeted judges and parole boards. As a result, discretionary practices simply moved elsewhere in the penal system—and seemed to have migrated from courtrooms to actual penal institutions. While a judge's hands may be tied by federal guidelines or an offender's sentence fixed by a state legislature, how and where time is served remains locally determined. Penal officials have enormous control over where inmates are channeled once in the system. They decide on inmates' risk classifications, which are crucial determinants of life behind bars.[27] They decide how to mark those risk classifications—through uniforms, wristbands, ward designations, and so on.[28] They decide how to punish bad behavior and where to transfer inmates who act out. They decide how to reward good behavior and where to locate model inmates. They decide who can work where. They decide who can study what. They decide who is eligible for special programs—many of which take years off a sentence once completed. Ultimately, local penal officials decide which state programs will be supported and which will become defunct.[29] Thus, key responsibilities are in fact being downloaded in the penal system, albeit in a jagged and uneven way.

A similar unevenness characterizes the processes of decentralization. At one level, it seems ludicrous to view the penal system as decentralizing. After all, in the last two decades, the system has undergone a stunning expansion in size and scope. Unparalleled in other state arenas, the penal system has grown to encompass millions of new citizens for longer periods of time. The rise in incarceration rates does indicate a move toward the augmentation of state control and the centralization of punishment. Moreover, the realities of prison overcrowding and warehousing add to the image of a centralizing system—with the concentration of more and more bodies in smaller and smaller spaces, the penal system is condensing control.[30] Then there is the massive concentration of state resources: as budget allocations for the penal system have ballooned, funds have been transferred steadily from other state sectors to the criminal-justice system.

So, at one level, decentralization seems at odds with this image of a big, bloated penal system. But herein lies a common misrepresentation of research on state reform: it tends to equate state restructuring with state withdrawal. However, as states decentralize and diversify, they do not always retrench. Instead, they can expand and augment. Or they can undergo qualitative changes in form, focus, and function. This is what has occurred in the U.S. penal system: recall that over seven million citizens lived under some kind of correctional supervision in 2006, with close to 75 percent of them regulated outside of jails and prisons. In a sense, it actually makes sense that an exponential increase in incarceration rates would necessitate some decentralization and diversification, as the system's boundaries need to stretch to encompass so many new bodies.

It also makes sense that new actors would be brought in to staff and manage this burgeoning system. Just as many welfare programs have been contracted out for administration, so too have penal facilities. In fact, penal institutions are often run by the same groups as other state hybrids—through contracts and grants, a similar mix of nonprofit, for-profit, and religious organizations have taken over control of state punishment. This change has been particularly dramatic in the area of policing, where a "mixed economy of public and private provision" has emerged since the 1990s.[31] Moreover, after over a century of severely curtailing the role of private and commercial interests in the penal system, there has been a sharp rise in the number of private, for-profit prisons. This comes on the heels of countless private companies setting up shop in state-run prisons as a way of tapping into one of the lowest-paid labor forces in the country.[32] Then there is the heightened role that religious groups started to play in this system. While religious programming has flourished in prisons for centuries, exclusively faith-based prisons have begun sprouting up across the United States, with the first one opening in Florida in 2004, followed by "facilities of faith" in Iowa, Texas, and Ohio.[33]

Of all the new actors playing the role of the penal state, perhaps the most prominent is the "community." As sociologist David Garland points out, some voluntary associations have been brought into the area of punishment in earnest, especially in the area of community policing and crime control.[34] Yet when it comes to actual penal facilities, many that claim to draw on the community actually operate quite conventionally: they rely on state employees who in turn rely on state funds to carry out state-mandated policies using clear state sanctions. Often called alternative-to-incarceration (ATI) programs, their main claim to community is that they operate outside the walls of traditional prisons—perhaps allowing their charges to maintain ties to family and community networks. But their form and focus can also end up replicating those of more traditional penal facilities. Nevertheless, the community continues to be touted as the "solution" to just about every problem of crime and punishment.[35]

The imperative to punish through community is usually articulated at the level of particular state governments. That is, state legislatures set forth proposals and reforms to bring the community into the field of corrections. California, for instance, has an especially long legacy of calls to decentralize its penal system. Stretching back for decades, support for "community-based alternatives" reached a fever pitch in the 1990s. This was also when the upper echelons of government weighed in: in 1990, the state-funded blue-ribbon Commission issued a report calling for more community-based programs. In 1994, the state legislature followed up on these recommendations by passing the Community-Based Punishment Act, which formed a state-local partnership to establish new "alternative punishments" and ATI programs. Yet the partnership was never funded. Instead, a few county-level pilot programs surfaced to "test" the ATI solution. Then in 2007, the legislature's Little Hoover Commission released its strongest call for community punishment: it demanded that the legislature shift "supervision and responsibility to communities," to extend resources to "expand local capacity," and to begin moving "low-level" and "nonviolent" offenders to community-based facilities.[36]

For the most part, these calls for community corrections remained just that—pleas for the creation of noncustodial programs or for increased funding for existing programs. Yet, at least in California, there was one area in which these programs took off: the field of drug treatment.[37] In 2000, California voters passed the Substance Abuse and Crime Prevention Act (Proposition 36) to expand the ATI arena for nonviolent offenders charged with drug-related crimes. Since then, Prop. 36 has diverted more than fifty thousand offenders to community-based facilities every year. This has dramatically altered the contours of the California penal system. In sharp contrast to the pages and pages of rules defining which offenders were eligible for Prop. 36, the law itself included no special regulations or guidelines for treatment facilities—except to say that all participating programs had to be licensed and certified. As a result, a wide array of programs were funded through Prop. 36; they ranged from Alcoholics Anonymous–inspired services to local community groups to faith-based organizations to medicalized treatment to private substance-abuse programs. This variation made Prop. 36 an example of state hybridity par excellence.

As in other state subsystems, hybridity in the penal system also led to a layering of institutions that defined themselves in opposition to each other. Those working in the penal system frequently represent it as having a bifurcated structure.[38] On the one hand, there is the centralized, coercive arm—characterized by rigid, retributive, and punitive institutions with little room for rehabilitative ideals. On the other, there is the decentralized, alternative arm—characterized by diverse, mixed, and hybrid institutions that form a rehabilitative enclave in the larger penal system. Yet even this may be an outdated representation of the terrain since, as I just outlined, many "alternative" facilities end up operating like their coercive counterparts. In addition, even the most traditional, centralized prisons also rely on community groups, nonprofits, and private companies to provide everything from education to counseling to health care to employment for inmates. Such mixtures can then lead to a collision of approaches, as a variety of organizational logics merge and conflict both across and within penal institutions.

Indeed, this is the critical issue to examine next: What has happened to concrete institutions in this state of hybridity? What does all the diversity imply for their operation and orientation? What challenges does it pose for their staff and clients?

EXTERNAL AND INTERNAL CHALLENGES OF SATELLITE STATES

Despite the inventive imagery used by scholars of state hybridity, their analyses often seem disconnected from social reality—in large part because their work is rarely grounded in the messy world of actual institutions. So while their images and metaphors help to conceptualize broad changes in governmental power, they reveal far less about actual institutional reverberations.[39] But these two levels of analysis can and should be linked: charting the institutional implications of state reform can provide more nuanced insights into the form, focus, and structure of contemporary government. In large part, this is because the two often diverge—as with their more traditional bureaucratic counterparts, state satellites do not always operate as planned or intended.[40]

Only the Promotable (and Fundable) Survive

In the world of devolved and spatially scattered states, public institutions often find themselves increasingly disconnected from a central political apparatus. Gone are the days when ties to the center were clearly tangible and discernable—or even when auxiliary institutions shared spaces with their sponsors. In this way, institutions now operate more like satellite states—like the institutional offspring of a centralized state body, encircling and hovering around it without being directly controlled by it. Yet this does not mean that satellites are autonomous, free-floating entities; or that, on a day-to-day level, they can set their own agendas or practices. Instead, with the increased geographical distance from the center have come new checks and balances. This regulation creates new external and internal dilemmas for satellite institutions.[41]

Externally, some of the most pressing challenges come from the new management practices and assessments now required of satellite state institutions. Once reserved for corporate and business organizations, external program evaluations and cost-benefit analyses are now applied to these state bodies. Guided by managerial models, these analyses employ tools like standardized performance measures, accountability scales, and ranking systems to rate institutional effectiveness. In the process, the definition of institutional effectiveness has shifted: instead of striving to ameliorate poverty, lower crime rates, or serve the needy, the goal has become to manage targeted populations in the most cost-effective way possible. For instance, penal institutions now fixate on internal measures of control, such as the rate of prisoner infractions, the ratio of "dirty" to "clean" drug tests, or the speed of inmate processing. As legal scholars Malcolm Feeley and Jonathan Simon point out, this focus deflects attention from more substantive social goals like inmate reintegration or rehabilitation.[42] It also insulates penal facilities from the empirical realities of poverty, crime, and the "messy, hard-to-control demands of the social world."[43] Yet one can hardly blame these institutions for obsessing about internal indicators; they are themselves evaluated and assessed in these terms.

What is more, the results of these assessments actually matter, especially for state satellites that operate amid considerable organizational and financial uncertainty. Since the 1990s, the orbits these institutions move in have become increasingly crowded. There are now a variety of recent spin-offs and downloads elbowing for room, which has created real competition among satellites—often over the wrong kinds of things. For example, instead of competing over whose inmates have the highest rates of GED completion or of finishing high school, they battle over who can make the largest and fastest cuts in the number of inmate infractions. Rather than competing over who better prepares inmates for reintegration upon release, they struggle over who can process more cases the fastest using the fewest resources.

For instance, take recent debates over the effectiveness of California's Prop. 36. In 2007, researchers from UCLA did the first large-scale evaluation of the legislation and arrived at some controversial findings: not only were drug offenders who were diverted to ATI programs under Prop. 36 less likely to complete treatment, but they were more likely to be rearrested for a drug offense than those who were not diverted.[44] While such findings could have prompted a serious reflection on the inability of state-funded treatment facilities to meet offenders' needs, they ended up leading to calls for increased surveillance of drug offenders under Prop. 36. They also prompted debate and discussion about how to best carry out this surveillance: Should offenders be forced to check in at street kiosks run by probation departments? Or should probation officers make unannounced visits to offenders' homes? With time, the report created even more competition over which programs could conduct this surveillance work in the most cost-effective way. In the process, little consideration was given to how Prop. 36 treatment facilities could be better regulated or to how the emphasis on cost-effectiveness may be undermining program effectiveness. Of course, none of this is surprising given the kinds of assessment protocols and evaluation measures these programs are themselves held accountable to.

These new modes of institutional assessment are consequential for yet another reason: they shape critical decisions about which programs get funded for how long. Gone are the days when state institutions can sustain themselves through fixed, long-term budgetary allocations from state legislatures. Far more common are agencies with mixed resource bases: they may have some fixed public funds, which they are forced to supplement with additional resources. The latter funds are increasingly allocated through competitive public contracts and grants, which can lead to the "tyranny of the RFP." These new funding imperatives then pit agencies against each other, creating rivalry and competition where there could be cooperation. They also create enormous uncertainty, since most grants run in one- or two-year cycles, constraining facilities from long-term planning or extended commitments. State satellites thus find themselves moving from funding competition to funding competition in order to stay afloat. This then pushes many satellites to expand in size and scope—hoping that they can guarantee some longevity and consistency by extending their tentacles into new areas and thereby diversifying their "funding profile."[45]

In this era of competitive state funding, the one factor that does seem to increase the likelihood of funding success is an institution's ability to prove it is not dependent on state resources;[46] or that it has the capacity and know-how to tap into private funding sources. The irony here is obvious: a facility is more likely to get state funds if it can demonstrate that it does not really need them. For instance, city and state governments frequently hold funding workshops and grant-writing seminars to help state satellites in the human and social services become more successful and savvy at securing outside funding. In these seminars, agencies are taught that, in order to be competitive, they cannot appear to operate like the big, bureaucratic state agencies of the past.[47] This means they cannot come across as reliant on public funds; they have to exhibit diverse "budgetary networks." In addition, the grant makers running these workshops often stress that competitive agencies should develop "lines" about themselves, to have a hook that sets them apart from the others. Each agency must seem unique and distinctive.

The imperative to appear unique leads to another external dilemma for state satellites: their ability to sustain themselves depends largely on marketing and publicity. Jamie Peck has found something similar in the welfare state—in the era of "fast policy" transfers, states and locales compete to be seen as the success stories that others strive to emulate.[48] The same is true of actual institutions. As they go up against each other in funding competitions, state satellites must sell themselves as special. Grant-writing experts are then deployed to advise them how to do this. Thus, glossy promotional materials and fancy Web sites become a way to get the word out. Again, the word each agency gets out must include a convincing line about what makes it distinct—whether it be an orientation, like "therapeutic corrections," or an approach, like "12-step wraparound services."

In fact, state satellites increasingly need a convincing line as they confront another form of competition: the battle for clients. In the early 1990s, the girls at Alliance had few choices in the ATI arena; if they wanted to do their time with their children, Alliance was the only game in town. Yet as the arena of "alternative" institutions began to fill up in the 1990s, inmates were given options. Take, for example, the new world of Prop. 36: it created hundreds of new treatment facilities all vying for the more than fifty thousand offenders eligible for diversion every year. These programs had to then gain a following and become known. Some did this recruiting through judges and justice officials—that is, they struggled to become the preferred programs of particular judges or parole officers, who could then guarantee a steady flow of clients and repeat offenders. Other institutions appealed to clients more directly, meeting with them while they were in jail or other treatment programs.[49] Such recruitment efforts made promotional materials and having a distinctive line all the more essential. The "marketization" of the state thus operates on multiple levels: facilities market themselves vis-à-vis each other while they sell themselves to sought-after clients.

To make matters even more complex, these external dilemmas can end up creating internal dilemmas for satellite state institutions. First and foremost, the structure of state satellites opens them up to enormous diversity in their clients and staff. One common way that satellites grapple with their organizational and financial instability is by combining different populations of clients. Without stable, long-term budget commitments, they must merge their funding resources; without a clear, long-standing organizational niche, they must combine their client pools. So it is not unusual to find different groups, with different needs, sharing the same institutional space. For instance, state satellites often serve both "private" and "public" clients—those who "pay" for their services through private sources or insurance companies and those who are publicly mandated to be in the program. Satellites also combine groups with an array of issues— from substance abuse to eating disorders to mental-health problems to homelessness to criminal records. The unifying mission then becomes the regulation of vice, broadly conceived—or, in their lingo, they target "hard-to-serve populations" with "wraparound services." Bringing these groups together into one facility can create unimaginable conflict. Among other things, it can breed animosity among clients as they compete for attention and acknowledgement. Eventually, it can lead to struggles over whose needs are the most pressing and whose vice is most threatening.

Similar challenges confront the staffs of state satellites. With the inclusion of all sorts of new actors playing the role of the state, staff practices have diversified; the tools that staffs use to interpret and respond to their institutional worlds have multiplied.[50] It is almost commonplace to point out how little job training an institution's staff receive or how much of their training occurs on the job. Those who staff state satellites also have different, and arguably weaker, ties to the institution than those who work in larger, more traditional state institutions, where commitment to the facility is often cemented through seniority structures, promotional/retirement ladders, and union membership. Few state satellites have clear seniority structures or retirement plans; even fewer are unionized. This can leave employees with fleeting connections to the facility and can also cause considerable variation in the staff's commitment to their work—without job security, it can be difficult to foster staff engagement. This is only exacerbated by the lack of guarantees for institutional longevity: in this satellite arena, facilities open, close, and merge at alarming rates. Thus, it is not surprising that the staff turnover rate in state satellites tends to be much higher than in traditional state institutions.

If all of this internal diversity were not enough, state satellites are also exposed to a variety of cultural and community influences. Here, too, their porous borders are the culprit. This actually makes perfect sense: less connected to a centralized apparatus, satellite states are more apt to pick up different interpretive frameworks along their journeys. It also makes sense that, as they compete and come into contact with each other, satellites become more permeable at the discursive level. All of this can then make them more connected to surrounding community and cultural contexts.

For example, there were countless ways in which the Alliance staff drew on the surrounding inner-city context as they regulated their girls. Sometimes this happened consciously, as when counselor Colorado brought in articles about then-rising rap star Queen Latifah, claiming the girls should emulate her as a strong, independent woman; or when schoolteacher Rachel created the Brennan Bucks Program to teach the girls to mould their behavior and respond to market incentives. Other times the influences seemed more unconscious, as when the staff unwittingly echoed Reagan-like arguments about personal responsibility and accountability; or when they drew on models and metaphors of community empowerment to make sense of the lives of disempowered women—thus mismatching political contexts in a way that enraged the young women they claimed to be serving.

None of this is to imply that cultural influences were not at work in state institutions at other historical moments.[51] Nor is it to suggest that similar influences are not at work in more centralized state facilities or national-level policy spheres in the contemporary period.[52] In the penal system, there is little doubt that California Department of Corrections (CDC) institutions like juvenile hall and CYA engage in culturally resonant practices. Yet, long-standing institutional rules and routines also create something of a buffer around these practices in a way they do not for state satellites. Thus, it is hard to imagine that Queen Latifah could become an icon for such a large and centralized institution as CYA. Quite simply, state satellites are constituted to absorb and institutionalize broader cultural scripts in ways that larger, more centralized state facilities are not.

This cultural absorption is itself something of a mixed bag. On the one hand, these influences can end up strengthening a staff's bond to their institution—what satellite facilities lack in financial and job security they might make up for in programmatic involvement. By giving their staffs the chance to draw on community knowledge as they form their practices, satellites may enable staff members to feel creative and innovative; by allowing them to draw on their cultural values and experiences as they construct the facility's approach, satellites may enhance their staffs' institutional commitment. Sociologist Nina Eliasoph demonstrates precisely this point in her revealing ethnographic account of community-based state youth programs—showing how staff members' allegiances to the programs arose from their commitment to multiculturalism and corresponding sense of civic pride.[53] And the programs gave the staff members just enough space to feel like they were meeting these ideals and respecting cultural diversity.

At the same time, opening the institutional door to various cultural influences can cause further diversification and fragmentation within state satellites. It can lead to divergent mandates and collisions of approaches. It can ensnarl everyone in misunderstandings and inconsistencies as different staff members hold clients to different cultural ideals. It can lead to conflicts among the staff as their cultures clash and community commitments diverge. This is precisely what occurred in Eliasoph's youth programs: from unhelpful volunteers to forced intimacy to messages that fell on the wrong ears, hybridity often bred misinterpretation and tension.[54] If mismanaged, internal institutional diversity can become divisive and corrosive. Indeed, this was what happened at Alliance in the early 1990s.

The Rise and Fall of a State Satellite

Given all the external and internal pressures confronting satellite state institutions, it should not be entirely surprising that Alliance closed in 1993, only a few years after it opened. Quite simply, the facility could not exist on such uncertain and contested terrain. Like many satellites, Alliance was sandwiched between two larger institutions—on the NGO side was the Fellowship for Change, and on the penal state side was the California Youth Authority. Alliance was thus held accountable to quite different modes of assessment and evaluative criteria; it was asked to emphasize both control and care, both retribution and recovery. Its staff were haunted by the onslaught of new checks and balances; they had no idea what to make of the performance measures and efficiency scales used to assess them. They were wholly unsuccessful at securing external funding. In its history, Alliance only received one grant from a public foundation—and it lasted only a year, after which time it was withdrawn due to accusations of organizational mismanagement. Although Alliance did try to use private charity, such assistance was limited. So Alliance was left to rely on old, traditional forms of funding, cobbling together resources from CYA and programs like AFDC and food stamps.

Then their girls turned on them. Infuriated by the mismatch between the program of dependency and the realities of their lives, the Alliance girls contested the core elements of the facility's program. As I described in chapter 2, the girls turned Alliance's hybrid structure on itself—bringing in outside state actors from CYA, the county rules and regulations department, and the city welfare administration to regulate what went on inside the facility. The girls drew on the complex layers of checks and balances to control the staff—telling other state actors whenever the Alliance staff violated a CYA rule, bureaucratic regulation, or licensing requirement. These battles not only left the staff fatigued and exhausted but also made Alliance appear unmanageable to the outside institutions upon which it depended. The Fellowship got too many complaints from too many of the girls Alliance claimed to be helping; CYA spent too much time dealing with too many problems from an institution designed to take some of the burden off of its officials. Eventually, CYA refused to renew Alliance's contract, and the Fellowship refused to appeal the decision.

In this way, the history of Alliance exemplifies many of the structural and institutional challenges discussed in this chapter. Alliance was an early form of state satellite at an early stage of state hybridity. It arose before social scientists had developed their complicated imagery, metaphors, and theorizations of government from a distance. It emerged before those working in the penal system had a clear sense of how the rules of the game were changing and what kind of survival strategies they needed to develop. To a large extent, the Alliance staff were not prepared or trained to deal with the challenges of state hybridity: they were products of the devolved, decentralized state but also were plagued by its internal and external dilemmas. Hence, while they had a clear sense of their alterative approach, the Alliance staff may have underestimated their uniqueness. Perhaps they were indeed harbingers of things to come: their discourse of dependence was on the horizon in many other state arenas as were the form and focus of their institution.

In fact, around the time that Alliance was falling apart, another state satellite, targeting a similar group of clients, was on the rise. The history of this network of institutions is equally telling. In a fashion typical of hybrids, the impetus for its development came from outside the actual penal system—it emerged from a group of feminist lawyers concerned about female inmates with children.[55] In the 1980s, when the problems of incarcerated mothers began to get some public attention, roughly 65 percent of all female inmates were mothers; close to two-thirds of them had been living with their children just prior to incarceration.[56] To address their plight, a San Francisco–based public-interest law firm, Legal Services for Prisoners with Children (LSPC), uncovered a long-forgotten statute in the state penal code of 1979 that allowed female inmates to serve their sentences with their children in community-based facilities.[57] Yet, in 1985, there were only three women in California doing their time in such facilities.

So LSPC took their fight to court: throughout the 1980s, they won a series of lawsuits on behalf of incarcerated mothers who wanted to use the state's Mother-Infant Program (MIP) and serve their time with their children in the community.[58] Yet the CDC remained uncooperative, refusing to inform inmates about MIP or process their applications. So, for most of the 1980s, the number of MIP participants hovered around a dozen. Then, in 1990, LSPC won a major settlement that required the CDC to comply with the 1979 statute and to begin to use MIP facilities.[59] Still, it was not until prison overcrowding became a serious issue in women's prisons in the mid-1990s that the CDC acquiesced and agreed to release eligible inmates to the program.

Once the CDC was forced on board, this network of penal institutions took off rapidly. After all, it promised to serve several interests simultaneously: the CDC would get some help with prison overcrowding, which had become a problem in female corrections; the foster-care system would get some institutional relief, since many female inmates fall back on foster care at some point during their incarceration; and progressive prison activists and lawyers would secure a route to channel women out of much-maligned women's prisons.[60] And, of course, the MIP came with a significant pool of resources for those facilities that won state contracts. The setup worked like this: each MIP facility would be contracted for twenty-five CDC inmates and their children. The CDC paid for the inmates at a cost of $25,000 per inmate per year, while the inmates' children were covered by food stamps and AFDC. Because there were no funds to cover setup costs, those facilities vying for MIP contracts needed to have existing infrastructures and developed resource bases—after all, they were housing CDC inmates, many of whom were convicted of quite serious felonies. So successful MIP facilities really could not be small, mom-and-pop operations. Instead, they had to be larger groups and NGOs—or smaller offshoots with access to the safety nets of bigger institutions.

In this way, MIP institutions were state satellites par excellence—if Alliance was an early form of state hybridity, MIP facilities were the advanced version. The community imprint on these facilities was clear: it was even encoded in the program's official name, which changed to the Community Prisoner Mothers Program (CPMP) in the 1990s. Like other satellites, CPMP facilities came up with clever names for their programs that drew on community metaphors.[61] They also had a variety of community ties. Some, like the CPMP facility run by Volunteers of America, had national connections to community groups. Others had links to local networks— like county drug courts, community-development projects, and substance-abuse programs. And, of course, all of them insisted on being located in "the community," since this was their main claim to institutional fame.

The funding structures of CPMP organizations were also textbook cases of state hybridity. They relied on a complex mix of state and private funding—most of them got support from big public programs, small foundations, and big businesses. For instance, one CPMP facility in Southern California had prominent business leaders and CEOs of national retail chains on its board of directors, which it proudly displayed on plaques in the facility's entryway. Some CPMP groups even had inmates contribute their own resources to support the facility. In the late 1990s, after many CPMP inmates were denied Temporary Assistance to Needy Families benefits because of new rules restricting the eligibility of women convicted of drug-related offenses and other felonies, some CPMP facilities began to require that inmates pay a daily contribution for their kids' room and board. Because the required contribution hovered around $10 per day, many women went into debt while at CPMP institutions—particularly because most of these facilities forbade them from working for wages while serving time.[62]

The CPMP clients and staffs also mirrored these organizations' hybrid structures. Because CPMP facilities were the offspring of larger, human-service NGOs, they often mixed their client populations to pool funding.

That is, they frequently housed CDC inmates with other "vice-afflicted" women—including women with histories of drug use, alcoholism, prostitution, and mental illness. A similar merging of backgrounds characterized the staffs at various institutions. Within their ranks, all sorts of communities collided and cultures met—from those staff members influenced by Oprah and Dr. Phil to Freud and Lacan to Alcoholics Anonymous and Narcotics Anonymous to L. Ron Hubbard and Scientology. Perhaps the biggest symbol of staff diversity was the requirement that CPMP facilities have at least one CDC official on site at all times. This bred even more institutional culture clashes, since the CDC official usually brought her own institutional culture with her and injected a good dose of penal discipline and punishment into these "alternative" facilities.

Needless to say, the diversity in structure, funding, staffs, and clients led CPMP facilities to experience many of the internal dilemmas characteristic of satellites. As I discuss in the following chapter, the majority of CPMP outfits collapsed under the pressure. To a large extent, the late 1990s were the heyday of the CPMP: when a total of six facilities operated across the state to serve close to two hundred inmates every year. By the time of my fieldwork in 2002, only two CPMP facilities remained.[63] Some facilities closed because they were unable to secure external funding. Others failed to develop distinctive "lines" about themselves and thus never carved out niches for their facilities. Still others fell out of favor with CDC officials, who then halted the flow of inmates to their programs. In this way, the history of CPMP organizations holds many lessons of state hybridity, demonstrating both the possibilities and limitations of this institutional form.

SETTING THE STAGE

The 1990s were a period of profound change in the practice of government. While not always coherent or consistent across time and space, restructuring processes altered the terrain upon which state institutions formed and transformed. At an abstract, systemic level, the holy trinity of devolution, decentralization, and diversification led to the vertical and horizontal distancing of state institutions from a central political apparatus. This, in turn, led to the downloading of political responsibility and conflict as well as the emergence of regulatory mechanisms to connect the core to its peripheries. While experienced in different ways in different state subsystems, these reform processes created states of hybridity characterized by unique mixtures of state actors, institutional logics, and governance strategies. At the more concrete, organizational level, hybridity posed external and internal challenges for state facilities. From new management practices to competitive bidding and RFPs to public-relations mandates to interagency rivalries to divergent cultural and community influences, state satellites began to confront a stunning array of threats to their institutional well-being and longevity.

So what does all of this imply for my ethnographic story of institutional narratives and the governance of gender? Quite a bit: by providing a structural backdrop for the case studies of Alliance and Visions, this analysis sets the stage for the second part of the story. While Alliance disappeared in this state of hybridity, Visions emerged from it. This difference helps to explain why Visions became even more closely connected to its surrounding community, culture, and context. It offers insights into how Visions managed its many tensions in order to survive—and why the development of a common institutional narrative became so important for its staff. It also provides a hint about why Visions chose to govern women the way it did—and why it decided on the regulation of desire as its unifying script.

PART TWO In a State of Recovery

FOUR

State Therapeutics

TRAINING WOMEN WHAT
TO WANT

It was a big day at Visions. The third-floor meeting room was filled to capacity, with more than thirty staff members and visitors sitting in front of a makeshift stage. They watched as the inmates of Visions performed readings and skits they had prepared with two local artists. Funded by a large public radio station, the artists had held classes during the summer of 2004 to help the inmates find their "voices" and perform their art. One after the other, women rose to recite poems and stories, most of which dealt with personal pain and turmoil. Each reading was more wrenching than the previous one, prompting many in the audience to bury their faces and break down in tears.

Midway through the performance, a surprise occurred when Tamika, a Visions staff member, unexpectedly took the stage. Unlike other counselors, Tamika rarely participated in events like this; she thought engaging in such emotional outpourings was unprofessional. Today was different. With a nervous smile, Tamika broke into a gospel rendition of "Some-where over the Rainbow." As her strong, deep voice filled the room, many inmates and staff members began to cry. Even Tamika started to choke up. In an attempt to regain her composure, she finished with a short sermon: "That was for all you mothers," she shouted. "To give you strength in your journey from dependency to independency." This was not an easy journey, she warned. The "road to recovery" would be long and hard. But they would make it. They would clear their minds, their bodies, and their souls. "You will cleanse the old and move from depen-dency to independency," she repeated. As she concluded, the weeping audience jumped up for a long standing ovation.

As I watched this performance, I was transported back to my previous work at Alliance, which had closed its doors over a decade earlier. The terms Tamika repeated, *dependence* and *independence,* had been keywords for the Alliance staff as well, forming the centerpiece of their discourse of need. Yet the meanings Tamika attached to them were strikingly dif-ferent. For the Alliance staff, in/dependence referred to women's social relationships, particularly with the state. Tamika deployed the words as therapeutic terms to reference women's emotional and psychological conditions. For her, in/dependence was a way to talk about the state of women's recovery from a variety of individual ailments. This was true even though the women's stories on stage that day had been full of social obstacles and inequities—from their failed attempts to find and maintain employment to their ongoing struggles to secure housing or education to their violent experiences with family members, spouses, and lovers. Despite this, at Visions the road to recovery bypassed the social, heading instead through women's minds, bodies, and souls.

Tamika was not alone in her understanding of recovery as an essen-tially therapeutic matter. Throughout the 1990s, this perception emerged in a variety of state arenas. In fact, one of its earliest expressions surfaced just down the road from Visions: the city's drug court was one of first and the most notorious examples of "therapeutic corrections." Its court-room operated like a big group therapy session, replete with personal confessions and appeals for love and forgiveness.[1] By the late 1990s, this approach became so ubiquitous that social scientists began to analyze it as "therapeutic governance." The rise of therapy culture in the United States is well documented, as are its effects on public institutions and discourse.[2] Yet its incorporation into the penal system has been particularly stunning: since 1980, the number of inmates engaged in psychological or drug treatment nearly tripled; the percentage of prisoners receiving therapy more than doubled, with the largest increase occurring in the early to mid-1990s.[3] These trends were even more pronounced in satellite institutions, since they are often staffed by clinical social workers trained in therapeutic practice and psychological counseling.

With its emergence in carceral settings, the therapeutic has clearly become a mode of state punishment. In addition to offering a template for making sense of the world, therapeutics serves as a technique of governance, used to manage psychological and emotional conduct in ways that align with the aims of government. To be sure, there is nothing new about subjecting wards of the state to therapeutic intervention. Such interventions have long histories as forms of state subjectification and individualization, what Foucault refers to as "technologies of the self."[4] Throughout the nineteenth century, a variety of political projects emerged to restrain the presumably out-of-control impulses of disorderly groups. In the United States, campaigns to address everything from sole motherhood to alcoholism to mental illness to poverty were premised on the idea that, with the right training, the undisciplined could learn to control their wills and lead well-regulated, "civilized" lives.[5] State institutions like reformatories, prisons, and schools thus became the sites for this retraining and resocialization.

Yet there does seem to be something distinctive about contemporary therapeutic governance. With roots in the self-help and AA movements, it problematizes particular kinds of vice and pathology. As Nikolas Rose suggests, therapeutics is now less preoccupied with managing social problems and more concerned with governing the "passions of self-identified individuals"—those who have fallen out of "citizen-forming" networks and into excessive lifestyles.[6] So the parameters of vice have widened to encompass not only the classics of sex, drugs, and alcohol but also certain personalities, associations, and identifications.[7] Related to this, the cause of these ailments is believed to be far deeper than ever before. As sociologist James Nolan documents, a "vocabulary of therapeutics" has emerged to reframe the scope of state policies and programs—as terms like *anxiety, trauma,* and *addiction* are used to explain why some "selves" are more distorted than others.[8] So the allure of vice has begun to reflect deeply ingrained choices and self-identifications. In addition, the path to rid oneself of such troubling impulses is less social and more psychological. As political theorist Barbara Cruikshank argues, therapeutics now aims at self-governance—forming the route to self-esteem, self-realization, and self-mastery.[9] So freedom from vice is equated with self-determination, while the refashioning of the self becomes a mode of empowerment.

Unlike nineteenth-century therapeutic interventions, which have been clearly linked to a variety of social and economic projects, we know little about the roots of contemporary therapeutics. Except for vague references to general cultural shifts—such as the erosion of a common moral order, the rise of the "risk" society, and a decline in the significance of religion—social scientists have avoided addressing why therapeutic governance so permeates the state arena.[10] Although cultural changes may help explain the salience and availability of therapeutic scripts, they cannot account for why these vocabularies were institutionalized in specific state spaces at specific moments. They rarely explain why these scripts framed some desires as prohibitive while normalizing others. And they give few insights into why these therapeutic idioms seem to resonate so strongly with those institutionalizing them—prompting women like Tamika to turn them into gospel.

In fact, Tamika's performance provides important clues about the source of the power of therapeutics. More precisely, her colleagues' reactions to her performance offer insight into the institutional roots of this discourse. For years, Tamika kept her distance from therapeutics, viewing it with discomfort and suspicion. Her reluctance was of grave concern to her colleagues, most of whom had developed strong attachments to a therapeutic script. They had good reasons for their attachments. This vocabulary was Visions's way of resolving many of its external and internal conflicts—tensions emanating from the advanced state of hybridity of the 1990s. Externally, it enabled Visions to situate itself in this crowded arena of the penal system, develop a seemingly distinctive institutional line, and increase access to coveted resources and funding. Internally, therapeutics allowed the staff to grapple with diversity in their ranks, as well as the resulting programmatic divisions and uncertainties. The standing ovation Tamika received was very much a celebration of her integration into the therapeutic community.

The first part of this chapter provides an account of how Visions's therapeutic community formed and how a discourse of recovery took hold to resolve the resulting organizational dilemmas. Instead of attributing therapeutics to some abstract cultural condition, I argue that it had concrete institutional roots: the script was linked to Visions's hybrid structure and the tensions inherent in it. I then analyze the specific practices the discourse of recovery gave rise to once it was institutionalized. Here I reveal how recovery came to mean the rehabilitation of the "self" through public exposure and confession. I also explicate how the regulation of women's desires became central to this rehabilitative process, with personal vice, addiction, and pathology as the main targets of this state of recovery.

THE INSTITUTIONAL ROOTS OF THERAPEUTICS

Although I did not realize it then, my ethnographic research at Visions occurred at a particularly revealing time. The facility was undergoing a significant transition that reflected larger shifts in the "alternative" arm of the penal system. Like other Community Prisoner Mothers Program facilities, Visions was born from progressive, feminist attempts to reform the penal system.[11] The late 1990s had been the high point of these programs, with as many as six CPMP facilities operating across California. By the end of the decade, three of them had been closed by the California Department of Corrections. Often these closings happened in a hasty, unexpected way. For example, one CPMP facility, located in the same city as Visions, was forced to close in a forty-eight-hour period—its staff was laid off without warning, while its twenty-five female inmates and their children were given one evening to pack up their belongings before being bused to other facilities across the state. Events like this reverberated throughout the CPMP network, serving as a clear warning to other facilities: there was to be no organizational stability or security for state satellites.

Along with a CPMP facility in Southern California, Visions survived this period of closings and reshufflings. In fact, these two facilities became CPMP flagships, and criminal-justice officials often presented them as model programs.[12] The favored status of the Southern California facility was connected to the visibility and prominence of the larger NGO of which it was an offshoot. Among other things, this financially secure NGO protected its underling from economic collapse and closure. Visions was also affiliated with a larger community-based group, the Recovery Project, but that relationship was far less lucrative for Visions. Although the Recovery Project had a long-standing community presence and an abundance of local ties, it was often plagued with financial difficulties. This left Visions with fewer material supports from its NGO sponsor, which required it to diversify its funding by drawing on a mixture of state contracts, welfare programs, public foundations, and private charities. In the process, Visions evolved into a classic state hybrid, combining divergent logics, orientations, and perspectives. It also merged its inmate population: half of them were CDC inmates convicted of a wide range of felonies; the other half were court-mandated clients sent to Visions as an alternative to incarceration; and a few came to the facility voluntarily, often directly from the streets.[13] At almost every level, Visions's diversity was both dizzying and dazzling.

Perhaps I was particularly sensitive to the diversity confronting Visions when I began working there in 2002. Having researched Alliance a decade earlier, at a less advanced stage of state hybridity, its example was never far in the back of my mind. I was expecting to encounter some diversity at Visions—but I never expected it to reach such a level. In my early interactions with the staff, I found myself constantly asking how they managed so many manifest differences. Over and over again, they told me that their unique program and orientation held the place together. Initially, I was suspicious; this explanation seemed too self-serving and consistent with Visions's need to appear distinctive. Over time, however, I began to concur, though probably for different reasons than the staff. Indeed, the Visions staff had developed a narrative about themselves, their work, and their inmates that allowed them to ease the organizational tensions destroying other state satellites. Gradually, I also realized that their narrative did not emerge naturally or even smoothly. Rather, it emanated from institutional struggles over how to structure the program and interpret inmates' problems.

The Upstairs/Downstairs Divide

The working conditions in satellite institutions like Visions were quite difficult. Unlike officers in traditional prisons, the staff of these facilities had little job security: they could be laid off on a whim, without justification or recourse. While California prison guards built one of the strongest labor unions in the United States, the Visions staff could not join it—officially, they were employees of the Recovery Project and not the CDC. This left them with limited bargaining power and collective representation. It also meant that they had few benefits and shockingly low salaries.[14] So, although their day-to-day work was not unlike that of correctional officers, it was not accompanied by the perks usually associated with criminal-justice employment.

The contrast between nonprofit and CDC employment was particularly stark in CPMP facilities like Visions, since their CDC contract required them to employ a correctional officer to oversee the inmates' activities and safety. The Visions CDC officer was Margaret, a no-nonsense woman in her early fifties. Margaret was one of the first female African American prison guards in the state and was quick to remind everyone she had paid her dues—she had spent years working in facilities where she was harassed by male prison guards. After more than two decades in the field, she was finally rewarded for her loyalty. At Visions, she set her own hours and wielded enormous authority over the inmates. She was also paid close to three times as much as other staff members. Moreover, her long CDC career gave her job seniority and security. Although she was not much older than other Visions staff members, her CDC pension enabled her to retire decades before her colleagues. In fact, Margaret spent much of her workday planning her impending retirement and searching the Internet for a mansion to buy in Texas.

While such material inequities were not lost on the Visions staff, they rarely surfaced explicitly. Nor did they become institutionally decisive or divisive. Instead, of all the potential sources of conflict, those experienced most acutely were related to programmatic approach. From my first day at Visions, it was apparent that the staff thought of themselves as at war. In this way, Visions was similar to Alliance; both facilities were engaged in struggles to define the form and focus of their programs. However, there was a central difference between their battles. At Alliance, the struggle was fought externally, in "us versus them" terms, while at Visions it was an internal struggle, fought out in "us versus us" terms. In part, Alliance's ability to externalize the struggle was rooted in their clearly defined "us." The staff viewed themselves as being on a common rescue mission to help girls escape from a destructive, dependency-producing penal system. The "us" was never as clear at Visions. Although Visions staff also considered their approach to be alternative, they were more divided over exactly what this meant.

Moreover, the Visions staff had a hard time pinning down exactly who was meant by "them." At Alliance the "them" was obvious: sandwiched between the larger, more centralized Fellowship for Change and California Youth Authority, the Alliance staff opposed "those" officials who ignored girls' needs. There was no equivalent "them" for Visions to go up against. Although it also operated in between two larger institutions—the Recovery Project and the CDC—there were countless other agencies operating in the mix. For example, Visions's funding structure was inordinately complex: its budget had more than seven general categories of funders, including federal, state, city, county, NGO, private, and inmate funding. Each funding category included several different subcategories—Visions's county funding alone encompassed six different sources, including assistance from public-health programs, mental-health agencies, drug/alcohol initiatives, and alternative-to-incarceration policies like Prop. 36.[15] This funding structure meant the demands placed on Visions came from many sources. And this made the staff's financial attachments equally varied: for some, employment rested on Visions's CDC contract; for others it was linked to funding from substance-abuse and mental-health agencies; and for others still, it was tied up with private foundations and charities. Amid such divergent loyalties and financial dependencies, there was no clear external "them" to oppose collectively.

Accordingly, the struggles at Visions were played out in internal, "us versus us" terms. The battle lines were clearly drawn. On one side were staff members committed to a "behavior modification" paradigm. They believed their job was to teach inmates the rules of acceptable social behavior and to force them to abide by these rules. For these staff members, following social norms was a choice that female inmates could and should make. Because of the inmates' personal weaknesses, it was also a choice that could only emerge after the administration of heavy doses of tough love. Few of these women on staff had had any training in corrections or the penal system. Instead, most had been involved in the drug-treatment, AA, and self-help movements. Some had even received certification in substance abuse or addiction studies. What these women lacked in formal training they made up for in life experience: they often came from backgrounds and communities similar to those of the inmates. They considered themselves a bit older and wiser than the inmates, which underlay their "been-there-done-that" attitude. Their commitment to the inmates was not abstract or theoretical; it was personal and experiential.

Most staff members at the lower end of Visions's hierarchy fell into this camp. Those who did the cooking, cleaning, child care, and administration tended to be the strongest adherents of the behavior-modification approach. This meant they constituted the majority of staff members. But whatever power they gained from their numbers they lost in influence— only a handful of those in counseling and management positions were on their "side." As a result, the divide became spatial: because these staff members tended to spend their days working on the first floor of the facility, where female inmates and their children resided, they became known as "downstairs" staff.

On the other side of the institutional divide were the clinical counselors. Their goal was to transform Visions into a full-fledged therapeutic community that reflected their educational background. Most of them had received nontraditional therapeutic training from local institutes and schools specializing in "alternative" psychological practices. Among other things, this meant that they came to Visions with psychological tool kits to promote "holistic healing" through self-discovery and self-understanding. It also meant that their treatment techniques included heavy doses of group therapy, drama therapy, art therapy, and somatic therapy. Well-versed in psychotherapeutic ethics, they had honed their counseling skills through years of clinical coursework and training. Not surprisingly, these staff members' life experiences were far from those of the inmates, but they insisted that they made up for this gap with education and knowledge. In effect, their legitimacy rested on exactly what their downstairs colleagues lacked: formal credentials, expertise, and training.

Although these women were the younger members of the Visions staff, they were at the top of the institutional hierarchy—again, mainly due to their education and training. Because their education also made them more expensive to employ, Visions hired fewer of them. The clinical staff bolstered their numbers by using a lot of interns, who tended to be even younger women from the counselors' alma maters who were in need of clinical experience. Moreover, what the clinical staff lacked in numbers they made up for in influence: the two women who founded the Recovery Project were deeply committed to a therapeutic community model, as was the clinical director, Jane, who eventually became the overall facility director. Since they tended to work out of the group rooms and private offices on the second floor of the facility, these counselors became designated as "upstairs" staff.

It would be easy to characterize the upstairs/downstairs split as only a racial one. Indeed, the divide did fall along racial lines: most downstairs staff members were women of color, while most clinical staff members were white. And, indeed, this is often how the split surfaced in practice; race became the most visible marker of staff divisions. Yet as frequently occurs in the social world, race also acted as a proxy for other differences between these women, such as class background, education, age, and life experience. These other divisions remained unacknowledged, as did the ways they overlapped with race. As a result, staff conflicts were frequently interpreted as racial conflicts, with the downstairs staff calling the clinical staff "touchy-feely white girls" and "visitors on our turf," while the counselors referred to the downstairs staff as "defensively uneducated."

The intersection of race and programmatic approach did make the staff conflicts all the more volatile. In the first months of my fieldwork, I observed countless exchanges that ended in shouting matches and tears. Discussions of everything from inmate problems to house practices to new hires became battles over which side would prevail—and thus whether the balance of power would shift. Take the time a clinical counselor, Lesley, visited a parenting class held by Tamika, the child-care coordinator and downstairs staffer. Outraged that the class consisted of everyone watching a *Barney* video, Lesley complained to the clinical director about the "passivity" being taught to the mothers. When the issue was raised at a staff meeting, a heated argument ensued, with Tamika defending videos as a way to teach women to relax with their children and Lesley insisting it was an "uneducated" and "lazy" approach to parenting. Debates about the *Barney* question continued for days, with each side coming up with new arguments for why it was in/appropriate for women to rely on videos for their childrearing.

These kinds of conflicts had a chilling effect on staff relations. In addition to keeping everyone on guard, they heightened the staff's fears that the facility would close—aware of CPMP facility closings across the state, they knew that too much institutional conflict could have very real consequences. This reality only exacerbated their fear of losing their jobs. The staff's sense of vulnerability was especially acute given their lack of job security and stability—many worried that saying the wrong thing to the wrong person could lead to immediate dismissal. Such worries were particularly pronounced for the downstairs staff due to their lack of formal education and training. These women often told me that they felt expendable and feared reprisals from the "higher-ups" when they voiced opinions or disagreed with the clinical staff. Although this fear rarely silenced them, it did cause them enormous concern and worry.

The depth of their concern became clear one afternoon when, on our way back to Visions from lunch, Margaret and I stopped at a nearby liquor store to buy some gum. While in the store, we saw May, the former house director at Visions, whose dismissal a year earlier had been very contentious. As one of the only African American staff members with influence, May had been a symbol for other downstairs staff. She had also been embroiled in an ongoing struggle with Jane, the clinical director, over the program's direction. A few days after a public disagreement about an inmate, Jane announced at a house meeting that May had been "let go," explaining that the conditions of her dismissal were confidential and would not be discussed. Immediately, rumors began to circulate that May had been punished for speaking her mind. "They just had to get rid of the one strong black woman with power," a downstairs staff member told me. "She was tough with them and the women [inmates], and they couldn't handle it."

The day we saw May, she was hardly recognizable. Once known for her snazzy outfits, May was wearing tattered clothing and missing most of her teeth. Her embarrassment at seeing us was visible as she stumbled through some niceties and shuffled out of the store. On the way back to Visions, Margaret was brought to tears. "Girl, did you see how she's fallen?" she asked me. "Oh, but for the grace of God go I," she repeated. In reality, Margaret had little chance of following May's path, since her CDC employment and seniority made her essentially untouchable. At that moment, though, she did not feel untouchable. She identified with May and shared her vulnerability, as did many other staff members when they heard of our encounter. Within an hour of our return, May was the topic of conversation downstairs; everyone was talking about how down-and-out she had become. By the end of the day, the story had been distorted to include tales of May's alcohol-induced slumber, bout with cancer, and recent stint in a mental hospital. As I left for the day, I heard one staff member remark to another that May's fall was a sign of what Visions "can do to us if we ain't careful."

Recovery to the Rescue

The upstairs/downstairs divide made life at Visions seem like a time bomb, ready to explode at any moment. It also led to a very high staff turnover rate, which then made the facility even more difficult to manage.[16] The staff members who remained often spent their days gossiping about who said what to whom and how it would affect the balance of power. Something had to give: either one side had to prevail or a compromise had to be struck. In this respect, the Visions staff differed from their Alliance predecessors: they were aware of the complex, competitive terrain upon which they operated and the pitfalls that threatened the facility's survival. Some of them also knew the importance of creating mechanisms to cope with these threats, or at least routes to bypass them. Ultimately, the Visions staff uncovered one such route: they came up with an institutional narrative to bridge their programmatic differences. This narrative was not achieved overnight, nor was it static or even secure. Rather, it was a tenuous truce that evolved out of several attempts to salvage staff relations after volatile eruptions threatened to tear the facility apart.

Over the course of my fieldwork, I watched the Visions staff develop a common discourse of recovery that encompassed elements of both sides of the upstairs/downstairs divide. This discourse constituted Visions as a space for women to heal from experiences of personal loss, trauma, and pain. The idea was to construct the facility not as a prison or a correctional institution but as a site for recuperation and renewal. In this construction, all staff members could contribute to the recovery process in their own ways: some through counseling, others through "experientially based sharing," and still others through tough love. These activities would all be considered valuable parts of their community of recovery. Importantly, this community was not to be confused with those focusing on rehabilitation—when talking to the Visions staff, I often used "recovery" and "rehabilitation" interchangeably, only to be corrected immediately. "That's what they do in prisons," Lesley once exclaimed when she overheard me make this mistake. "We aim for a deeper, real transformation."

Visions's discourse of recovery was premised on a shared interpretation of the source of the inmates' problems. Since the inmates were complicated women with complex backgrounds, there were a slew of potential problems the staff could have targeted. Yet the staff came together to form a metanarrative that reduced all of the women's issues to one: they were addicts. Many inmates were said to have gone astray because of their addictions to substances, most notably to drugs and/or alcohol. While some of the women at Visions did have serious drug and alcohol problems, many did not. Never mind: they were addicts too. They were just addicted to other things. Those convicted of fraud, burglary, and other property crimes were addicted to money, as were those incarcerated for selling drugs. Others were diagnosed as addicted to destructive and unhealthy relationships. Women with long histories of domestic violence were thought to be addicted to abusive men, sex, or male attention. Most generally, there were those who were addicted to a way of life—to the energy, sounds, and sensations of street, or "gangsta life." What united all these women was an inability to resist destructive impulses and to develop enough self-awareness to understand what caused them harm.

Once constituted as addicts, these women could then be parceled out to different staff members for treatment. Instead of inspiring fights over which programmatic approach would prevail, Visions's discourse of recovery allowed everyone to contribute in their own ways. This institutional division of labor first became clear to me during a staff meeting concerning Jacinta, a thirty-three-year-old mother of four incarcerated for assault. Jacinta was a lightning rod for staff conflicts, with both sides claiming her as their "case." Her tough demeanor and "badass attitude" prompted the downstairs staff to claim familiarity with her "type" and the methods to deal with her. These same attributes made her a challenge for the clinical staff, who struggled to get her to drop her "defensive mask" and expose her "vulnerability and pain." On this occasion, Jacinta had been brought in because of a fight she started with an inmate who accused her of stealing a bag of chips from the kitchen. Jacinta repeatedly denied the charges, claiming the assault was justified since the other inmate had fabricated the story. One staff member suggested that even if this were true, Jacinta should "turn the other cheek" and transform the false allegations into "positive energy." Jacinta would have none of it: "In my life I've learned that if you let someone run over you once, they'll keep doin' it. You fight if you've been wronged."

The staff then dismissed Jacinta from the room so they could decide how to address her "acting out." A turf war immediately surfaced: Evelyn insisted that Jacinta had broken the "no fighting" rule and should be punished swiftly, while Lesley contended that Jacinta's "emotional pain" needed to be treated first. Just before this familiar battle escalated, Collette, another counselor, jumped in to derail it. She suggested that both approaches were essential to Jacinta's recovery. Yes, she needed to be taught the importance of rules and the value of abiding by them— even those rules that seem unfair or unjustified. Yet she also had to learn to transform a sense of injustice into "positive energy to make herself a better person." Both lessons were key to ending Jacinta's addiction to "attitude" and "conflict." Collette's words were met by approving nods; she had clearly struck a chord with her colleagues. A solution was then proposed: Evelyn would do some "experientially based sharing" before giving Jacinta extra work hours in the kitchen, while Lesley would step up her counseling in an attempt to treat the source of Jacinta's anger. "At Visions, we can't change the world and all of its problems," Collette later explained to me. "But we can give [the inmates] the psychological tools to cope and be in the world in a healthy, nonaddictive way."

Collette's comments perfectly encapsulated Visions's discourse of recovery. Not only did this discourse provide a way to accommodate staff members with varying orientations, it also united them in a common cause with common assumptions about inmates' problems. It implied a clear sequencing for the treatment of these problems: only after women recovered psychologically would their social relationships improve. The goal was to bracket all external relationships in the treatment process so the women could focus on internal self-awareness and discovery. Thus, social relations of family, work, and community were all to be sidelined as the inmates delved into their personal experiences of pain and trauma—with the ultimate goal of finding and increasing their "self-esteem." In fact, the template of self-esteem was so central to this treatment program that it acted as both an independent and dependent variable. Low self-esteem emerged as the cause *and* the outcome of the inmates' behavior: the women at Visions were thought to have become addicts because they had little or no self-esteem, while their addictions were said to have chipped away at their self-esteem.[17]

In short, Visions's discourse of recovery offered a clear, easy-to-follow interpretation of the inmates' problems: low self-esteem led to addiction, which then led to even lower self-esteem. It also led to a clear, easy-to-follow model of treatment: reflection and introspection heightened self-esteem and thus ended addiction. On the surface, this institutional narrative may seem like a victory for the clinical staff. After all, it was solidly therapeutic in its diagnosis of the ailments of the self and in its curative program. Yet the narrative also drew on ideas that were near and dear to the downstairs staff: Visions's recovery discourse was infused with 12-step notions of treatment phases, cycles of progress and denial, and references to a "higher power." It bundled all kinds of issues together and linked them to one addictive source. And it left room for a bit of tough love, overt coercion, and direct surveillance. In this way, Visions's therapeutic ethos was itself a hybrid: it was a mixture of AA and EST, a combination of Dr. Phil and Dr. Freud.

In fact, this mixture was precisely what made Visions's program of recovery seem like such a brilliant response to its internal and external dilemmas. Internally, it gave the staff a framework for dealing with the enormous diversity in their ranks. By bracketing all social relations and inequities, this discourse allowed the staff to sideline exactly what divided them; it enabled them to put aside their potentially divisive differences in age, class, education, race, and professional background. Once they siphoned off everything social, they were left with the individual psyche. Moreover, by emphasizing internal psychological struggles, the staff found new ways to align with each other—after all, what woman was not recovering from something? Who was not dealing with some self-esteem problem? At the same time, their discourse of recovery allowed the staff to grapple with inmate diversity. The Visions inmates not only came from divergent backgrounds, they occupied different positions in the penal system. With a one-size-fits-all narrative of recovery, these differences could be obfuscated and collapsed into one metaframe. In effect, this institutional narrative allowed the staff to stitch together a community they thought could overcome the facility's internal uncertainty and diversity.

It also proved to be an externally useful narrative. While other CPMP facilities were scaling back or closing, Visions was launched into a period of growth. Its expansion was due to the influx of new funds and inmates, both of which were linked to Visions's ability to position its program as unique. By defining itself as a therapeutic community—or, as it claimed in its promotional materials, a "community of recovery"—Visions could develop a distinctive "line" to give itself a competitive edge. It could then tap into new funding sources. The tentacles of addiction could spread out in all sorts of directions, drawing in funds earmarked for public health, mental illness, and substance abuse. There were also Prop. 36 funds, which Visions was perfectly situated to access with its addiction frame.[18] Other federal and state grants also became available, like the National Institutes of Health grant that Visions received to treat "dual diagnosis" clients. With the new funding, Visions expanded in size and diversity: it brought in more "clients," as opposed to CDC inmates, while it hired more grant-dependent workers, as opposed to stable, salaried employees.

Herein lies the irony of Visions's institutional narrative. While the staff grasped onto therapeutics in response to the pressures of state hybridity, this discourse ended up further diversifying the facility. In doing so, the potential for future problems only deepened. With the mixing of different groups of clients and CDC inmates, the possibility of internal conflict increased; with the merging of different funding sources, the possibility of future staff cutbacks heightened. And the looming threat of downsizing only increased the overall sense of vulnerability. So, in one sense, the discourse of recovery had indeed come to the rescue. In another sense, it became an additional source of organizational uncertainty and strife. Yet none of this stopped the Visions staff from forging ahead with the building of a therapeutic program of recovery.

RECOVERY AS SELF-DISCOVERY AND EMOTIONAL EXPOSURE

The discourse of recovery that took hold at Visions not only encompassed abstract arguments about the source of the inmates' problems.

It also gave rise to concrete institutional practices that reflected those interpretations. During my time in the facility, I heard no discussion of programs to enhance women's legal or social rights. Nor was there much talk about addressing women's needs—not even the kind of discussions that had characterized the institutional battles at Alliance a decade earlier. Unlike the girls at Alliance, the inmates at Visions received no formal schooling or education, even though many of them did not have high-school degrees or GEDs.[19] The Visions women had virtually no access to books: the facility's small library, which was a small bookshelf in a counselor's office, included only a few donated novels and self-help books. These women could not attend job-training courses or employment counseling.[20] Legal services were nonexistent, even though many of the women had cases pending with Child Protective Services and/ or the state welfare department.[21] Although many inmates would be denied social assistance upon release due to their criminal convictions, no one ever sat down with them to explain these reforms.[22] Whenever the women asked for these services, they were told they had "deeper" issues to address first.

In some respects, the program of recovery constructed at Visions looked like a textbook example of contemporary therapeutic governance: its script of addiction relied on a vocabulary of therapeutics to emphasize what was going on inside women's heads with their sense of self. Yet it was not just any "self" that was problematized—it was a self riddled with dangerous desires and cravings. It was a self that lacked the strength to resist destructive impulses and urges. It was a self unable even to recognize which desires were damaging and painful. Most of all, it was a self that continually confused want with need—by insisting that it needed illegal substances to give pleasure, men to get by, or street smarts to survive. "I'm so tired of these women talkin' about how they need this or they need that," Evelyn once declared in a staff meeting. "They are sick. They are addicts. What they *need* is to stop thinkin' they *need* everything."

In this way, the Visions program of recovery operated through the regulation of desire. Or, in Evelyn's terms, it tried to convince the women that what they thought they needed, they really just desired. Once needs had been redefined as pleasures, they could be managed and controlled. This training began with the reigning in of the women's runaway desires and ended with instruction on how to enjoy healthy pleasures.

Where There's Smoke, There's Fire: Reigning in Dangerous Desires

Before the inmates at Visions were ready to participate in this desire training, they had to unearth their dangerous desires. But before they could do this, they had to master a new language—what the inmates called "program speak." From the moment women entered the facility, they had to refer to it as the "house" and/or "community." For instance, the weekly facility-wide meeting was called "community awareness," while excursions were "house outings" or "house activities." The women also had to refer to one another as "sisters" and to the staff by their first names. Those staff members with the most authority had "Miss" attached to their first names. So there was "Miss Jane," the house director, and "Miss Margaret," the CDC officer.[23] In addition to new words and designations, the inmates were taught new ways of expressing themselves and their feelings. Most importantly, they had to begin to use what the staff called "I statements"—sentences that positioned themselves as the central actors. Instead of using the passive voice, inmates had to start their sentences with "I." According to the staff, "I statements" not only allowed the women to claim their own feelings, the phrase stopped them from blaming others for their emotional state and actions.

An inmate's first expression in this new language was the twenty-page autobiography she had to write upon entering the facility. Constructed in conjunction with the counselors, these texts were essentially confessions, designed to account for how and why the self had become so distorted. The narratives went into excruciating detail about painful moments in these women's lives: they discussed horrific experiences of child abuse, sexual assault, and domestic violence. They recounted all of the ways in which the women had wronged others. They listed the many vices the inmates had developed over the years. An autobiography or "auto," as the women called it, was not considered complete until it included such detailed accounts. Because of this, some inmates had a difficult time writing their autos; those who were new to the penal system and/or drug-treatment programs often struggled for weeks with these texts.[24] But there were real incentives to finishing them: a variety of "house privileges" were tied to moving through the program's phases, and completion of the auto was the first of these phases.

Once an inmate's counselor deemed her auto acceptable, it was ready for public presentation at the weekly house meeting. Every inmate was required to read her auto aloud to the entire "community." Not surprisingly, this often provoked considerable anxiety, leading some inmates to delay their readings for weeks. Here, too, there were incentives for completion: the second phase of the program depended on the outcome of these readings. As inmates read their autos to the group, a few "older sisters," acted as recorders and turned the narratives into personal mantras, or what Visions called a "safe-to-speak." These mantras were abridged versions of the inmates' auto couched in program speak. Since most autos were written in the women's own language, they had to be translated into the vernacular of the facility.[25] Once constructed, an inmate had to memorize her personal mantra and recite it when in the presence of a staff member. This was to be done for a designated amount of time, anywhere from a few days to a few weeks, after which time the staff decided she was ready to become a full member of the "community."

The first time I encountered an inmate's mantra occurred within hours of my arrival at Visions. I was walking down the hall, still trying to acclimate myself to the environment, when a young African American woman approached me. "I am an addict," she proclaimed. "Love the attention and life of the streets. Beaten and abused. Found comfort in the arms of crack. Made choices that destroyed me and my child. Now I'm ready to find real comfort. Safe to speak?" I stood there stunned, without a clue as to how to respond. The inmate was equally confused as she stared at me, expectantly. Finally, a counselor ended our perplexed standoff when she walked by and whispered in my ear, "You need to answer 'safe.'" Once I did, the inmate smiled and moved along. Later, I was educated about safe-to-speak etiquette and told that the ritual was a way to show inmates they were in a "safe place" where they could "speak from their hearts."

Of course, the safe-to-speak ritual taught the women much more than this. These exchanges encapsulated one of the most important aspects of Visions's program of recovery: public exposure. The entire facility was organized around airing the intimate details of one's life, experiences, and addictions. At Visions, "working the program" was synonymous with one's willingness to engage in these airings. Full and unrestrained participation was key to a woman's ability to progress and move closer to release. Those who refused to immerse themselves in these confessionals were considered to be "withholding" and "maintaining a mask." At a minimum, "withholders" could be dephased, which meant the withdrawal of house privileges and freedoms. If the withholding went on, an inmate could be deemed unfit for the program altogether—which, for the CDC inmates, not only meant going back to traditional prison but returning their children to relatives or the foster-care system. There was a lot at stake here: an inmate's institutional future as well as her children's well-being depended on her willingness to create a script of the self and to perfect it publicly.

These imperatives then had interesting effects on the staff's assessments of different groups of inmates. For instance, the staff often noted that African American inmates were more expressive and apt to share their feelings. They applauded them for this—for not being fearful of self-disclosure, confession, or "keepin' it real." These problems were often attributed to white inmates, who were frequently described as emotionally restrained and psychologically guarded. African American women were said to be candid about what they felt, while white women had to be coerced into exposing themselves. But African American women received their own form of disciplining. They had to be trained how to express their emotions more productively—or, as one staff member put it, to "take responsibility for their lives" and "stop blaming everyone else for their problems." For both groups, this retraining was to occur in public, in front of the community of sisters.

For all of the staff's talk about therapy, the women at Visions spent very little time in one-on-one sessions with their counselors. Instead, their days were full of collective meetings and classes, which they called "group." On any given day, the women attended three to six groups on topics ranging from anger management to alcohol/drug prevention to art/drama therapy to life skills to general "recovery issues." These groups were run like combinations of AA meetings and talk shows, with counselors acting as the hosts and the women as both guests and audience members. The idea was to push one another to divulge and reflect. The inmates were to divulge quite specific things, though—they were not encouraged to discuss the details of their crimes or why they landed in prison. In fact, when they did talk about this, counselors accused them of "detouring."[26] Rather, the women were to come clean with all their addictions so the group could dissect what had caused them. Good group sessions were those in which the staff thought the women had "gone deep"—that is, exposed the details of their past abuse and present feelings about it. The number of tears shed was usually a reliable indicator of how "deep" the group had gone. Again, failure to attend groups or to participate fully in them could lead to dephasing and even removal from the program.

Every Tuesday afternoon, the level of public exposure reached new heights at the Visions community-awareness meeting. These gatherings not only included the reading of autobiographies, but also the chance for inmates to air grievances about one another and the program. Because the former often ended up taking all the allotted meeting time, the staff created a format for inmate confrontation: the focus seat. Any staff member or inmate could call for someone to enter the seat, an effort that was usually coordinated earlier in the day; those who were targeted were rarely notified beforehand. It worked like this: a chair was placed in the center of the huge circle everyone sat in for the meeting. The targeted inmate took the seat and, for an indeterminate amount of time, everyone waged complaints at her. All kinds of dirty laundry were aired—from things the inmate had said or done to "vibes" or "energy" she was giving off. Amid all of this, the targeted inmate could not say a word; the point of the focus seat was for her to sit silent. As the onslaught progressed, it frequently got out of control, with women angrily jumping up as they hurled their accusations at the woman in the seat. The staff would sit on the sidelines, only occasionally intervening to remind the women to use their "I statements." Eventually, a staff member would call an end to the focus seat, usually only after the targeted woman became hysterical.

The purpose of the focus seat was to get the targeted inmate to come undone. For the most part, this was precisely what happened. Like the time Mary, a forty-year-old mother of three, was forced into the seat because some of her sisters believed she was talking behind their backs. As soon as the confrontation started, Mary began to break down, trembling and fidgeting in the chair. "Look at me," one inmate yelled as she moved her chair directly in front of Mary's. "You're talkin' shit about me to others 'cause you're too weak to say it to my face. Now what ya' gonna do?" Another inmate jumped in to suggest that Mary's "wimpiness" caused her husband to have affairs and "beat on" her. "He knows he can walk all over you," she exclaimed. This prompted Mary to sob and shake uncontrollably. Then another inmate entered the fray and accused Mary of taking her anger out on her young son, which was further evidence of Mary's weakness since the boy was "defenseless" and "innocent." At this point, Mary ran out of the room, ending her focus seat. She refused to leave her bedroom for the rest of the day.

The inmates at Visions were simply not permitted to retain any privacy or to maintain any personal boundaries. Exposing all aspects of their lives to the "community" was a key part of the treatment process. There was even a physical dimension to this exposure. All the women at Visions were forbidden from wearing makeup; the CDC inmates were also required to wear their hair completely off their faces, either in a ponytail, a bun, or braids. The hair rule came from the CDC, which prohibited female prisoners from wearing their hair down, supposedly for "hygienic" reasons.[27] Of course, as with all CDC rules, Visions could have applied a loose interpretation of this one. In fact, during public performances and special occasions, the staff did allow inmates to wear makeup and loose hairstyles. On a daily basis, though, the staff policed the restrictions. They did so because, as a counselor once noted to me, "the rule works for us." In effect, the hair and makeup restrictions became a way to force the women to drop their "masks" and not hide behind a façade of femininity. "It's good for them to really face themselves, who they are for real," another counselor explained. "I mean, all the worry about physical appearance detours and lets them escape their real problems."

The enforcement of the hair and makeup rule leads to another critical aspect of Visions's program of recovery: it subjected the women to continual surveillance and supervision. What is more, this policing was often carried out by other inmates. In part, this was out of necessity, since it would have been nearly impossible for the staff to oversee the comings and goings of the more than fifty women in the facility. Such surveillance was made particularly difficult since, for a carceral institution, Visions allowed considerable freedom of movement both within and outside its walls. Although CDC inmates had to stand in front of their rooms to be counted five times a day, they were otherwise given the run of the "house."[28] Moreover, as long as they got staff approval, inmates could exit the facility on their own—those with school-aged children walked them to a nearby school every morning, while those who had "phased" could go to doctors' appointments or attend to other official business.

Initially, all this movement among inmates struck me as a bit risky—that is, until I realized that the women leaving the facility usually had to be accompanied by their "older sisters." The idea was to "delegate" supervisory responsibilities to women who had already proven themselves in the program, those who the staff believed could be trusted to reign in a fellow inmate's behavior if she got out of control. These women had to report back if a "younger sister" used a banned substance, went to an unauthorized location, talked to strangers, made a phone call, or engaged in one of her "trigger behaviors." Over and over again, the staff presented such delegation as an important lesson in "self-governance." As Carrie, a clinical counselor, once explained to me: "It's good for them to see their sisters out there resisting the temptations and acting in healthy ways. You know, to learn by example."

Visions also expected inmates to learn by example while within the facility. It did so by creating an environment of perpetual monitoring, or "mirroring," where the women were encouraged and expected to regulate one another's actions. Most of those who had been caught engaging in inappropriate behavior had been turned in by their sisters. In fact, many inmates were continually on the lookout for those breaking the facility rules. Sometimes news of such transgressions would reach the staff directly, with some women turning in others. More often, violations came out in community meetings, especially during the focus seat, when the women's emotions were high and their guards down. "It looks to me like them staff come to community awareness just to get the goods on us," Devon, a CDC inmate once revealed to me. "That's why I just sit silent. Don't want to spill no beans or anything." Indeed, there were a lot of "goods" to be gotten at these meetings: inmates were quick to reveal who had consumed banned substances like drugs, alcohol, and caffeinated coffee; they pointed fingers at those who sneaked food from the kitchen; they exposed those who watched too much television; and they reported on illicit affairs and sexual encounters among the women.

Of all the out-of-bounds behavior reigned in at Visions, the most contentious was smoking. When I began my work at Visions, the staff allowed the women to smoke in the back of the facility four times a day; these smoking breaks were even written into the daily class schedule. Conflicts arose when inmates reported that some women were smoking outside the designated areas at unscheduled times. "The smokers are out of control," Jen, an older sister, once proclaimed at a meeting. "They light up whenever and wherever they like." The conflict then escalated when the staff decided to add tobacco to its long list of unacceptable substances, thus banning smoking from the facility altogether. At a meeting to explain their decision, the staff argued that smoking was not only a dangerous addiction but also acted as a "trigger" for more detrimental impulses. "It keeps you tied to substances," Jane, the clinical director, explained. "That is not acceptable or healthy. It signifies deeper problems. 'Cause where there's smoke, there's usually a fire." Once smoking had been banned, a full-fledged war broke out—with some nonsmokers following smokers around the facility to police their every move. Eventually, tensions got so high that the staff intervened to "solve" the problem: they created the "Smokers' Support Group" to discuss the women's personal relationships to cigarettes and what this attachment signified about other destructive tendencies.

In addition to reigning in desires for certain substances, the women were expected to control one another's personality problems and "inner demons." When they encountered someone who was not working the program, the women were expected to call her on it. These were referred to as "pull-ups"—instances when one sister accused another of exhibiting an unacceptable trait and suggested an alternative way of acting. Pull-ups could happen anywhere at any time, which led to a sense of constant surveillance. They also produced an environment in which inmates were to act as minitherapists, always there to interpret one another's psychological problems and issues. "Sharon has issues with control," Nadine, a twenty-two-year-old inmate, once proclaimed at a house meeting. "When she works in the stock closet, she treats house stuff as her stuff. She won't let no one in and won't give us the stuff we ask for. It's like it's her space." Then there was Rochelle's analysis of Jacinta's problematic personality, which mimicked the staff's explanation: "She's a master of denial. Once I sat and watched her sneak into the kitchen and take cookies. So I pulled her up, telling her that ain't right. But then she got up in my face and told me I didn't see nothing. It's like this mask comes on her face, you can see it comin' on. Like it's not even her anymore. She yells and denies and denies. There's no gettin' through those defensive shields of hers." The staff applauded Rochelle for attempting to pull up her sister.

In this way, although the women at Visions had to participate in practices of control and confrontation, the staff remained the main orchestrators: they led the programs, meetings, and groups that mandated these practices. Whenever they deemed the house to be veering from the path of recovery, they were quick to regain control of it. The most direct way they did this was to put the house on a "freeze"—essentially locking down the facility and suspending all normal activities. During a freeze, the staff forbade all inmates from leaving for any reason; they canceled visiting hours so no one could come in from the outside; they banned all talk among the women; and they halted all groups and meetings. Since freezes could last from several days to a few weeks, they were the ultimate punishment—akin to collective solitary confinement. While at Visions, I observed five different freezes. Some were initiated because the staff sensed the entire house was "off the hook"; others were called to deal with specific conflicts among inmates. In all cases, the staff determined that the program of recovery had broken down and needed repair.

The ways the staff went about making these repairs were telling. All of the freezes I observed involved rituals designed to remind inmates of the central components of Visions's program of recovery. In effect, these rituals were heightened and condensed versions of Visions's everyday practices of recovery. For example, the first freeze I observed occurred over a two-week period during which every inmate was brought up to the group room, one by one, to find the entire staff, including the CDC officer, seated in a long row of chairs. Facing us, each woman was told we were there to "help" and "support" her. A counselor then instructed the woman to begin by telling us about her "role in the house." Within minutes, the encounters became confessionals in which the woman was required to reveal everything about herself, past and present. And we sat there until she did—or at least until she broke down in tears. Evaluations followed: Was she digging deep? Was she really trying to understand her "self"? Was she ready to change it? The freeze ended after every inmate had faced the confessional and had written out personal "commitments for change" to herself and her sisters.

Connected to this, the rituals of the freeze reminded the women— again, in an accentuated way—that they were not permitted to maintain any privacy or personal boundaries. Attempting to retain either would not only have negative implications for the individual woman but also for the house as a whole. To relay this, the staff often ended the freezes by having the women perform collective skits. Because these were to be done together, the whole group went down if even one woman refused to participate—which could prompt the staff to prolong the freeze until everyone "came around." As a result, there was enormous pressure for every woman to capitulate. Most eventually did.

Almost without fail, these performances involved women acting out what the staff expected of them. Replete with "I statements," the skits demonstrated that the women understood and accepted Visions's definition of recovery. One particularly memorable skit perfectly illustrated this lesson: in it, a group of CDC inmates performed what their lives were like before coming to Visions. They acted out all of their supposed pathologies and addictions, from their "badass attitudes" to urges for drugs, alcohol, men, and money. Then they showed how their bad behavior had landed them in prison—and how, after being arrested, they had sat in their jail cells dreaming about their vices. Finally, they concluded with life at Visions, where they had learned how "messed up" they were and how to get their acts together. In recognition of just how well they captured the program of recovery, the women received a standing ovation from the staff, and the freeze ended.

In this way, yet another message was embedded in the rituals of the freeze: despite all the gestures to self-governance and collective supervision, the power in the facility was firmly in the hands of the staff. This became particularly clear during a freeze initiated to deal with what the staff considered the women's fixation with "accumulating useless stuff." The previous week had been marred by inmate conflicts over who had used whose hair products and toiletries, and the staff concluded that the women's attachment to material objects was getting in the way of their recovery. The staff called a freeze in which they would conduct secret room searches. Both the downstairs and upstairs staff gathered early one morning to prepare for the search while the women were on a house outing. Margaret was on hand to distribute the official CDC list of allowable items—guidelines for how many articles of clothing, toiletry items, and children's toys each woman was permitted to have in her room. Once the staff received the checklists, off they went to search the rooms.

My search partner was Lesley, the yoga teacher and a main pillar of Visions's therapeutic community. I agreed to hold the trash bag as she rummaged through the women's belongings, which she did with a surprising lack of restraint. She made her way through every nook and cranny of the rooms. She laughed when she found an inmate stocking up on shampoo in preparation for her impending release, giggled when she uncovered hidden boxes of snacks, and sighed with exasperation when she repeatedly discovered women with far more things than the CDC permitted. "Unbelievable," she groaned. "They just accumulate and accumulate." By the end of the morning, trash bags full of women's belongings lined the walls of the facility. When the women returned, they were livid. Perhaps they did have too much stuff, but wasn't it their right to decide what to keep? A lecture followed, with the staff stressing the importance of "cleaning out your closet" to make sure "the past doesn't weigh you down." Their clever metaphors were lost on the women, who kept insisting they had been violated and treated like kids.

Indeed, they had been infantilized, but this was the point of many of Visions's practices of recovery: to position the women as not yet capable of controlling their urges and as needing help managing their desires—for only after these desires were under control could they be replaced by healthy ways of being.

Let Them Eat Cake: Teaching Acceptable Pleasures

Even in its colloquial use, *recovery* connotes some sort of recuperation—or, ideally, the evolution into a new, better way of being. At Visions, this aspect of recovery was given short shrift, emerging almost as an afterthought. Day in and day out, the staff sought to convince women of the dangers inherent in certain physical and mental desires and to acknowledge their dependency on these impulses. To achieve this, the staff relied on techniques to break down the self through confrontation and exposure. Yet when it came to rebuilding the self, Visions's desire training was far less developed. It was as if the staff hoped the women's dangerous desires would simply disappear once exposed. In this way, Visions's program was marked by another cultural imprint—although they rarely used the term, the staff seemed to fall back on the promise of "magical thinking."[29] If the inmates just transformed themselves internally, the external world would follow suit; if they changed what was in their heads, their lives would alter accordingly.

Occasionally, the Visions staff acknowledged that magical thinking might actually be wishful thinking. They also admitted that it might be helpful if they not only cleansed inmates of their dangerous desires but also steered the women toward socially acceptable activities. In doing so, the staff set out to convince women that they could satisfy their urges in new, healthier ways. The goal became to shift the objects of desire—away from those the staff saw as risky and toward those they considered safe.

When it came to physical pleasure, yoga, meditation, and "spa days" were all presented as healthy ways to experience one's body. For instance, counselor Lesley came in early on weekday mornings to offer yoga classes to the women—although very few of them took advantage of her classes. Moreover, after the staff banned smoking in the facility, they replaced the designated smoking breaks with scheduled times for "meditation"—claiming that women who used cigarettes to "get their heads together" could now use meditative techniques for similar ends. There were also the spa days held as rewards for good behavior. Although the inmates could only afford to provide self-administered pedicures, facials, and massages, the staff thought these services gave women a taste of how to take care of themselves. Like yoga and meditation, spa days were also thought to have emotional payoffs: by triggering calmness and tranquility, they gave women new ways to "heal" and "moderate."

Food consumption was another activity held out as physically pleasurable and gratifying. It was actually the one sensory arena that the staff allowed the women to retain some control over. All inmates participated in food preparation—in conjunction with the full-time cook, they planned, cooked, and served three meals a day. The women took this job very seriously; for some, food preparation became an obsession. The inmates planned quite elaborate meals and demanded that the staff purchase just the right ingredients for them. Food also became something of a fixation for those consuming it: the women talked about food incessantly and often structured their days around it. "I make sure I eat all three meals everyday cause there ain't nothing else to look forward to around here," Rosa once explained to me. Meal times were real events, with women anxiously awaiting to be served and devouring their portions as if they were starving.

I rarely saw the women at Visions as happy as they were when they ate—as they took in the smells and tastes of food, their faces expressed a rare look of joy. I recall one incident when, after completing my fieldwork, I returned to Visions for a meeting with a group of inmates who were working with me on a writing project. I brought along a chocolate cake and served it just before we started working. After the first bite, silence fell over the room as the women devoted all their attention to the cake. They said nothing until the cake was gone, its sensory effects enjoyed completely. The following day, when word got out about the cake, tensions rose among the inmates: How could these women have eaten an entire cake? Didn't they think of saving some for their sisters? Were they so selfish?

While the staff did allow the women the sensory pleasure of food, it was a double-edged sword. Almost without exception, inmates gained a lot of weight while at Visions. Some gained so much weight that they reverted to wearing maternity clothes after a few months in the facility. The changes in their bodies caused considerable anguish and despair, particularly for white inmates, who often talked about how "disgusting" and "gross" their bodies had become. In response, many began to act out on their bodies in painful ways: they binged during meals, purged after them, and fasted for days before family visits. The staff never seemed to notice, much less problematize, such behavior—or to see it as a compulsive replacement, even displacement, for other desires.[30] The inmates were thus left experiencing the intersection of pleasure and pain; what Visions held out as acceptable pleasures ended up causing them pain and suffering.

This intersection between pleasure and pain also characterized another of Visions's acceptable pleasures: motherhood. The program gave scant attention to the women's lives as mothers—even though their status as mothers had brought them to the facility in the first place. It often seemed like the staff would have preferred to have the women to themselves, particularly since children presented a challenge to the bracketing of inmates' social relations. Unable to cordon children off, the staff transformed them into a potential pleasure. Children were considered physically and emotionally pleasurable; holding a child was thought to be the best way to fulfill a healthy desire for closeness, while watching a child develop was said to be emotionally gratifying.

Yet unlike yoga or food, motherhood was not merely a replacement for other, less acceptable desires. Instead, it was a pleasure the inmates could enjoy only after they had rid themselves of other negative impulses. Over and over again, the women were told they could reap the full benefits of motherhood once their addictions had been treated. Enjoying caretaking and childrearing became a telltale sign of recovery, an indication that a woman's diseased self was in remission. Yet the reverse was also true: women who voiced maternal ambivalence were told their addictions were to blame; inmates who felt conflicted about their children were told they were acting out their sicknesses.

There was something insidious about positioning motherhood as a sign of recovery. It negated the very real ambivalence and conflict some inmates had about mothering, reducing these feelings to addiction and pathology.[31] It also obscured all the ways that life at Visions actually undercut women's ability to enjoy their children. On a daily basis, children watched as their mothers were punished and ordered around. The children were often present in meetings when their mothers were infantilized and brought to tears. "My mommy is in trouble," five-year-old Malik said to me one afternoon. "She's been bad and can't leave her room today." When faced with such a comment, it is hard to imagine how Shanika, Malik's mother, could then reestablish maternal authority or respect.

Yet Shanika was hardly alone in her struggle: many women at Visions insisted that they had lost control of their children in the facility. They claimed their children no longer respected them, listened to them, or took their reprimands seriously. They also reported that their children developed severe behavioral and psychological problems while at Visions. It was not uncommon for children to cry for weeks after entering the program. In fact, many children eventually ended up with their own diagnoses, from hyperactivity to depression to autism to psychosis. Some of them also underwent therapeutic counseling and treatment. With no private space to retreat to in order to cope with such problems, the inmates were forced to deal with them publicly, which often provoked even more stress and anxiety. All the while, they were instructed to find pleasure and enjoyment in their mothering—those were signs of recovery, after all.

The inmates' sense of maternal anxiety was exacerbated by the guilt many of them felt for bringing their children into a penal facility that curtailed their children's lives and freedoms. Their guilt increased whenever new restrictions were placed on their children's movements or activities, like those that occurred when the house went on a freeze. As kids often do, the children at Visions absorbed and articulated the unspoken. At times, this led them to act out or say what their mothers could not—like three-year-old Mario, who made countless attempts to escape from the facility by making mad dashes to the backyard fence, scaling it while screaming, "I go home. I no like it here. I leave NOW." Other times, the kids played on their mothers' guilt—like five-year-old Stephen, who frequently told his mother how much he hated his new life in prison. This is how his mother, Samantha, expressed it in an account she wrote in my writing class:

> One day [my son] Stephen started crying and said to me: "Mommy I am going to stay here with you in the program. But I don't like it here. I am only staying because you have to and I don't want you to go back to prison if I leave." When he said this, I was touched by his loyalty. He was so strong for such a little guy. He was becoming aware of what the sacrifices were going to be for him, from his inability to going outside to play with friends to watching what TV programs he wanted when he wanted. Life was about to become very different. And he was doing it all because he loved me. I felt terrible. How could I bring him here?

Of course, to rid the inmates of this pain and guilt, Visions offered its biggest pleasure of all: self-discovery and public exposure. "Didn't that feel good?" a staff member once said to a sobbing inmate after an hour in the focus chair. "It may hurt now, but your mind will feel clear before you know it." More than anything else, from yoga to cake to children, the women were expected to find pleasure in the therapeutic practices of recovery. If done properly, therapeutic practice would lead to everything from self-awareness and self-understanding to self-fulfillment and self-empowerment. Juanita, a thirty-eight-year-old CDC inmate and mother of four, summarized these promises in a reading she did at one of Visions's public performances: "When I'm outta of here, I'm gonna be the bomb. I'm gonna have my head straight. So I can get all my shit together. I'll be ready to find me a big house that I'll decorate real nice and fancy. I'll chill in that house with my kids and people—havin' cookouts and movin' to the groove. And I'll hang there with a big, strong man who knows how to treat a lady. Yea, you know, I'm gonna have it goin' on."

GOVERNING DESIRE

The public performances organized at Visions were opportunities for the inmates to demonstrate their understanding of its program of recovery. Juanita's performance nailed this perfectly: her "reading" of her life after

Visions not only stressed the changes made in her head but also the internalization of new pleasures. Juanita's imagined future clearly encapsulated the central aims of the facility. First and foremost, Visions's goal was to move the programmatic focus to women's internal lives, thus excluding the external, social world. The idea was to establish inmates' problems as rooted in their psychological cores, in their inner selves. Only after getting to the core and exposing its pathologies could inmates rid themselves of their bad impulses and implant new desires. These aims then congealed into an institutional narrative that emphasized the transformative capacity of therapeutics and its ability to reign in unacceptable behavior. And this narrative gave rise to institutional practices designed to secure such behavior—from focus seats to personal mantras to program speak to encounter groups to inmate pull-ups to spa days.

Visions's program of recovery clearly had cultural imprints. It merged aspects of U.S. therapy culture with elements of the AA movement— while also adding in a bit of local community flavor. But exposing the program's cultural influences is not the same as explaining why this particular version of therapeutics so permeated this penal facility. Here I turned to the institutional environment surrounding Visions. This was an environment in which state hybridity had gone wild: the internal and external problems facing state satellites were especially pronounced at Visions. Not only was the facility plagued with financial woes and organizational uncertainties, but its staff and inmates had divergent backgrounds and different ties to the penal system. Therapeutics offered a way around the potential conflicts posed by all this diversity. Its roots were thus institutional, related to the constraints placed on state facilities that worked at the margins and dealt with the marginalized. And the roots of these constraints were structural, connected to state devolution and decentralization. In this way, Visions's trials and tribulations reflected broader changes in the form and focus of contemporary governance.

To conceptualize Visions's program of recovery as a form of governance does not necessarily condemn it as conspiratorial, conniving, or controlling. Nor does it imply that Visions's institutional practices could not also be productive. This is one of Foucault's more enduring insights about governance: as strategies of control close off some options, they can open up others; as some forms of behavior are forbidden, others are sanctioned. This was certainly how therapeutics worked for the Visions staff.[32] In many ways, therapeutics was a productive narrative for Visions. It enabled the staff to salvage their institution amid considerable conflict and strife—even as it also robbed members of that community of any sense of social or systemic inequity. Therapeutics allowed the Visions staff to stitch together a community with different roles for different people—even as it also denied the uniqueness of anyone's contribution. And it led Visions to branch out and fund-raise—even as it ended up further diversifying the facility and adding to the potential for conflict. In short, therapeutics closed off some ways of being while opening up others. Of course, therapeutics was not the only discursive means to these institutional ends. It was, however, the one available script that seemed to offer the staff a way to survive and even thrive.

This was also how the Visions staff hoped it would work for the inmates. They insisted that their program of recovery was designed with the best of intentions. It had worked for them, so when they imposed it on the inmates, they did so with commitment to its transformative potential. Perhaps therapeutics would be a bit uncomfortable at first— as the inmates' old ways of being were challenged and disrupted. But eventually the Visions program would train the women to want different things; it would teach them to engage in healthy pleasures. At the end of all this training lay the promise of empowerment and a life free from addiction, vice, and pathology.

So did the training work? Did the Visions inmates internalize new wants? Were they able to turn the regulation of desire into a productive narrative for themselves?

FIVE

The Empowerment Myth

SOCIAL VULNERABILITY
AS PERSONAL PATHOLOGY

On a summer afternoon, a group of inmates gathered in Visions's art room for the first meeting of one of my creative-writing classes. It was the third such course I had offered at Visions, so I began with a writing exercise that worked with the other groups: I asked the women to list ten emotions or sentiments, which I then wrote on the blackboard. "Sorrow," Rosa yelled. "Grief, fear, and depression," Chanel added. "No, you've got to put anxiety and frustration at the top," Melissa demanded. "No way," Claire interjected. "Guilt and regret should be up there." The list concluded with "disappointment" and "loneliness." Their list was strikingly similar to those produced in the previous classes so I raised an issue I resisted mentioning to the others. "These are all negative emotions," I noted. "What about positive . . . " Before I could finish my sentence, Rosa jumped in. "Girl, I thought you knew this place. Didn't you learn anything? This place is all about depression and guilt. What positive feelings do you want from us?"

These were hardly the sentiments one would expect from the "empowered" selves Visions claimed to be producing. The promises the staff made to their charges were exceptionally lofty: if they worked the program, the women would lead lives free of addiction. Once freed from addiction, their self-esteem would soar. And once full of self-esteem, personal empowerment and transformation would soon follow. Nowhere in this formula were the fears and anxieties expressed by the women in my writing class.

The Visions staff members were not the only ones with high hopes for their program. Social scientists, activists, and journalists often look to facilities like Visions as promising alternatives to punitive corrections.[1] Their optimism comes from two main sources. First, some see hope in the structure of these programs. Located outside the confines of traditional prisons, alternative-to-incarceration programs have become a model for progressive penal reform and a way to get inmates out of the much-maligned formal penal system. The assumption is that serving time in the "community" is necessarily better than living behind bars because community-based facilities are thought to be less punitive. This assumption also underlies many analyses of women in prison, which often presume that penal institutions become more "women friendly" as they move outside the official boundaries of the state.[2] As a result, these analyses almost invariably conclude with calls to place female offenders in community settings where their needs will be understood and addressed.[3] Even those scholars who are otherwise suspicious of recent shifts in governance remain optimistic about such programs, with one suggesting that they can breed a "radical politics of rights and empowerment."[4]

Second, there are those who have high hopes for the therapeutic aspects of penal programs like Visions. For decades the U.S. penal system has been accused of warehousing inmates and giving lip service to the idea of rehabilitation.[5] Such accusations tend to be coupled with calls for penal programs that address the deeper problems leading inmates to offend—problems that are often linked to substance abuse or psychological trauma. This linkage is particularly pronounced for female offenders, who are more likely to suffer from physical and emotional abuse and to be convicted of drug-related offenses.[6] Given this, it is not surprising that community-based therapeutics is frequently presented as the alternative to correctional punishment for women; or that so much research on women in prison points to therapeutics as a progressive, palliative measure to treat female inmates' specific needs;[7] or that so many feminist therapists have begun working behind bars—so many, in fact, that the journal *Women and Therapy* devoted a special issue to women in prison to document the therapeutic potential in everything from 12-step counseling to art therapy to boot camps to inmate-led encounter groups.[8]

Yet there are very real dangers involved in pinning all hopes for reform on community-based therapeutics. Most notably, such optimism is rarely based on serious empirical inquiry into actually existing programs. Far too many calls for community-based therapeutics are premised on myths about what such programs could deliver—or idealized images of the "community" and what might happen if inmates moved outside the formal confines of prison into it.[9] So while we can hope that community corrections would give rise to a "politics of empowerment" or "women-friendly" programs, the real effects of this approach require real empirical investigation. We can also hope that doing the opposite of what we know does not work might end up working—so if inmate warehousing were replaced with community-based therapeutics, perhaps the penal system would become responsive to inmates' needs. But that, too, is an empirical question.[10]

In this way, the challenge Rosa posed to me in our writing class was on target: indeed, I did learn something from my time at Visions. First and foremost, I learned that community-based therapeutics can actually disempower those it targets. The fear and anxiety expressed by the women in my writing class were far from exceptional states of mind at Visions; these emotions were conveyed everyday, in a variety of ways, by an array of inmates. I also learned that this sense of disempowerment came from precisely those aspects of Visions's program others were so optimistic about: its community-based structure and therapeutic focus. The inmates complained incessantly about Visions's hybrid structure, claiming that its gestures to the community covered up the facility's pervasive control and led the staff to abdicate their own responsibility for the inmates' recovery. In effect, these women taught me how governance through community can become what criminologist Pat O'Malley calls a strategy of "responsibilization"—that is, a way for state actors to shift all accountability to those under their control.[11]

In addition, the Visions inmates taught me about the deflective capacity of therapeutics. Day in and day out, they complained about being forced to participate in the facility's therapeutic practices. As with claims to community, some inmates saw these practices as a cover up for the facility's intrusiveness and invasiveness. Others indicted therapeutics for ignoring the economic and social realities of their lives. Still others questioned the personality traits and characteristics exalted by this therapeutic model, arguing that they were out of touch with who the women were, who they needed to be, and who they wanted to become. So, as occurred a decade earlier at Alliance, the inmates' words and actions exposed the facility's myth of empowerment—this time suggesting that the myth was individualizing, debilitating, and ultimately threatening.

This chapter documents the disjuncture between the promises of Visions's program of recovery and the experiences of those subjected to it. I first analyze how the *context* of the program ended up controlling the inmates. I also explore how governance through community left inmates open to endless evaluation, which exacerbated their sense of vulnerability. I then discuss how the *content* of Visions's program of recovery further undermined the promise of empowerment. By turning injustice into an emotional issue, Visions's therapeutics transformed social vulnerability into personal pathology and left the inmates less able to protect themselves on the outside. In the end, Visions's community-based therapeutics made the inmates' "recovery" and "empowerment" more myth than reality.

CONTROL THROUGH COMMUNITY: THE CONTEXT OF RECOVERY

While Visions's hybrid structure posed organizational challenges for the staff, these challenges paled in comparison to those confronting the inmates. Visions's institutional hybridity drew on an unusually diverse inmate population. Unlike other Community Prisoner Mothers Program facilities, Visions's inmate population was mixed, which meant that women's paths to the facility followed different routes.[12] First, there were California Department of Corrections inmates who arrived directly from one of California's three large correctional facilities for women. Although a few of them had heard about the CPMP on their own, most had been "recruited" into the program while in prison. The inmates told stories about how CPMP representatives showed up in the prison yard to tell them about the program. Those women thought to be eligible then received invitations to an information session where representatives sold them on the program through a promotional video. The recruiters never made any mention of drug treatment or substance-abuse counseling in these sessions.[13] Instead, CPMP representatives emphasized motherhood—they promised an environment in which women could bond with their children and work on their mothering, while the video showed a suburban-style home full of women happily caring for their kids.

Interested inmates were then instructed to apply for the program. This involved a complicated assessment of each woman's past, including her health history, criminal background, and marital status.[14] It often took CDC officials several months to complete these assessments; only the select few were eventually deemed eligible. Then more waiting ensued as eligible inmates frequently remained in prison before space opened up in a CPMP facility.[15] During all the waiting, inmates' expectations rose— as they recalled the promises of the program and their struggle to gain access to it. Their expectations heightened further as they anticipated being reunited with their children, sometimes after years of separation. By the time they finally reached Visions, some had been fantasizing about their "new" lives for years.

So imagine their shock when the prison van pulled into the driveway of an old, dilapidated building on a busy inner-city street lined with drug dealers and the homeless.[16] Or when they walked through Visions's doors, usually in shackles, to encounter another group of women that no one had told them would be there. These other women traveled their own route to Visions: arrested on a variety of drug-related charges, they came to the facility directly from county jail through a hodgepodge of alternative-to-incarceration and diversionary programs—in the lingo, they were so-called perinatal clients or Prop. 36ers. Because their eligibility for ATI programs had been established by justice officials at the time of arrest or sentencing, these women had not been subjected to the same level of screening as CDC inmates. So although many of them spent time in jail while awaiting their placements, they had not been incarcerated very long before coming to Visions. Among other things, this meant that more of them were coming off recent bouts with drug or alcohol abuse; those who came straight from the street often suffered withdrawal symptoms. Moreover, the streets they came from tended to be local: unlike CDC inmates, these women had more ties to the surrounding neighborhood, with some claiming to have bought drugs and frequented crack houses in the area.

This group of women also tended to be more familiar with facilities like Visions. Since most ATI programs gave clients three attempts to get clean before sending them to prison, many of these women were experienced "programmers." In fact, some had even done time at Visions before: there was something of a revolving door through which perinatal clients came and went until they had used up their three strikes. Visions's diverse funding structure created an incentive to keep readmitting these women after relapses. Unlike the CDC contract, which paid Visions a fixed amount for twenty-five inmates no matter how many CDC inmates actually resided in the facility, perinatal clients were financed on an individual, per case basis. This piece-rate system made it in Visions's economic interest to admit and retain as many perinatal women as possible. So of the fifty women at Visions at any time, roughly 60 percent were supported by state or county ATI programs.[17]

In this way, the women at Visions reflected the facility's hybrid structure—they differed according to their positions in the penal system, histories of substance abuse, and ties to the surrounding community. Not surprisingly, they also differed demographically. The CDC's vetting system led it to send a higher percentage of white women to CPMP facilities: roughly 60 percent of Visions's CDC inmates were white, 20 percent African American, and 20 percent Asian or Hispanic.[18] The reverse was true of perinatal clients: about 60 percent of them were African American, 20 percent white, and 20 percent Asian or Hispanic. Yet once these women entered Visions, all of their differences were to be wiped out. They were promised new lives, in a community of recovery that operated according to its own norms and ideals. But it did not take long before both groups of women questioned these promises and pinpointed how the program's context left them feeling vulnerable and exposed.

Discipline Disguised as Freedom

Visions's insistence that it constituted a "community" of recovery was meant to convey to all its inmates, both the perinatal clients and CDC inmates, that they had entered an environment free of coercion and force. As soon as an inmate arrived at Visions, she was enmeshed in a series of rituals designed to "free" her from the coercive constraints experienced in prison or jail. For instance, all CDC inmates came to Visions wearing short, checkered nightgowns, which, according to CDC officials, deterred escape attempts.[19] The Visions staff saw it differently, claiming that the gowns were a final attempt to humiliate and debase the inmates. So the first thing they did with CDC inmates was to get rid of the gowns. "We need to free you from this horrible costume," Mildred, the head administrator, always said. "We won't treat you like that here." The perinatal women also had to be freed, but for them this meant getting rid of heavy makeup and revealing clothing—what Mildred called their "ho look." The removal of makeup and street attire was presented as a freeing act, a way for these women to drop their protective armor and to "be real" in this accepting, coercion-free community.

Similarly, the language all the inmates learned in their first days furthered the community-as-freedom message. By instructing the inmates to call one another "sisters" and the facility a "house," the staff attempted to instill a sense of trust and safety in the inmates. Then there were the safe-to-speaks that all new inmates had to produce and perform as a way of marking their inclusion into Vision's "community of sisters."[20] In fact, integration into this community was so important that the staff often made the women wait for weeks, or even months, before their children could join them. When I asked Jane, the clinical director, about these long waiting periods, she explained that some of the women needed time to "unlearn institutional ways of being" and learn to live productively in a "real community free of control and force."

Yet Jane's comment missed one of the most basic of sociological insights: communities also exert discipline and control over their members. And these forms of control can be just as constraining as those at work in more formal organizations. This was not lost on the inmates, however, who complained constantly about how their lives were curtailed by the community. They pointed out how their space and movements were under perpetual surveillance—through everything from the rigid daily schedule to the inmate body counts for CDC inmates to the room searches to the complicated procedures for entering and exiting the facility. They remarked on how their consumption patterns were supervised—through restrictions on everything from caffeinated coffee to cigarettes to snack food to clothing to toiletries. They noted how closely their money and resources were monitored—through everything from the "money calls" they had to undergo before withdrawing funds from their accounts to the "needs lists" they had to submit to the staff before making any purchases for themselves or their children. And they commented on how their social interactions were regulated—through everything from facility-wide freezes to the focus seat to the insistence on "I statements" to the surveillance at community meetings. "They'd be more in your business here than they were in Valley State [prison]," Devon, a CDC inmate, once remarked.

In and of itself, there is nothing unusual about the control exerted over these women—after all, Visions was a penal facility; the inmates were official wards of the state. Although the women hated all the control, they rarely found it perilous or unmanageable. What they did find debilitating was the facility's lack of safety. There is a difference between feeling controlled and feeling out of control. The inmates at Visions experienced both, but it was the latter that seemed to trigger a sense of vulnerability and anxiety. The therapeutic practices the staff forced them to participate in required safety; the inmates needed to trust those around them before revealing intimate details of their lives. Yet, almost by definition, carceral environments lack safety and trust—even those staffed by women and located in the "community." In fact, the public, communal nature of Visions's therapeutic practices made them more unsafe than traditional therapy for many women. All the safe-to-speaks in the world could not deflect from the very real forms of power and discipline underlying Visions's program of recovery.

The Visions staff, particularly the counselors, had unimaginable authority over the inmates. For CDC inmates, a negative evaluation from a counselor could lead not only to the withdrawal of house freedoms but also to their return to prison. Although this was not unlike the authority wielded in other total institutions, there was a key difference at Visions: here the staff also determined the fate of the inmates' children. Sending a CDC inmate back to prison or a Prop. 36er back to jail implied an incredible disruption in the lives of their children, many of whom then went to unsafe or unstable foster-care placements. So when inmates like Devon claimed that their counselors "had all the power in their hands," they were not overstating their case. Yet Visions also expected female inmates to confide in their counselors and to tell them their deepest and darkest secrets. What is more, the counselors made it clear that they based their assessments on an inmate's willingness to divulge her innermost thoughts—or, as they often put it, "to go deep." This left the inmates struggling in ways that paralleled those confined to other total institutions: Visions women had to walk a tightrope, managing their own needs for self-preservation and the institution's demand for self-exposure.[21]

The Visions tightrope was even more difficult to walk given the high turnover rate among the staff. At a minimum, therapeutic relationships require consistent, ongoing interaction. Yet the inmates at Visions could not count on such consistency given the perpetual staff reshufflings. During my time at Visions, the facility director, clinical director, house director, and half the clinical staff were replaced. Among other things, this meant that the program's focus always seemed to be in flux. And this meant that the inmates received varied and even contradictory messages about what was expected of them. Many inmates then became ensnarled in these inconsistencies. Claire, a thirty-five-year-old CDC inmate, was told for months "to learn to grieve as a victim of abuse," only to be faulted months later by a counselor for "wallowing in her pain." Mabel, a twenty-seven-year-old Prop. 36er, was told repeatedly to view her dependence on crack as a "disease" entirely outside her control, only to be evaluated months later by the clinical director as unable to take personal responsibility for her out-of-control impulses.[22]

While these entanglements certainly exacerbated inmates' feeling of vulnerability, they could also lead to disastrous outcomes. This was what happened to Keisha, a twenty-three-year-old Prop. 36er. I first met Keisha in the summer of 2003 when she came to Visions for the second time after an arrest for drug possession. Like so many of the Visions women, Keisha had a troubled past. Her parents were musicians who introduced her to drugs at an early age, only to be killed in a drug-related shooting when she was a teenager. Keisha then moved in with a series of older men, supporting herself through prostitution and drug dealing. In the process, she developed a serious crack addiction, which eventually landed her in jail and then at Visions. After she spent two months in the facility, struggling to get clean and to care for her five-year-old son, Keisha disappeared from Visions one day. A few months later, Keisha resurfaced after another drug arrest. Weary of returning to Visions again, she was convinced to do so by a "deal" the Visions director offered her: if she returned, Visions would credit her for time served, thus requiring her to remain in the program for only eight months.[23] Keisha accepted the deal and returned to Visions, ready to take her recovery seriously. In addition to working the program, caring for her son, and attending all her Narcotics Anonymous meetings, Keisha accomplished what no other woman at Visions had: on her own, without any institutional support, she prepared for and passed her GED exam. She had become the shining star of the program.

When I met Keisha again in the summer of 2004, she proudly showed me her framed GED certificate and described all her future plans. But then things began to unravel. When she asked a staff member to help her secure Section 8 housing for what she believed to be her impending release, she was told that she had over five months left on her sentence. She then took the matter to the new director, only to be told that there was no record of Keisha's time-served deal; her new counselor also claimed to know nothing of the promise. After a series of meetings in which all her appeals were rejected, Keisha fell apart. She spent a week walking around the facility, crying. Then reports came in that she had broken house rules: inmates found her smoking, stealing food from the kitchen, and leaving her son unattended. With each new violation, the staff withdrew Keisha's house privileges and questioned her recovery. "Getting a GED is fine," her counselor stated in a meeting. "But it's not the same as true recovery. . . . The way she's dealing with disappointment tells me more about her state of mind." Eventually, Keisha went AWOL again. The last I heard, she was back on the streets. Having used up her third strike, another arrest will get Keisha sent to prison and her son to foster care.

Surveillance Disguised as Sisterhood

For women like Keisha, the staff inconsistencies had very real consequences; they turned Visions into a highly unstable and unsafe environment. Yet Keisha's story also exemplifies another central aspect of Visions's context of recovery: the facility made it close to impossible for inmates to escape therapeutic evaluation. All actions could become fodder for the therapeutic mill; all behavior could signify something about one's state of mind. Thus, Keisha's smoking was interpreted as evidence of a deep emotional problem, while sneaking food became a sign of serious psychological distress. Both transgressions outweighed all the progress she had made to obtain her GED and kick her crack habit.

In effect, Visions's all-encompassing approach meant that even the smallest, most insignificant act could call into question an inmate's commitment to recovery. This then put the inmates on a high state of alert, exacerbating their fear of doing the wrong thing in front of the wrong person. Whenever they articulated this fear, the staff lectured them about how they should be grateful for Visions's counseling and the opportunity to heal. After listening to these lectures for months, I asked Jamie, a counselor who claimed to have been "saved" through years of therapy, how she would have felt if forced to live with her therapist. "Gee, I never thought of it that way," she responded. "I guess I would have gone nuts. I'd be so worried about what she was seeing and thought of me."

Indeed, the inmates at Visions were worried about how others saw them. Their concerns were even more pronounced since they did not have just one therapist to worry about—they lived among fifty minitherapists, many of whom insisted on flexing their newly formed therapeutic muscles. In this way, the relations of power operating at Visions not only shaped staff-inmate relations but also influenced interactions among inmates. The Visions staff expected the inmates to provide information about one another; recall that the reports on Keisha's smoking and stealing came from her "sisters." Most inmates could recount an incident in which she was outed by a sister: Tiffany could pinpoint exactly which sister told the staff that one of her Sunday visitors was not her cousin (as she had claimed) but a man she had met at an AA dance while incarcerated. Marika knew precisely who informed her childrearing counselor each time she smacked her son on the behind in anger. Nicole was aware of who provided the kitchen staff with a list of the food she snuck during her late-night snack attacks. Rachel and Brenda could identify who notified the Visions director about their afternoon sexual trysts.[24] All of these women were fully aware of the rewards of snitching—from feeling like a staff insider to gaining special house privileges to having their own rule violations ignored.

Even when inmate snitching was not done so explicitly, the women often unwittingly doled out damning information about their sisters to the staff. This was particularly true in community meetings when, as the inmates voiced their complaints about one another, they frequently revealed who was violating the house rules and norms; or when, as their emotions ran high in focus seat sessions, inmates unintentionally exposed their sisters' secrets. Given such lapses, it is easy to imagine how unsafe these women began to feel with one another. This was what happened to Adrian one afternoon when one of her closest friends unintentionally exposed her past experiences with prostitution. It was toward the end of Adrian's focus seat session, and the crowd had begun to get particularly rowdy—accusations flew about Adrian's lying and two-faced behavior. Then Jean stood up to accuse Adrian of having "no inner strength" or "realness." In an attempt to defend Adrian, Mabel jumped in: "Look who's talkin', Ms. Crack Ho. . . . You'd be giving it up for the juice for

years. . . . But Adrian, she only did that a few times." Adrian's face immediately went pale as she looked at Mabel in horror. "Oh shit, girl, you
done outed that bitch," another inmate yelled. Adrian's focus seat ended
soon thereafter when she broke into tears. For their part, the staff sat back
and observed the upheaval, with satisfied smiles on their faces. They
seemed to enjoy such lapses of confidentiality, while being careful to
assure Adrian that her secret would be kept safely "in the family."

Yet it would be far too simplistic to attribute inmate "outings" to staff
intervention alone. These breaches also reflected the very real power
struggles underway among the inmates. While such struggles often
characterize total institutions, as the regulated take it upon themselves
to regulate each other, such instances were arguably more pervasive
in a facility like Visions.[25] Because of the constant public exposure, the
inmates knew a tremendous amount about their sisters' problems and
traumas. So when fights broke out, the inmates had a huge psychological
arsenal to draw on; they knew exactly what buttons to push and the fastest way to access them. Even the smallest quarrel could escalate into an
all-out psychological war, implicating everything from the combatants'
emotional weaknesses to their histories of deception to their criminal
behavior. Not surprisingly, these escalations only intensified the inmates'
sense of danger with one another.

Of all the accusations the inmates leveled against each other, the ones
that seemed to make them most desperate were arguments about their
failings as mothers. In this way, while other research has revealed that
prison officials evaluate female inmates according to their commitment to
mothering, at Visions mothering also served as a source of power among
the inmates.[26] This should not be surprising given the context: most
Visions inmates were very insecure about their parenting, yet they had to
mother under the watchful eyes of fifty other inmates. This made allegations of bad mothering common and particularly painful. "We all make
mistakes with our kids," a sobbing inmate screamed after her time in the
focus seat centered on her parenting problems. "I could point to any one
of you and tell what you're doing is wrong. I don't deserve this."

To make matters more difficult, the inmates frequently offered up
evaluations of one another's children. Just as the inmates lived under

a therapeutic microscope, so did their children. When a child was per-ceived as unruly or troubled, the mother often got stigmatized—other inmates interpreted the child's behavior as signifying something about the mother. This was precisely what happened to Rosa, whose three-year-old son Mario spent his first six weeks at Visions screaming at the top of his lungs, often throughout the night. Eventually, Rosa's sleepless roommates turned their frustration on her, calling her an uncaring and inexperienced mother. At one community meeting, the inmates held a collective complaint session about Mario's outbursts and Rosa's "bad mothering" that lasted for more than an hour. It took Rosa months to rid herself of this stigma. Even after she did, she claimed that she never felt safe or comfortable at Visions again. "I just couldn't believe this shit they were talking. Like it was my fault or something . . . like their kids weren't traumatized too. After that, I just knew to keep my distance . . . like there's no way to trust those women."

There were also cases when the stigma attached to the children them-selves, which created even more panic in their mothers. This was what happened to Samantha, whose five-year-old son Stephen was taken away in an ambulance one afternoon after experiencing what the staff described as a "nervous breakdown." As soon as the shock of the inci-dent wore off, the evaluations started: Did the others see how crazy the boy was? Did they notice how he would break down for no reason and hyperventilate? What about how he beat up on the smaller kids? Later in the week, after Stephen's return, some inmates began referring to him as "the little crazy." Others refused to let their kids play with him, claiming that Stephen could make their kids "sick" as well. In an effort to shield Stephen, Samantha kept him by her side for weeks. She also took to standing literally in between him and the other inmates, thus forming a wall of protection around him. When coupled with her own psychologi-cal exposure and maternal insecurities, it is easy to imagine how unsafe Samantha felt with her "sisters."

When faced with this sense of vulnerability, women like Rosa and Samantha yearned to retreat—to escape the perpetual surveillance and "get their heads together."[27] Yet Visions gave them no way to do this; there was no place to retreat, even temporarily. This lack of space for individual reflection was an ironic aspect of Visions's context of recovery. Because therapeutic practices stress the importance of reflection and contemplation, one might assume that Visions would diverge from other carceral institutions by giving inmates access to a bit of private space. After all, how can self-esteem and self-realization emerge when the internal "self" has no space to develop? Yet the Visions staff constructed a facility devoid of any such space. The architecture of the facility left no room for women to escape even for a short respite: the three large common rooms left their inhabitants subjected to the watchful eyes of others. Surveillance cameras kept an eye on the facility's hallways, entrances, and exits. Even the inmates' rooms were public—because they housed three to four inmates and their children, there was no way to retreat to them for privacy.[28] "Your room ain't really *your* room," Devon once explained to me. "It's not the place you go to relax. Usually, it's a place you gotta escape from."

Moreover, when inmates carved out small spaces of privacy, the staff found ways to close them down—thus forbidding the inmates from having unexposed internal lives.[29] In a sense, this was what the smoking breaks had provided many women; they gave the women an excuse to sit and reflect a few times a day. But this ended with the smoking ban. The same was true of the other tiny cracks and crevices the inmates pried open to retain a bit of privacy. While on room searches, the staff often discovered these cracks: like the small pictures that women pinned to the sides of their bunk beds so they could look at their loved ones before falling asleep; or the letters they taped to the top bunks so they could read them while resting. The staff took down the pictures and the letters, deeming them an "improper use of facility furniture." According to Rosa, there was only one space left to retreat to: "Some days I sit with Mario in the bathroom. We spend hours in there. It's the place I can be alone with him. I can calm him down in there when it's just us." Or, as Samantha wrote in an account for my writing class:

> The walls have ears here; the saying you can run but you can never hide took on a new meaning for me [at Visions]. We spent a lot of time hiding in bathrooms, trying to deal with Stephen's punishment. Other women and children would just stand outside the door, laughing when he was in there with me, which only made him angrier. He would scream out

louder; the language he began to use became more "colorful." He would throw things around the bathroom and at me. But this was the only place I could be with him and deal with his problem.

The image of Rosa and Samantha huddling with their kids in the bathroom encapsulates the fear many inmates experienced in this program of recovery. Visions required inmates to participate fully in its therapeutic practices. Yet its institutional context consistently undermined the safety and trust needed for such participation. Out of this tension emerged an acute sense of vulnerability, both for the inmates and their children. This sense of vulnerability deepened as the inmates realized that their future well-being rested on their conformity to Visions's therapeutic ideals.

INJUSTICE AS AN EMOTION: THE CONTENT OF RECOVERY

Working from a more traditional carceral context, sociologist Jill McCorkel has revealed how the physical layout of prison therapeutic communities can replicate their paranoid focus.[30] Often organized according to panoptical designs, these facilities give inmates the sense that they are always being monitored, which, in turn, pushes them to self-regulate and self-govern. Despite Visions's community-based setting, something similar occurred behind its doors. The staff's narrative of recovery positioned the inmates' out-of-control desires as the root of their problems, so it made sense that Visions put the women under perpetual surveillance— the staff worried that these desires would wreak havoc if left unregulated. It also made some sense that the staff refused to allow inmates any privacy or internal life—they did not trust the women to live responsibly once outside the therapeutic gaze. In this way, Visions's *context* of recovery was linked to the *content* of its agenda for recovery.

The Visions staff could not have been any clearer about what this agenda implied: first, inmates had to reign in their out-of-control desires for everything from drugs and alcohol to money to men to conflict to "street life." Once controlled, these urges could be replaced by desires for healthy substances and behaviors. Then, voilà, their lives would change for the better. Any issue or problem that complicated this formula could, with a bit of work, be subsumed within it. This was even true of the one issue that seemed to pose the most serious challenge to the formula: social injustice. In addition to bracketing all things social, the Visions staff tried to convince the inmates that the injustice they sensed was simply in their heads—thereby transforming inmates' social problems into emotional, psychological problems. Then, if this did not work, the staff tried to convince the inmates that they could end this sense of injustice by simply developing new habits and/or personality traits. Yet these techniques collided head-on with the inmates' ideas about the world and their strategies for surviving in it—a collision that ended up leaving the inmates feeling more vulnerable and disempowered in this program of recovery.

"The System is in Your Head"

Since the 1990s, a lot of attention has been devoted to the shift away from a rehabilitative model of corrections in the U.S. penal system.[31] With this shift, the penal system has largely lost any focus on social reform and reintegration—although never fully oriented toward rehabilitation, once upon a time penal institutions did stress the need for social work with prisoners and for preparing inmates for their reintegration into the institutions of social life.[32] To the extent that contemporary penal institutions even attempt rehabilitation, their approach tends to be quite individualized, emphasizing personal responsibility and self-reform. In large part, this shift reflects a more general discrediting of social explanations for crime and criminal behavior: from politicians to media pundits to justice officials to criminologists, notions of social rehabilitation have been deemed ineffective and unproductive.[33] Even worse, such social explanations have been accused of deflecting attention away from individual responsibility and providing offenders with an "excuse" for their offensive behaviors.[34]

While Visions's discourse of recovery also sidelined notions of social rehabilitation, this was not primarily because the staff was politically opposed to it. If anything, the Visions staff insisted that their plan for recovery resulted in a more profound change than social rehabilitation offered. Their goal was to "go beyond" the social determinants of behavior to reach a "deeper" understanding of inmates' impulses and motivations.[35] At the everyday level, this led the staff to bracket off the social or structural aspects of inmates' lives. Most often, this bracketing occurred indirectly, through the type of programming available to inmates. Of the dozens of groups offered by Visions, not one was devoted to GED preparation, education, or job training—despite the inmates' repeated requests for these groups. Of the many Alcoholics Anonymous and Narcotics Anonymous meetings the inmates could go to outside the facility, not a single inmate was allowed to attend classes at a local community college or job skills courses at the nearby job fair—despite the fact that many inmates had researched, applied to, and been admitted into these programs.[36] And of the countless counseling hours inmates endured, not a single one was devoted to release preparation or reintegration issues— despite the many problems the women encountered resolving legal cases, applying for social assistance, and securing public housing, health insurance, and public assistance prior to release.

The inmates complained vociferously about these gaps in the program, claiming that they needed far more "practical help"; or, as Chanel put it, "Give us the shit we'll need in the real world." Whenever the inmates raised these issues, the staff countered that they were receiving longer-lasting help at Visions. Jane, the facility director, always responded to such arguments by telling the inmates that if they wanted practical skills, they should have stayed in prison. "You can get education and job training at Valley State," she would remark. "Would you like to go back? We help you to get better, to recover, and to deal with your concerns and stresses." Of course, the inmates' lack of formal education and job training did cause them enormous concern and stress. Most of them were quite aware of their social and economic marginalization; all of them were worried about the discrimination they would face once released. Neglecting these concerns did not make them disappear—if anything, it just allowed them to deepen and fester.

The depth of these concerns became clear to me during a résumé course I held for the inmates. The class resulted from a house meeting in which the staff received an onslaught of requests for "practical help," so I agreed to hold the class for those who wanted it. When I announced the class at the next house meeting, everyone in the room signed up for it. Then, the day before the class, a few inmates asked me if I could hold individual sessions rather than a group class. Perplexed, I agreed to the one-on-one meetings. After a few sessions, I understood their request: the inmates were embarrassed by their limited work experience and educational backgrounds. Few of them had completed high school or obtained a GED; even fewer had worked in anything other than service-sector jobs. They did not want their "sisters" to know their backgrounds or to see their embarrassment when discussing them. "The work part is gonna be empty," Jacinta warned me as she nervously sat down to construct her résumé . "I don't have anything to put down there."[37] Or, as Claire said with a look of trepidation on her face: "I never finished high school. I had a few classes left but just couldn't do it. Shit, this is what I should be doing in here. I've been asking, but no one listens or cares."

In addition to asking for more "practical" help, inmates often questioned the accuracy of Visions's addiction model, suggesting that the source of their problems lay elsewhere. Those who did this most openly were the CDC inmates incarcerated for drug-related offenses. Although their drug-related convictions got them labeled "addicts," many insisted that they were dealers not users. So they resisted the required substance-abuse classes, claiming that their connection to drugs was purely economic. They explained how drug dealing was an irresistible way to make ends meet and support their families. They insisted that they began dealing for a living when their Temporary Assistance to Needy Families benefits had been cut and they had nowhere else to turn. And they argued that the punitive drug laws they had been convicted under were unjust and unfair. "It's off the hook out there," Juanita once proclaimed in a meeting. "You get put away forever for selling [drugs]. If I murdered someone, I would have gotten less time." In making such arguments, the inmates tried to draw into view the social and political realities of their lives—and to link their illegal activities to those realities. But the staff would have none of it. Whenever the inmates advanced these arguments, the staff shut them down, calling them "tactics" to avoid the deeper issues and the hard work of recovery. The goal was to bracket inmates' social and economic marginalization in order to target their psychologies.

At times, the staff did more than simply sideline inmates' social marginalization: they actively denied it by insisting that such experiences were in the inmates' heads. Lesley, an influential clinical counselor, had a refrain that she repeated: "The system is in your head." When she first began saying it, "the system" referred to the penal system—it was her way of pointing out how prison left its mark on inmates' thinking. So whenever an inmate did something Lesley did not like, she would blame the woman's "institutional thinking" on "the system." Yet, with time, the saying became Lesley's personal mantra; she repeated it all the time to inmates. Realizing that it was a quick way to shut down discussion of social inequality, she used it to refer to other "systems." It was a tactic to refocus attention from the external to the internal and to undermine inmates' claims to injustice. Then other counselors began to deploy it— sometimes even using "the system" and "inequality" interchangeably. This was particularly true when the inequalities being discussed hit close to home—or were related to Visions's program of recovery.

One of the best examples of how Lesley's mantra was used occurred during a special community meeting called to address the firing of May, the house director. Because May had been the inmates' favorite staff member, her dismissal angered them. So they began the meeting by accusing the staff of a grave injustice. The staff let this go on for a while. "They just need to vent," Jane whispered to Collette. "So let's let them." Eventually, Gloria, the facility director, had enough and jumped in to defend the decision. She argued that she had to fire May for financial reasons: her budget had been cut by the "big guys in Sacramento," which left her no choice but to cut back on the staff. "I feel my intelligence is being insulted," countered Karrina, an outspoken CDC inmate. "You fired her cause we liked her and she helped us." In response, Gloria did something she never did: she broke down in tears, asking the women to understand the "deep emotional pain" this caused her. The inmates fell silent, stunned at the sight of their sobbing director who had always been a model of distanced professionalism.

Eventually, Karrina ended the silence by suggesting that everyone at Visions participate in a letter-writing campaign to convince the "Sacramento bigwigs" of May's importance to the facility. Maybe they could even go to the state capital to testify so that the legislators would "know we aren't shitn' them and really believe us."[38] While the other inmates nodded in agreement, Lesley jumped in with her "the system is in your head" mantra. Then she proposed an idea: they should all form one big circle, hold hands, and let their feelings of disappointment come to the fore. As the other staff members moved the chairs into a circle and grabbed the inmates' hands, another silence fell over the group. This one lasted for over fifteen minutes, interrupted only occasionally by Lesley: "Feel the strength of the women next to you," she chanted. "Let your feelings take you over. It will all be okay." The meeting ended soon thereafter.

If the cultural imprint on these practices is not already clear, Devon astutely pointed it out a few days later. It was late in the afternoon, after a long day of meetings and focus seats, and a group of inmates had gathered in the TV room to relax. The *Oprah Winfrey Show* was on in the background. The show commemorated the anniversary of some horrible trauma for a suburban family—perhaps the day their child disappeared or the day they discovered one of them was terminally ill. What the actual trauma was did not much matter. Oprah's mode of addressing it was what caught the inmates' attention: after a lot of crying, Oprah had everyone on stage sit in a semicircle and hold hands. As they bowed their heads, Oprah mumbled something about forgiveness, strength, and healing. "Look, it's a black Lesley," Rosa shouted out. As the others laughed and began mimicking Oprah, Devon walked into the room. She shook her head as she corrected them: "Shit, you all got it reversed. Oprah's the famous one. She's who all these chicks wanna be like. Lesley is the white Oprah."

Eating Luna Bars and Dropping the Mask

There was yet another way that Visions's therapeutic agenda ended up turning injustice into an emotional issue: it led the staff to insist on a recipe for change that was purely individual and internal. The recipe was easy to decipher. Once inequality had been relocated into the inmates' heads, all the women needed to do to end it was to change their heads. The ingredients for change were equally clear. Certain habits and personality traits were idealized as essential to the recovery recipe, while others were pathologized as ruinous. Here it is important to remember that this plan was not optional. In order to prove they were on the road to recovery, the inmates were required to abide by it. This was true despite the fact that most of what the staff idealized was inconsistent with the women's own ideals—leading, once again, to the inmates' sense that the content of Visions's recovery model was debilitating and disempowering.

The actual list of habits and traits that Visions encouraged ran the gamut from the seemingly mundane to the clearly significant. On one end of the spectrum were the everyday habits the staff tried to induce in the women. Many of these habits were designed to steer the women away from their dangerous desires for drugs, alcohol, money, men, and "street life" toward "healthy" ways of being. So instead of retreating to the TV room to "space out," inmates were encouraged to exercise or meditate.[39] Rather than unwinding with a cigarette or a drink, the women were urged to play with their children or to take walks. Instead of rewarding themselves at the end of a difficult week by spending money or hooking up with a man, the inmates were told to cook themselves a good meal or to treat themselves to a spa day. "If we can get them to take healthy lifestyle options, the possibilities are endless," counselor Collette once explained to me. "They will begin to transform themselves in all sorts of other ways."

When faced with such encouragement, the inmates' responses ranged from subtle avoidance to quiet annoyance to outright resistance. Although some of the women did go through the motions, few seemed to accept Visions's "healthy lifestyle options" as replacements for their own routines and habits. "Here I go to do that yoga thing again," Shavon once proclaimed, rolling her eyes. Given her impending release, Shavon admitted that she had stepped up her yoga routine to impress her counselor. Then there was the Top Ramen war, a moment when the disjuncture between Visions's lifestyle choices and those of the inmates erupted into an intense battle. The conflict started one day when, during a community meeting, Karrina wrote "Top Ramen" in large letters on the meeting blackboard.

She then launched into a lecture about how this was her favorite snack food; she had grown up on it and had socialized her son to enjoy it. Other inmates jumped in to agree. "I've been eating it since I was a kid," Rosa noted. "I miss it in here." The staff members in attendance made faces with each inmate comment. Finally, counselor Lesley broke down. "I'm sorry but that stuff is terrible. . . . There's not a single vitamin in it. Just lots of preservatives and salt. You shouldn't be feeding it to the kids." Her colleagues corroborated, claiming that Top Ramen was equally unhealthy for the women, especially for those with diabetes and high blood pressure.

As the discussion got heated, counselor Collette proposed an alternative. Worried that her colleagues were "playing the guilt game" by making the inmates feel bad about their "culinary choices," Collette suggested that Visions offer them Luna Bars instead. She gave a long speech about the benefits of Luna Bars: they had plenty of flavor, packed in the nutrients and vitamins, and included "good calories." They symbolized the "healthy lifestyle options" the inmates should learn to desire. At one point, Collette pulled a bar out of her bag, showing everyone the picture of a jumping woman on the wrapper. "See, it's made for women and women's needs," she insisted.

The Luna Bar alternative only upped the ante for Karrina. What began as a suggestion to expand the facility's snack options snowballed into an angry debate about the politics of lifestyle. Some inmates mentioned the prohibitive cost of Luna Bars. "How much is one of those?" Chanel asked. "I could buy me a whole meal for that." They thus blamed the staff for being out of touch with the economic realities of their lives. Then the inmates moved on to question the availability of Luna Bars in their neighborhoods. They claimed they would not know where to buy them on the outside—maybe they were sold in the fancy health-food stores in the staff's neighborhoods, but surely they were not available in the areas the inmates would be living. So it did not make sense for them to "get hooked" on something they would not have access to later. Finally, the inmates concluded the discussion by returning to where it began: declarations about what gave them pleasure and what they found desirable. Karrina ended the exchange, saying, "It's simple. You can give us all the arguments for why we shouldn't want it, but we still do. The fact is that we want Top Ramen. We like it and we want it. So just let us have it. That's it."[40]

Of course, as the inmates knew all too well, it was not so simple: the Visions's program was oriented toward changing what the women wanted and found pleasure in. While the Top Ramen example may seem frivolous, the staff tried to instill other traits that were far more consequential. Visions's program of recovery sought to create women ready for self-disclosure and exposure; it idealized those prepared to reveal the most intimate details of their lives. The staff wanted women willing to expose their "inner demons" and to "go deep" in order to excise those demons. They valorized those who seemed unafraid to cry, unfazed by emotional outpourings, and undaunted by their sisters' traumas. These were all signs of a successful recovery, indicating that the inmates were becoming better, healthier women.

As they idealized these characteristics, the staff never stopped to consider if they were desirable or viable for the inmates. More precisely, staff members ignored all indications that their ideals were inconsistent with the inmates'. On a daily basis, the inmates questioned the staff's visions of what they should become. In groups, when they were instructed to "share" and "go deep," some countered that they were uncomfortable divulging so much. They claimed to have been socialized to keep to themselves and wanted to remain that way. For instance, whenever Veronica was asked to expose and disclose, she launched into long descriptions of how she survived her abusive family by staying tough and strong. When the staff and her sisters prompted her for details about the abuse—or, as they put it, to take off her "emotional armor"—she simply stated that she never opened up to her family members or "let their shit get to me." In effect, she indicated that she had no desire to remove her well-used armor for any family, real or imagined.

Similarly, in community meetings when inmates' emotions ran high, I observed some inmates struggle to stop themselves from crying— despite the staff's constant urging to "let go" and "allow the emotions to flow." Here, too, inmates questioned the desirability of the staff's emotive ideal. They claimed that they did not want to become the kind of women who acted like "blabbering idiots" or who, as Jacinta put it, "can't get a grip on themselves." In fact, whenever Jacinta found herself in meetings that turned into crying sessions, she would close her eyes and whisper something to herself. During one such meeting, I sat next to her and heard her chanting "Never let them see you cry." Realizing I had heard her, Jacinta later explained to me that her mother and grandmother always warned her to beware of crying; her female kin had cautioned her that once "they see you cry, they got you." Since this mantra had worked for generations of women in her family, Jacinta had no desire to change it now. She held firm despite the staff's attempts to get her to question her desires or to believe that what she may dislike or feel uncomfortable with were good for her.

In addition to questioning the desirability of the staff's ideals, inmates questioned their viability. Given the realities of their lives, the inmates warned that these ideals may be dangerous to them. The inmates knew quite well that they were expected to drop their "masks" and "badass attitudes" as signs of recovery. Yet when instructed to do so, some inmates began talking about how their masks and attitudes had been key survival strategies for them, allowing them to withstand abusive family members and lovers; this armor helped them to navigate tough, inner-city neighborhoods and enabled them to maintain a degree of self-preservation and protection. "Where I come from, we learn to watch out for ourselves," Towanda once explained to me when I asked why she spent so much time in our writing class staring out the window and analyzing who went where on the neighboring streets. "It's like an instinct I have. Make sure you never get caught with your guard down and never open yourself up. So you always need to know who's where and who's planning what." Given such representations, did it really make sense to convince her to let go of her "defensive masks" and expose her "emotional pain"? Would Visions's therapeutics end up leaving inmates like Towanda ill-prepared to protect themselves on the outside and in the communities they were about to return to?

As she so often did, Karrina answered these questions most forcefully one afternoon in a community meeting. And, as was so often the case, her answers emerged in response to attacks on her mothering. This time, the attacks came from the parenting coordinator, who claimed

Karrina was too tough on her son. She accused Karrina of refusing to comfort him when he hurt; she said Karrina made him responsible for things no six-year-old could handle; and she recalled times when Karrina rewarded him for "copping an attitude" and "acting all tough." As the accusations flew, Karrina got progressively agitated. She kept her cool—until another childcare worker argued that Karrina was teaching her son to act like a "gangster from the hood." Then she responded: "My reality ain't your reality. I'm a single mother from South Central [Los Angeles] and I'm just trying to prepare myself and my son for our reality. It ain't gonna work out there like it does in here. . . . He can't be a pussy. He needs to learn to be independent and tough. For his survival and for my survival. If you like it or not, that's how I'm going raise him. Just watch me." The discussion concluded with the staff shaking their heads in disapproval.

Exchanges like this were not simply abstract debates—they had real implications for the inmates' lives. Just as Keisha's AWOL story exemplified the effects of Visions's context of recovery, Mary's story personified the consequences of its therapeutic content. Unlike many other inmates, Mary seemed to thrive in Visions's community of recovery. She came to the facility after numerous convictions for drug possession and immediately latched onto its addiction narrative. In meetings, she often launched into stories about how her whole family was addicted to something and how much she wanted to break the cycle for her two kids, both of whom resided with her in the program. After close to a year, the staff rewarded Mary by moving her into the "transitional group," thus allowing her to spend much of the day outside the facility searching for work and housing. It was at this point that Mary ran into problems. With little education and almost no work experience, she could not find stable employment; with a long list of drug felonies, she found herself ineligible for most welfare programs and housing subsidies. The Visions staff encouraged her to "stay strong" and remember her "12 steps."

Then one of her random drug tests came back positive for cocaine. Within hours, the staff removed Mary's children from the facility and sent them to live with their father.[41] Mary panicked, claiming that their father had a history of drug use and domestic violence. Adding to her panic, a judge ruled that she had to return to jail immediately to complete her original two-year sentence. "Then she just went nuts," counselor Collette recounted to me. "She was bouncing off the walls like I've never seen." To calm her, Collette gave her a walkman with a tape of inspirational poetry. As Mary sat in the corner listening to the tape, nervously rocking back and forth, Collette had an epiphany. While the outcome would be devastating for Mary in the short run, she saw a silver lining: "I looked at her and realized that she wasn't the same woman who entered [Visions] a year ago. This time she couldn't make it but maybe next time she will. . . . My job is to make the women aware of their psychological pain. She's aware of it now. So in some way, it was kind of a victory."

SOCIAL VULNERABILITY AS PERSONAL PATHOLOGY

It is hard to imagine that Mary shared Collette's optimistic view. While I never saw Mary again, I did observe how other inmates reacted to her downfall. Just like the Alliance girls had done a decade earlier when one of their mates, Maria, escaped from the facility, the Visions women saw in the incident evidence of everything they had been complaining about. For them, Mary's downfall was symptomatic of gaps in Visions's program: of how its lack of practical help would leave them unprepared for employment upon release, how its denial of social inequality would leave them without the tools to combat the real challenges in their lives, and how its inability to understand who they needed to be to survive would leave them weak and vulnerable. Of course, this was not the only occasion the inmates had to make these points. On a daily basis, their words and actions exposed the myths of the facility. And the myths upon which Visions operated were many: there was the myth of the coercion-free community context, the myth of the community of sisterhood, the myth of the all-encompassing addictive desire, and the myth of the psychological origin of all problems and conflicts.

Of all these myths, perhaps the most dangerous was the myth of empowerment—the promise that everything would be okay in these women's lives if they just dropped their masks, let their pain come to the fore, held hands, and wished inequality away. The danger came from the myth's bracketing off all things social. By not discussing the inmates' concerns about social marginalization and discrimination, Visions allowed the women's anxieties to fester. And the staff could also avoid the harsh realities of reintegration that most inmates would confront—realities that included ongoing legal cases, broken familial bonds, political disenfranchisement, economic discrimination, and restrictions on public benefits. Rather than giving inmates the tools to grapple with these realities, Visions's therapeutic practices forced the women to take responsibility for problems that were largely outside their control. This, in turn, seemed to set the inmates up for failure. If they became angered by an injustice they confronted, it was because they could not control their "addiction to conflict." If they relapsed, it was because they lacked the will to resist their dangerous impulses. If their lives did not improve, it was because they were not smart or strong enough. This is why Mary's story was so resonant: it exemplified how the Visions approach to recovery held women accountable for personal *and* societal failings.

Of course, it may be unfair to hold state institutions up to grandiose ideals such as female empowerment. After all, can we really expect penal facilities, no matter how "alternative" they are, to lead revolutions? Actually, in this case, we can, since these are the ideals Visions held for itself—it promised nothing less than female empowerment. So if community-based therapeutics failed to deliver, we must interrogate this failure. Perhaps even more importantly, the Visions program did not just fail to live up to its own ideals but actually deflected attention from them by refusing to acknowledge social obstacles to empowerment. The staff did not have to educate the inmates about structural inequality; they were already quite aware of it. All the staff had to do was acknowledge the women's own diagnoses of the social problems they faced and provide tools to cope with them; or simply to recognize the emotional costs of inequality and the psychological effects of the difficult lives most of the inmates had led.[42] The staff's failure to contextualize inmates' lives and their insistence on draining the women's experiences of all social content are arguably what led to so much conflict at Visions—and to so much anxiety among the inmates.

SIX The Enemies Within

FIGHTING THE SISTERS
AND NUMBING THE SELF

Whenever I entered through Visions's large, steel doors, I never knew what awaited me. More often than not, it was some sort of conflict or crisis. The facility always seemed to be in turmoil: fights between the staff and inmates were commonplace, as were facility-wide breakdowns and freezes. Rarely a day went by when there was not an emergency to be managed or a problem to be resolved. Sometimes it felt like the daily rhythm of the facility revolved around such crises; they energized and charged both the inmates and staff.[1] The inmates were tough, outspoken women; when something disturbed them, they immediately acted on it. The staff were equally tough and outspoken; they had become very committed to their model of recovery and therapeutic diagnosis. But they were also exhausted by the constant flow of inmate complaints. By the end of my fieldwork, many staff members claimed the facility had become impossible to run.[2] In this way, Visions's institutional relations were not unlike those that characterized Alliance a decade earlier—full of volatility and strife.

At another level, the relations at Visions were strikingly different from those of Alliance. This was especially true when it came to relations among the inmates. At both facilities, the inmates developed astute analyses of their surroundings and of the ways each program bred a sense of danger and vulnerability. But while the Alliance girls used their shared analysis to develop a collective plan of action and to launch into a unified struggle with the staff, almost the opposite occurred at Visions. Rather than leading them to form a united front, the Visions women's discontent spewed out in all directions. Instead of taking aim at one common target, their anger was directed at each other. The Visions inmates responded to their sense of disempowerment and injustice by turning on each other and on themselves: in effect, they transformed what could have been an external struggle with the staff into an internal one—waging an "us versus us" war on themselves and other inmates.[3]

This chapter in the Visions story is not an easy one to tell. In large part, this is because it is not the kind of story that sociologists like to tell. As Loic Wacquant has argued, ethnographers are particularly averse to telling such stories—our commitment to those we study can unwittingly seep into our analyses, narrowing what we are willing or able to reveal about them.[4] Consciously or not, our proclivity to sympathize with our subjects, many of whom come from marginalized and stigmatized groups, leads us to downplay their more unflattering behavior and unseemly qualities.[5] So we accentuate the valiant responses of the oppressed to deplorable conditions. We search for what sociologist Erving Goffman called "secondary adjustments," the underlife of a total institution in which the subjugated resist their ongoing abasement, humiliation, and degradation.[6] In the process, we often insist on our subjects' fundamental goodness, respectability, and decency.[7] And we emphasize their agency in moments of collective, common struggle—however few and far between those moments may be. In short, we prefer to tell resistance tales, whether they be of the "power of the powerless" or the "weapons of the weak."[8]

The lure of the "romance of resistance" seems especially strong in accounts of the penal system.[9] And it is even stronger when the inmates under examination are women. Although analyses of women still constitute a small portion of prison research, such studies are strikingly similar in their representations of prison life. These accounts tend to portray the lines of prison power in dualist, dichotomous terms: the prison staff has power, while female inmates are subjected to it.[10] As a result, the former become victimizers and the latter victims; the former become the actors, the latter the acted on.[11] When female inmates are shown as actors, they are usually of the noblest sort—exhibiting keen insight into the nature of carceral power, while maintaining spectacular distance from its underside.[12] Yet, as sociologists Candace Kruttschnitt and Rosemary Gartner remind us, women develop different approaches to doing time.[13] Clearly, many of them are victimized by prison staff; some of them respond by developing networks of support and friendship.[14] But many also survive their sentences by isolating themselves and keeping their distance from others. Some do time by maintaining a hostile stance toward those around them. Some even become emotionally and physically abusive to themselves and others. Yet such variation is often absent from accounts of women's prison life: seldom do we see how offensive institutional environments can lead women to act in offensive ways.

In this chapter, I suggest that this empirical gap has conceptual consequences. By not examining female inmates' responses to confinement in all their complexity, we miss important insights into how power and punishment operate.[15] By smoothing over the contradictions in their responses, we end up obfuscating an important way that inmates are governed. At Visions, when we examine the more painful aspects of the inmates' behavior, the imprint of the facility's power relations is clearly discernable. The inmates' sites of struggle mirrored the sites of institutional power—the women also fought over the self and mobilized discourses of desire. They often divided to conquer, found pleasure in pain, and psychologized the social. So although the inmates complained about the context and content of community-based therapeutics, their responses were deeply affected by them.

The convergence between Visions's therapeutics and the inmates' struggles thus had the unintended effect of legitimating the facility's program of recovery: the inmates reacted in ways that seemed to confirm the staff's diagnoses. As the inmates fought about the best place to shop or the best way to mother, they appeared to become void of all reason—thus bolstering the staff's claims that the women needed to control their urges and passions. As the inmates took advantage of their sisters' weaknesses, they seemed to become psychologically brutal—thus strengthening the staff's arguments that the women needed to learn to channel their emotions in "positive" and "productive" directions. As the inmates repeated stories of trauma in lurid detail, they appeared to become numb—thus reinforcing the staff's impulse to push the women to "go deep" and excise their "inner demons." In this way, Visions's power relations reproduced themselves: the inmates' responses to Visions's program of recovery ended up confirming the need for therapeutics and justifying its mode of governance.[16]

This chapter outlines two of the most common ways the inmates responded to Visions's program of recovery. First, I describe how the inmates often reacted by turning on each other and transforming their many differences into sources of conflict. I also reveal how, of all the possible divisions, the most explosive were those that involved Visions's acceptable pleasures. I then turn to the second common inmate response: to become emotionally numb and disengage from their surroundings. Here I chart how many women reacted to Visions's program by competing with each other in an "emotional pain game" and by withdrawing into their own heads. In the end, I argue that these responses embedded the inmates in a vicious cycle through which their actions seemed to confirm Visions's recipe for recovery.

FIGHTING THE ENEMIES WITHIN

Whenever the Visions staff tried to make sense of all the turmoil in the facility, they always returned to the same representation: the house was

split into two warring factions—the California Department of Corrections inmates and the perinatal clients. The staff traced this split to the
different rules and regulations that applied to the two groups, claiming
that the legal basis for their incarceration differed, which created conflict.[17] This representation then structured the kind of solutions available
to address the problem of rampant unrest. Since the facility's financial
survival rested on the merging of these groups, getting rid of one of them
was not an option. Instead, the staff debated the possibility of physically
separating them—that is, keeping both groups at Visions but housing
them in different living quarters and providing them distinct programs.[18]
Yet the staff's addiction narrative ultimately won out: the staff's insistence that the inmates had similar problems and treatment needs led
them to reject the idea of separation. So the staff developed other ways to
try and bridge the gap separating the inmate populations. They created
encounter groups, organized collective outings, and established a "big
sister" program to get women from each group to bond. Through such
bonding experiences, the staff hoped to lessen the conflict in the facility.

The staff's assessment of the source of inmate unrest did illuminate
a real dividing line in the facility. The CDC and perinatal women were
indeed enmeshed in different parts of the penal system and subjected to
divergent rules and regulations. And, indeed, these differences did give
rise to conflicts—as when the perinatal women accused CDC inmates of
stealing their belongings because the CDC women were "prisoners." Or
when the perinatal clients argued that they did not want their children to
live among "convicted criminals." For their part, the CDC women waged
their own assaults against the perinatal group—as when they made fun
of those who were "dosing" as they came off of drugs.[19] Or when the
CDC inmates argued that they did not want their children to live among
"crazy druggies."

Yet the staff's image of the CDC/perinatal split also obscured the
countless other divisions plaguing the house. At Visions, anything could
become a potential dividing line. The inmates spent much of their time
exposing the enemies within their ranks and subjecting them to harsh
treatment. In doing so, it was almost as if the inmates forgot about the
critique they had developed vis-à-vis the Visions program: instead of

stressing their common experiences of discrimination as they did in their struggles with staff, they accused one another of psychological failings; rather than emphasizing their collective marginalization, they focused on their sisters' individual problems and pathologies.

Attention, Target and Wal-Mart Shoppers

The house divisions at Visions ran the gamut from the mundane to the serious. There was the schism between the good and bad cooks, with some inmates refusing to eat food cooked by certain women. This split frequently erupted into screaming fights as some women accused others of making them sick. There was the divide between the soap opera and the talk show watchers. This war often led to yelling matches in the TV room over whose viewing choices were more worthy and credible. There was the rift between the slow and the fast showerers. The stakes were particularly high here, since getting stuck behind a long showerer could mean missing the morning meeting and thus facing a staff reprimand. Making this split even more charged was its intersection with another division—the gulf between the short and the long haired and the grooming routines that hair length implied. This split then circled back to overlap with the CDC/perinatal divide: because all CDC inmates had to wear their hair back, perinatal women argued that CDC inmates did not need to wash their hair everyday and thus should not be allowed to take so much time in the shower.[20]

Of all the divisions that preoccupied the Visions women, two schisms surfaced with particular consistency and intensity. The first mobilized their roles as consumers. Once a month, the house went on what was called a "needs shopping"—the staff piled all the inmates into vans and headed off to a nearby store, where the women purchased basic necessities for the month. The decision about which store to go to was a hot-button issue. Some inmates demanded to be taken to Target, while others insisted on Wal-Mart. Initially, this seemed like a good-natured debate, with the women of each side joking about why their preferred store was better. With time, however, these two factions evolved into full-fledged interest groups; they even began to lobby the staff and their undecided sisters in favor of their preferred store. Eventually, each side started coming to community meetings ready to do battle. Armed with evidence of the lower prices or better selection at their store, the women spent hours debating the relative merits of Target and Wal-Mart. In one instance Shanika, a strong Target supporter, brought in an old pair of pants she had purchased at Wal-Mart to show how they had come apart. Holding them up for her sisters to see, she pointed out all the holes and tears. "I'm not gonna waste my money on this shit," she proclaimed.

When the staff finally decided that the needs shopping would be done at Target, the conflict escalated. Some Wal-Mart supporters accused the other side of using unfair tactics to influence the staff's decision, claiming that a group of senior sisters with more access to the staff had pressured them to decide in favor of Target. In retaliation, they boycotted the Target trip. Then accusations surfaced that the Wal-Mart women were secretly destroying or stealing the goods their sisters had purchased at Target. This led to a special meeting to address the conflict. But that failed to end it: the Wal-Mart/Target war continued for months, with each side spontaneously launching into speeches about the superiority of their store in the middle of house meetings and discussions of other topics.

While this conflict may seem superficial, it touched off a lot of rage in the Visions inmates. In part, this was because the struggle drew on consumer identifications that were full of race and class signifiers. It was not simply that one side of the divide included more African American or white women; in fact, these groups were equally represented on both sides. Nor was it that the women on one side were poorer than those on the other; most of the women at Visions were impoverished. If anything, the Wal-Mart/Target split replicated a suburban/urban division in the house: supporters of Wal-Mart tended to come from suburban areas, while those in the Target faction were from cities.

Yet race and class did factor into this conflict through the arguments deployed by each side to defend their choices. Over and over again, Wal-Mart defenders insisted that their store carried a brand of children's clothes sold in Macy's. This, they believed, gave them access to middle-class style and quality. "I ain't gonna be embarrassed with my son wearing some unknown brand," Karrina once argued. "I want him to have what the kids who go to Macy's have." For their part, Target supporters mobilized their own signifiers—repeatedly calling Wal-Mart a "ghetto store" and referring to commercials that represented Target as a place for affordable, high-level design. The implication was that the Wal-Mart women were too unsophisticated to appreciate truly good quality and high-level design. In this way, the women's struggles over consumer choice were bound up with larger identifications and aspirations.

Another set of associations was activated in the second major inmate division: the spilt between the mothers of older children and the mothers of younger children. When I began my work in Visions, I was struck by how motherhood seemed to be a strong point of alliance among the women. The inmates took care of each other's children and enjoyed playing with all the kids in the house. During community meetings, it was often difficult to tell who a given child belonged to since all the women acted like mothers to all the children, fawning over the babies and disciplining recalcitrant toddlers. But this changed after a house meeting in which a group of inmates announced the formation of a special group for the mothers of "big kids." In explaining their group, the women claimed that older kids experienced discrimination at Visions. "All the outings are for little kids," proclaimed Samantha. "Most of the house activities are just too immature for our kids." What is more, these women argued that their kids had special needs that were not being addressed by the facility. "My son's becoming a little man," Karrina announced to the group. "He needs more privacy and more space and more control over his environment. We need to make room for kids like him and stop treating them like babies."[21]

These arguments prompted an explosive debate among the inmates—a debate that usurped several meetings and eventually devolved into screaming matches. Then, a few weeks after the formation of the "big kids" group, another group of inmates came to a house meeting to announce the formation of new group for the mothers of young children. To the sneers and heckles of the older-kids' mothers, they explained that their children were in fact the ones being discriminated against—they claimed the big kids ran over their children on the playground, knocked them over in the hallways, and stole their food at mealtime. They also argued that the Visions program favored older kids: "Of all the house outings I've been on, my son only enjoyed one," asserted Tasha, the mother of an eight-month-old. "So where's this discrimination you all are talkin' about?"

With time, these two groups coalesced into warring factions. They met in secret to plot how to carve out more space for their children and to convince the staff to be more responsive to them. Although these meetings did give the women in each group a platform upon which to ally—and even some institutional space to support each other as they mothered in prison—the split also became a source of enormous strife and division. Some mothers refused to let their children play together; others stopped delegating childcare responsibilities to members of the opposing group. This ended up limiting the women's ability to participate in activities within and outside the facility. After the childcare staff left for the day, inmates had to rely on their sisters for childcare, using official "childcare agreements" to delegate childcare responsibilities to one another. These agreements became increasingly difficult to enter into once the motherhood division surfaced—since the women refused to entrust their kids to inmates in the other faction. This then constrained the inmates from leaving Visions or attending classes after working hours.

For instance, after the formation of these two warring maternal groups, many of the women in my writing workshop started bringing their babies to class, claiming that they were unable to find other inmates to watch their kids during class time. Eventually, the class began to feel like a nursery and writing became close to impossible. So I set out to find childcare for the children. After a long search and a lot of coaxing, I located two inmates who were free during class time and willing to watch the babies. "No way," Tasha exclaimed when I proposed the arrangement. "Those women hate little kids." Then Rosa added, "Ain't no way I'm leaving Mario with them cause they'd beat on him and neglect him just to get at me." In the end, Tasha and Rosa realized they could not focus on their writing while caring for an infant. Even though they were two of the most engaged writers in the group, they decided to stop coming to class until they could find mothers from their faction to care for their babies.

It was not a coincidence that the two main house divisions surfaced over the inmates' roles as consumers and as mothers. Recall that Visions had positioned consumption and motherhood as acceptable pleasures and held them out as healthy desires.[22] In this way, the inmates' responses to Visions's program of recovery was clearly influenced by the form and content of the program itself—an influence that becomes even clearer when we consider the inmates' responses to Visions's therapeutic agenda.

The Pleasure of Pain

The divisions separating the women at Visions not only revolved around their daily activities and routines. They also impinged on the inmates' psychological state and composition. The level of psychological brutality the inmates could inflict on each other was shocking. At times, it seemed like the inmates took stock of their sisters' problems and vulnerabilities just so they were ready to pounce when necessary. And pounce they did—like when Jacinta and Stacey tormented Mary during a focus seat session, calling her an uncaring mother and a wimp whose husband repeatedly cheated on her. Or when Mabel made fun of the panic attacks Samantha began to suffer after her son had been taken from Visions in an ambulance and admitted into a psychiatric hospital.

Then there was what happened to Irene, a forty-year-old heroin addict who came to Visions for her fourth attempt to get clean. The staff enrolled Irene in a nearby detox program, which meant that she often came to house meetings "dosing" from methadone. This made her the butt of many jokes. "Hey, Irene, can you hear me in there?" her sisters would query. After a few weeks at Visions, the staff allowed Irene's five-year-old daughter to join her in the facility. This exacerbated Irene's anxiety, leading to more taunting from her sisters: "Is Irene getting nervous?" or "Does Irene need some smack to calm herself down?" Then, one day while on a doctor's visit, Irene disappeared. She resurfaced late that night, clearly high and in a manic state. When the staff refused to let her into the facility to see her daughter, she became even more manic. Apparently, she spent the night on the street, screaming and pounding on Visions's front door. This then became a common inmate refrain: mimicking Irene's slurred speech, the inmates would yell, "Let me in! I need to see my daughter!" and "I'm not high, I just want to see my girl!'"

In addition to taking advantage of their sisters' vulnerabilities, the inmates were quick to blame one another for their problems. When it came to their own lives, the women could offer quite sophisticated socio-logical explanations for their troubles. But when one of their sisters had problems, they became unforgiving. In fact, the inmates tended to be relentless in assigning individual blame for their sisters' past and pres-ent transgressions. This was particularly true of the older sisters in the house, who frequently took a been-there-done-that attitude with newer inmates. They also claimed hazing rights over their younger sisters. These initiation rituals were actually built into the Visions's program. Once an inmate had been in the program for a certain amount of time, she became eligible for election into "Women of Vision," a small group of inmates whose job it was to oversee the progress of newer residents and to deal with house conflicts. Women of Vision met once a week to come up with recommendations to the staff on a wide range of issues—from which sister should be moved up to the next stage in the program to where to go on house outings to how to reprimand an unruly inmate.

Women of Vision took their disciplinary work very seriously. Other inmates often told me that they dreaded being called up to explain their actions to the group. For good reason: Women of Vision were known to deliver the harshest reprimands and reprisals for errant behavior. "She's the worst mother I've ever seen," a Woman of Vision once proclaimed after reviewing a case of an inmate who left her son in the house play-ground while she took a nap. "Dephase her immediately. There's no excuse for that kind of neglect." Although the group's deliberations were conducted in the absence of the staff, they often sounded like excerpts from the staff handbook—replete with speeches about their sisters' addictions, out-of-control impulses, and lack of personal responsibility.

Perhaps the strongest adherent of this approach was Karrina, who reigned as the head of Women of Vision for months. Outside Women of Vision meetings, Karrina was known for her collective activism and leanings. But inside these meetings, she changed her tune: "Take her house privileges away until she admits responsibility for acting like a fool," she once ruled in a case of stolen potato chips. Then there was her statement to an inmate accused of starting a fight: "You need to go on a freeze until you personally accept blame for this. Stop blaming others for your behavior." While other inmates also blamed Karrina for her harsh treatment of them, its source was clearly institutional: because Visions made it a privilege for the Women of Vision to administer punishment and pain, the chosen few began to find pleasure in this privilege.

It was not only the Women of Vision who relished the spectacle of pain. A few times a month, these hazing rights were allocated to the entire inmate population through the notorious focus seat. In an almost perverse way, inmates looked forward to these public displays of anguish. They would remind each other who was targeted on a particular day; they would arrive to these sessions with food and drink on hand; and they would argue among themselves to secure the best seat for the event. Focus seat sessions became forms of entertainment. These spectacles had a particular rhythm: as the momentum built, the onlookers became increasingly excited. Then call and response would start, with one inmate shouting an accusation, followed by the cheers and approvals of the others. The whole thing culminated in crying and hysteria. "You missed an off-the-hook focus seat today," Rosa once noted to Keisha. "Mary was taken out and called on everything. And she bawled like a baby. You should've seen it."

The inmates' tendency to find pleasure in their sisters' pain was hardly surprising. The program of recovery they were enmeshed in had clear, mandatory prescriptions for them. And it would be naïve to expect the inmates to remain unaffected by these imperatives. Instead, the inmates' responses bore the Visions's imprint: when targeted and treated as individuals, the inmates became individualized; when denied their commonalities, they turned on each other; and when taught to find pleasure in pain, they transformed their sisters' punishment into an enticing spectacle.

In social research, as in everyday life, exceptional events can illuminate the normal and taken for granted. This occurred one morning at Visions when an advocacy group for incarcerated mothers paid a visit to the facility. The group had tried to break into Visions for months to meet with the CDC inmates and finally got one of its lawyers in while many staff members were on summer vacation. Despite the lack of advance warning, every CDC inmate showed up to the meeting—good and bad cooks, slow and fast showerers, Target and Wal-Mart shoppers, mothers of older and younger kids. The lawyer began by explaining that she had come to inform them of their legal rights and the laws structuring their incarceration. She also wanted to hear about their experiences at Visions. A silence fell over the room as the inmates looked at each other in disbelief. "Is she for real?" Keisha asked Jacinta. "Shit, I think so," Jacinta hesitantly responded.

The floodgates opened. The women spoke about how Visions denied them education and job training; they revealed how scared and vulnerable they felt in this "therapeutic community"; they recounted how the facility violated CDC rules governing the terms of their confinement; and they asked about how welfare reform would change their access to income support, housing subsidies, and health care. Most of all, the inmates began to talk as if they had social rights and entitlements—even if those rights and entitlements were attached to the stigmatized category of the "prisoner." They also struggled to turn this talk into action, asking the lawyer how they should go about fighting the injustices around them. Should they use legal channels and sue the facility? Or should they take a more political route and write letters to state legislators? When addressed as a collective, the inmates responded as a collective.

I never saw the CDC inmates as energized and emboldened as when they left that meeting. Unfazed by having missed lunch, they grabbed a snack and went directly into the previously scheduled community meeting. They then proceeded to take it over. Seated in a long row on one side of the room, they spoke for the first time in a completely unified voice. "We are prisoners," proclaimed Karrina. "And we have rights. They may be violated here all the time but we have them. And we're gonna claim them now." The others proceeded with their long list of problems and complaints. "You say this is our community, but that's just bullshit," Rosa stated. "What am I supposed to do when I disagree with your diagnosis of me?" Then Claire interjected, "That's right. My counselor tells me I'm addicted to men and male approval. And that she's a trained expert and I'm not. So am I just supposed to shut up? How can this be our community?" These comments were followed by countless accusations of how the facility violated their rights to everything from familial contact to education to legal representation to financial assistance. "Are you writing this down?" Karrina yelled at the staff as her CDC sisters continued down their list of violations. "How are you gonna remember what we're saying if you don't write it down?"

After about an hour, Jane, the house director, insisted that they move on to other topics. In particular, they still had to decide where to go for the monthly needs shopping. As soon as this notoriously contentious issue was on the table, the CDC alliance began to crumble. Suddenly, the Wal-Mart/Target split took over, dividing women who had only minutes before been allied as entitled prisoners. By the end of the meeting, some CDC inmates were no longer speaking to each other. A few weeks later, I asked them what became of their plans for a letter-writing campaign. They shook their heads in disillusionment, explaining how "some of those bitches" started to steal their belongings after the needs shopping and to discriminate against their kids. "They can't be trusted," proclaimed Karrina, referring to her CDC sisters. Life at Visions had returned to normal.

BECOMING UNCOMFORTABLY NUMB

The conflict and turmoil at Visions took its toll on all the inmates. Day after day, they were embroiled in struggles with the staff and their sisters. In such an environment, it is hardly surprising that many women began to withdraw. Over time, a numbness seemed to set in: although the timing of its onset varied, most inmates eventually became afflicted by a creeping detachment and disengagement. In this way, the inmates at Visions were not unlike their counterparts in traditional prisons. As criminologists have documented, female inmates frequently respond to the harshness and brutality of incarceration through some form of withdrawal—whether by isolating themselves from the prison community or subjecting themselves to painful practices like self-mutilation.[23]

Given the nature of the Visions program, it was nearly impossible for inmates to withdraw through physical isolation. Their days were full of required groups, meetings, and counseling sessions; refusing to attend these groups could result in dismissal from the facility. Instead, inmates expressed withdrawal in other ways. First, some disengaged from their surroundings and became desensitized to its brutality. These inmates participated in the required groups and sessions, but they did so in a mechanical, almost robotic way—as if they were present in body but not in spirit. On the surface, this response did not seem like withdrawal at all, since these women continued to participate in Visions's rituals of self-disclosure and public exposure, albeit impassively. But the second form of withdrawal was far more recognizable: many women checked out into a state of semiconsciousness. Those inmates who could opted to medicate themselves into numbness with legal drugs and medications. Those who were not able to self-medicate sought solace in sleep, using every chance they could to exit into a slumber. These forms of withdrawal were actually two sides of the same coin—they evidenced an alienation from oneself and others. Thus, both reactions could be exhibited by the same women, even during the same day.

The Competitive Confessional

Of the many things Visions demanded of its inmates, the most non-negotiable was participation in the confessional. The moment a woman entered the facility, this expectation was made clear to her: the first act she had to perform was the construction of an autobiography, her testament of the "self" and plan for remolding it. From this testament came her safe-to-speak, an abridged version of her autobiography that she recited publicly until she had been "phased" into the community. Even after this phasing, the confessionals continued. The entire facility was organized around these public airings; the groups, meetings, and focus seats were geared toward "going deep." At any moment, inmates could be asked to engage in an outpouring of emotion. And their institutional fates rested on their willingness to oblige—their progression through the program and movement toward release depended on their participation. So although some inmates complained about having to divulge so much so often, the reality remained: if they wanted to survive at Visions, they had to take part in the confessional.

Yet the actual content of their contributions could not be prescribed. Over time, as I got to know the inmates better, I began to see their participation as increasingly scripted, even rehearsed. It was almost as if they had learned to break their life stories into pieces and to package them for public presentation when called on. Since most inmates had spent time in other correctional institutions and 12-step programs, it is possible that the women came to Visions with these scripts already prepared. Wherever they originated, the scripts were rarely developed on the spot. This was clear from the women's faces: in groups, I rarely saw an inmate struggle to come to terms with her past. Instead, most seemed to respond to the staff's calls to "go deep" by pushing a button to play a recording of what was expected of them. The recordings even appeared to be catalogued. Some buttons led to specific topics, such as substance abuse, family violence, or sexual assault; others led to an emotion, such as outrage, hurt, or remorse. The repetitive nature of the staff's requests only enhanced the recorded quality of the inmates' responses, forcing the women to replay the tape several times a week. It also led the women to appear numb to some horrific experiences—from gang rapes to suicide attempts to drug overdoses to incest.

As they recited these scripts, the inmates faced a real dilemma. Clearly, it could not be obvious that they were performing a prepared text; it could not look like they were "wearing a mask." After all, one of the main purposes of the confessional was to elicit a reaction—not only in the confessor but also in the audience. With few objective indicators of when an inmate had "gone deep," the audience's reaction to her became critical. So the extent to which a confession provoked tears, shock, or anguish in those hearing it was an indication of its power and depth. Among other things, this resulted in an insidious competition among the inmates: Whose lives were the most shocking? Whose stories were the most lurid? In this competition, the worst outcome was to tell a chapter in one's life to the uninterested faces of the staff and sisters.

To avoid this, the inmates began to tell increasingly wrenching stories. They also became increasingly vivid in their storytelling. It became no longer enough for a woman to discuss being gang-raped—she had to detail how, when, and where the rape happened, as well as how it made her feel. Then, the next time she confessed, she had to be even more revealing to have the same effect. Eventually, this spiraled into a one-upping of pain and suffering in which the inmates competed against their sisters—all the while trying to keep emotional distance from their surroundings and what it took out of them.

I first noticed the competitive confessional in the writing classes I held with the inmates. From the very first class, the women were surprisingly eager to "tell their stories." As soon as word got out that this was what we were doing in the classes, I was overrun with interested participants. On the first day of class, nearly all the women arrived with a clear sense of what they wanted to write about. At the end of the first week, most of them enthusiastically gave me their texts and asked me to read them over the weekend. I recall that weekend vividly: since it was early on in my fieldwork, I was unprepared for the openness with which the women revealed experiences of trauma and turmoil. I then spent much of that weekend rethinking my plan for making the class a writing workshop and worrying that the inmates would not want to share such personal, painful texts with the others. I feared that, come Monday morning, there would be silence when I asked them to read their accounts out loud.

How wrong I was. That morning, the women came to class geared up to read their work. In fact, they spent the first minutes of class arguing about who would be the first to share. "I want to go first," Rosa yelled. "Cause my story is off the hook. You just wait." After they agreed on an order and began recounting their stories, another concern set in—I worried that the women's reactions to the texts would be so intense that I would be ill-equipped to deal with them. Again, how wrong I was. With few exceptions, the stories I found to be so unsettling did not seem to move the others. In fact, they did not provoke much of an emotional reaction at all. Instead, responses like Rachel's were common. "Now let me go next," she jumped in as Tamara finished a story about her years as a prostitute. "My story is more deep." As I discovered in the months to follow, this was a common dynamic. In my subsequent writing classes, participants insisted on engaging in competitive confessionals. It was a constant struggle for me to convince them I did not expect competition or confessionals from them. But I always lost the struggle. Even if I did not ask this of them, the inmates expected it of themselves and others.

At the individual level, the competitive confessional created a situation in which the women felt like they had to one-up themselves with each retelling of their story. This often left them unable to rework or revise their stories—and, in some cases, they became completely alienated from the story itself. This was what happened to Claire, a quiet, forty-year-old CDC inmate who began as one of the most engaged writers in my class. She came to every session, spending the entire class furiously writing in the back of the room. It took her over two weeks to share her story with the others. But when she did, it was explosive. Her story captivated the other inmates in a way I had never seen. On a hot afternoon, she softly read a harrowing account of giving birth in the state prison. Claire's face was blank and expressionless as she recounted how the prison transferred her to the mentally ill ward just prior to the birth. Convinced that her cell mate was incarcerated for incest, she spent the week before the birth in a corner of the cell, refusing to move or speak to anyone. Her terror then led her to wait three hours into her labor before calling the medical staff to inform them that she needed to be moved to a delivery room.

> When that crazy woman [cell mate] heard I was givin' birth, she came at me. Like she lunged at me, and all I could think about was how I needed to protect my baby from this maniac. All I could think of was how she was gonna take him and abuse him. Then I became like a crazed animal who'd do anything to protect her young. I started to growl at that woman, to warn her off. Maybe I was even drooling from my mouth. When the medical staff arrived, they found me in the corner, all bloody and convulsing on the floor. They had to tie me up to get me out of that cell. Like a crazy animal, they had to rope me up. That's what I had become. An animal giving birth.

The imagery of Claire as a flailing animal made the other women gasp. As soon as she finished, they let out a collective scream—like they had all just been through labor again. Immediately, they deemed Claire's the best, most "off-the-hook" story in the group.

Initially, Claire seemed quite proud of this. But with time, it created problems for her. At nearly every class, the other women asked Claire for a "new installment" of the story. Initially, she provided them with revised pieces and additions to her account. But these follow-ups never produced the same cathartic reactions in her audience, which seemed to disappoint Claire. At times, it appeared as if Claire resorted to fabrications to get a reaction out of the others—throwing unbelievable or inconsistent details into the story to get a rise out of her listeners. Then writer's block hit, and Claire announced that she needed to take a break from writing. Despite our encouragement, she eventually stopped coming to class and writing altogether. After that, whenever I saw her around the facility, she would bring up the story, promising to get it to me soon. Even after I left Visions, Claire continued to send me notes in the mail. "I promise I'll get my story to you by early November," her last note read. "It's been hard . . . thanks for your patience."[24]

In addition to creating an internal one-upmanship, the competitive confessional produced external rivalries. Like so many aspects of life at Visions, the confessional became another source of conflict and strife among inmates. The women feuded over who was willing to confess more details of their past traumas and thus who had lived the hardest, most difficult lives. Such rivalries were totally consistent with the nature of the confessional—the goal was to elicit a reaction in those listening to it, so confessors quite naturally vied for the most memorable response. This dynamic also got played out in my writing classes, with some inmates writing dueling accounts of their lives. For instance, two of the inmates in one of my classes, Brandee and Keisha, had similar backgrounds: orphaned at young ages, they were abused by foster parents, kicked onto the streets during adolescence, and turned to prostitution to support themselves. Instead of uniting over these similarities, Brandee and Keisha seemed threatened by them. It was as if finding someone with a parallel "story" somehow negated their own experiences. So they turned their commonalities into an intense rivalry. Each time one of them wrote about a memory, the other countered in the next class with a similar memory that included slightly more detail about past cruelty and abuse. This went on for weeks. Finally, Brandee conceded defeat and decided to focus her writing on how she lost her children to Child Protective Services—something that had never happened to Keisha.

In the summer of 2004, these rivalries reached a new level in a series of public performances organized by two local artists. Funded by a large public radio station, the artists held four week-long workshops designed to help the inmates "find their voices." Each workshop ended in a public show of the inmates' work. The first performance was low-key and limited to Visions inmates and staff. As the inmates performed their skits, poems, and stories, they were touchingly uncertain and nervous. It was the staff's reaction that proved critical: at the end of the performance, the staff launched into a long evaluation of it. In doing so, they responded to the women's performance as confessionals and assumed the inmates had performed literal representations of their lives. The staff decided which portrayals were the most meaningful; they dissected why some vignettes were more powerful. Not surprisingly, they were most impressed by women who shared lurid details of trauma, applauding these inmates for their bravery and willingness to expose themselves to others.

After this initial performance, the tone was set: the next three would become more revealing. They would also become far more public as the staff decided to invite larger audiences to showcase the women's work. As the performances became more public, they became even more confessional. Both individually and as a group, the inmates felt the need to top their previous performances through new levels of exposure. So in the next two performances, as group skits were replaced by individual readings, new rivalries formed and old ones deepened. The whole thing culminated in the workshop's grand finale, for which an audience came from far and wide. Those in charge of the workshop's funding, who happened to be a group of men in suits, were seated in the front row. The women then performed twenty vignettes, every one of which was a personal confessional. The degree of exposure increased with each vignette—concluding with Elizabeth's long, detailed account of how she had been molested as a young child by her step-father, followed by Xena's angry letter to all the men who had abused her. The usual debriefing followed, with the staff proclaiming how proud they were of the inmates' courage. "Thank you for putting my troubles in perspective," remarked a sobbing audience member. "When I look at you, the troubles with my kids and husband don't seem so bad."[25] In the end, director Jane summed it up best:

> It is hard for me to express all the emotions I am feeling right now. Most of all, I just feel privileged to work with women like you. You have experienced so much pain and yet still confront it with such courage and strength. You should feel very proud of what you achieved today, letting the pain out of you and ridding yourselves of it. If you don't already, you will feel cleansed and freed from the pasts that hurt and disrespected you.

Given the intensity with which the inmates participated in such public exposure, it may seem erroneous to view the women's displays as examples of withdrawal. But withdrawal was exactly what came from the competitive confessional. Whether the inmates recounted their stories in group meetings, writing classes, or public performances, the women expressed a numbness to the most painful moments in their lives. Having been told so often in so many contexts, these stories no longer produced an emotional charge. The repetition with which the inmates had to air these experiences ended up emptying their pasts of meaning and draining their histories of personal significance and resonance. Instead of holding onto their backgrounds as experiences to work through or as histories to learn from, Visions had the inmates offer up their pasts for public consumption. It had the inmates turn their lives over so the staff could feel proud of the program's work and onlookers could feel better about their own problems. Given this, it is hard to imagine how the inmates could have remained sensitive to their experiences; or how they could not have felt alienated them from their selves and their stories. In this way, Claire's inability to continue writing was completely understandable. The same was true of Xena's reaction to her much-heralded performance at the grand finale: instead of basking in the glory, Xena retreated to her room for days, refusing to talk about the performance or to explain why all she could do was cry.

Sleeping through the Sentence

It was clear that Xena sank into a deep depression after the grand finale. Instead of coming out of the performance feeling cleansed as Jane promised, Xena became despondent and dejected—as did so many of her sisters. Although this does not indicate that such performances were inherently debilitating, it does highlight the importance of the context in which women like Xena had to expose themselves. First and foremost, Visions was a penal facility. Its inmates had little say in the terms of their exposure. They could not decide to keep their stories to themselves. Once they let them out, the inmates had little control over what would happen to their accounts. Quite often, their accounts were consumed by those around them and used to confirm their listeners' own lifestyles and choices. Other times the stories were appropriated as psychological ammunition in the facility's battles. And other times the issues raised simply remained unaddressed, almost hanging in thin air. According to the staff, the transformative part of the process was the simple act of releasing the story; that alone would be healing. But without a way for the inmates to make sense of their stories or to channel the aftershocks, this rarely occurred. The competitive confessional tended to breed more pain and an impulse to withdraw further.

Yet when inmates experienced the impulse to withdraw, there were few spaces to retreat to. In fact, it was quite unusual for an inmate like Xena to be allowed to disappear into her room for several days. In most cases, depressed or isolated women were forced back into the community through mandatory classes and groups. In response, many of them proceeded to check out internally; they used whatever means at their disposal to enter into states of semiconsciousness. When I began my fieldwork, I was struck by the inmates' lethargic and enervated behavior. Many of them wandered aimlessly around the facility, with glazed-over looks on their faces. My early fieldnote descriptions are of an almost zombielike atmosphere. They include a litany of inmate complaints about being tired, weary, and worn-out. With time, I also saw the women activated, energized, and engaged in struggles. By the end of my fieldwork, a polarized picture of inmate life emerged: long periods of lifelessness

were punctuated by intense outbursts of conflict and confrontation, followed by long, robotic lulls.

For some inmates, entrance into this robotic state was facilitated by
medication. Upon entering the facility, many perinatal clients were put
on legal drugs to sedate them (not an option for the CDC inmates). The
array of drugs prescribed by the staff was stunning: it was not uncommon for women to take handfuls of pills two or three times a day. The
drugs ranged from antidepressants like Prozac to sedatives like Valium
to more serious drugs like Lithium. In fact, sedation was so common that
the facility's rhythm correlated with the dispensing of medication. The
women got their medications up to three times a day at "med calls," and
the mood of the facility often underwent a dramatic change a few hours
after these calls.[26] At the start of the day, the emotionally charged morning meetings were followed by long post-med-call lulls of withdrawal
and retreat. The same was true in the afternoon and evening—the hours
leading up to med calls were always the most intense and fraught with
conflict, only to be followed by a medically induced calm and quiet. So
dramatic were these shifts that it often seemed like the staff used medication to control the mood of the facility, timing med calls to follow house
meetings, counseling sessions, or focus seats.

Similarly, it often seemed like the staff used medication to control
the moods of particular women. It was possible to chart the rhythm of
some perinatal clients through their history of medications.[27] The newer
a woman was to Visions, the more combative and resistant she tended
to be. Those women who questioned the program of recovery, fought
the confessionals, and refused to participate in the therapeutic practices
were usually the program's more recent arrivals. Over the course of a
few weeks to a few months, acquiescence would set in. What once provoked anger in an inmate slowly became commonplace and routine. For
some, the change was clearly a sign of resignation. But for many it was
resignation aided by medication. And as with other drugs, the women
began to need more medication to achieve the same desensitizing effect.
So they would often insist on getting their meds more often or at higher
doses. Or the women would demand that the staff extend the range of
meds prescribed to them.

For instance, over the course of one summer, I watched as the drug cocktail of Shanika, a perinatal client, increased to include daily anti-depressants, afternoon sedatives, and nightly sleeping pills. Yet no one seemed troubled by what appeared to be a contradiction between Visions's addiction narrative and the staff's dispensing of large quantities of mind-altering substances. In part, this was because the staff refused to see legal medications as drugs, which might have been related to their own reliance on these same medications.[28] After noticing Shanika fall into zombielike state by the end of the summer, I asked a counselor about her dosage. The response was typical: "Oh, but she's so much calmer now. . . . Those long, angry tirades she went on in meetings have almost stopped. She seems happier, more content now."

While withdrawal through medication may have "calmed" some perinatal clients, this route was not available to the CDC inmates. Before being released to Visions, the CDC had to give all inmates a clean bill of health, which meant they could not be on medication.[29] Moreover, due to legal constraints on the use of medication while at Visions, few CDC inmates could take antidepressants or sedatives.[30] So they found other ways to withdraw, the most common of which was sleep. While the perinatal clients took their meds, the CDC inmates went to sleep. In between meetings and scheduled activities, a stampede of CDC women would run to their rooms, crawl into bed, and check out. It seemed like they spent all their free time under the covers, dozing off. Many CDC inmates walked around Visions like they had just woken up, no matter what time of day it was.

Moreover, all inmates spoke of sleep constantly. They quantified exactly how much of it they needed, backing up their numbers with scientific research. This was particularly true of those inmates with young children. Since room assignments were often made according to the age of an inmate's child, those women with babies tended to be especially sleep deprived. Inmates complained vociferously about this, pleading with the staff to move women with sleep-challenged kids to other rooms. But it was also clear that sleep had taken on a heightened significance for other reasons. For some, it was the one time they believed they could experience the joys of life in a free, unrestrained way. It was the one activity they could engage in to escape and retreat. Most of all, it was the one area in which they thought the staff could not dictate their feelings.

As with so many of the lessons I learned at Visions, this last point was made clear to me in my writing classes. From the first class, I noticed that the inmates relied quite heavily on dreams in their stories. Since this is a common literary device, initially I did not make much of it. But, with time, I began to see that sleeping and dreaming had special meaning for the women. In their writings, the only time the inmates appeared willing to fantasize and move outside the first-person "I" was when they wrote about dreams. Those sections of their prose were always the least confessional and most creative. It was almost as if they were able to imagine a different way of being when sleeping. In fact, a few inmates even kept journals of their dreams, which they then used to inform their writing. In class, they would eagerly open up their journals, anxiously recalling where their unconscious had led them the night before. They seemed to believe that through the realm of escape, or the arena of the unconscious, an authentic, truer version of their "stories" would emerge.

Whether through medication or sleep, withdrawal became the ideal. For the women, escaping their surroundings was a way to stay sane, maintain their identities, and "keep it real." Of course, these were not the lessons the staff wanted to be teaching. But the facility's call for self-awareness morphed into a need to check out; the imperative to get in touch with one's feelings created an impulse to go numb; and the mandate to expose oneself transformed into an urge to withdraw. While Visions could limit the inmates' modes of escape to medication and sleep, those limitations would obviously be lifted upon their release. This was when the real test would begin. Once the inmates had learned their lesson about the need for escape and withdrawal, it was only one small step for the women to turn to drugs or alcohol as quicker, more effective escape routes when those routes became open to them again.

As occurred a decade earlier at Alliance, this point was made clear to me in one of my final interactions with a group of Visions inmates. It was the fall of 2005, and I had returned to Visions for a final visit with a group of inmates who were about to be released. With some negotiation, the staff allowed me to bring in a cake to celebrate. The sight and smell of the cake produced euphoria in the group, which then prompted a conversation about what the soon-to-be-released inmates planned to do once "free." Keisha said she planned to go someplace by herself and smoke an entire pack of cigarettes in one sitting. Smiling, Claire described her plan to drop her son off at her mother's house and then go for a long, uninterrupted sleep. "I think I'll sleep for a week," she proclaimed. Then Rosa interjected: "Oh, get real. I'm gonna down a six-pack of beer with my homegirls. . . . I'm gonna kick it on my block with my girls and forget all about this place." The others nodded in agreement.

TRAINING WOMEN WHAT TO WANT

Like their Alliance sisters, the women at Visions had learned their lessons well. While doing time, many of them learned exactly what Visions wanted them to unlearn; they solidified attachments to old ways of being and modes of enjoyment. As they walked out of Visions's doors, they went off to escape however they could, whether through cigarettes, sleep, sex, or drugs and alcohol. This outcome was hardly surprising, since power often operates in such a fashion: its route from intentions to outcomes is rarely straightforward. Instead, this path is usually full of twists and turns and detours that lead its subjects to places they do not want to go. As Visions reduced inmates' problems to personal addiction, so the inmates arrived at a similar diagnosis of their sisters' ailments. As the staff emptied the inmates' lives of all social content, so the inmates competed over their confessionals and found pleasure in one another's pain. As the staff denied women their shared experiences, so the inmates found little common ground upon which to ally for longer than a moment.

Through the twists and turns of power, something else quite significant occurred: the inmates began acting in ways that seemed consistent with the staff's construction of them. In the inmates' attacks on each other, one could find evidence for the staff's claim that the women needed to channel their impulses in more productive directions. In their medicine-induced slumber, one could find evidence for the staff's assertion that they needed to overcome their escapist ways. In their quest to maintain some modicum of enjoyment, one could find evidence for the staff's insistence they needed to reign in their desires. Although the staff may have wanted the inmates to unlearn these behaviors, the women's failure to do so was actually quite useful for the staff. It was what led the inmates into an "us versus us" war that let the staff off the hook. On bad days, when life at Visions put me in a conspiratorial mood, I saw Visions's program of recovery as self-perpetuating, as a way to turn inmates into "cases" that the staff could then treat. Obviously, the staff would not have done this intentionally. But this often seemed to be the outcome; like the afternoon when counselor Collette turned to me after an especially brutal focus seat session and commented, "It's such a tragedy that powerless women don't know how wield power responsibly. We have so much work to do with them." Indeed, it was tragic: the inmates seemed stuck in a vicious cycle in which therapeutics pushed them toward behavior that corroborated the staff's diagnosis of their pathologies and Visions's recipe for recovery.

It is hard to know just how long these women will be stuck in this cycle or how long its effects will last. This is a limitation of ethnographic research—even when done over several years, it is difficult to trace long-term patterns and outcomes. Like Alliance, Visions kept no systematic data on what happened to its perinatal clients or CDC inmates after release. Yet recent quantitative studies of those who have done stints in similar alternative-to-incarceration programs reveal shockingly high recidivism rates. For instance, the first major evaluation study of California's Prop. 36 found that those offenders who served time in diversionary treatment programs were more likely to be rearrested on new drug charges since Prop. 36 took effect.[31] Of those convicted of drug-related offenses who completed a treatment program, 40 percent had new drug arrests within thirty months of their prior convictions. The numbers are even worse for those who failed to complete treatment: 60 percent of them were rearrested within the same time frame. Perhaps most damning of all, this study found that offenders who never went to rehab were actually less likely to be rearrested than those who spent some time in a treatment facility.

These quantitative data are consistent with the postrelease experiences of Visions inmates.[32] Many of the program's "stars" returned to jail within months of their release—like Shavon, the yoga queen, who was sent back to prison almost immediately for drug possession; or Rochelle, the budding therapist, who went back within months of her release for a parole violation. Others remain "free," but are hanging on by a thread. Through e-mails and telephone messages, many have kept me posted on their lives, trials, and tribulations. Some of them continue to recite the 12 steps and motivational phrases they learned at Visions, but without much passion or conviction. Others ditched such slogans long ago, realizing they were not going to work for them—like Karrina, who moved back to South Central LA with her son, got a job in a fast-food restaurant, and continues to talk about suing Visions for "all the shit they did to us."

Yet one thing does seem to unite the inmates I have kept in touch with: they all express extreme disdain for therapy of any sort. They all view it as punitive, intrusive, and controlling. Even those women struggling with serious emotional problems claim they will never turn to therapy for help. Rosa, for example, told me that she cannot even watch Oprah, much less Dr. Phil, without being brought back to Visions. "Whenever I see that crap on TV, I think I'm back there [in Visions]. My mom watches it and I just leave the room. . . . I can't stand it."

The inmates' rejection of all things therapeutic may be one of the most long-lasting outcomes of Visions's program of recovery. It also may be one of Visions's biggest disservices to its charges—in the end, Visions may have made a mockery of important, otherwise commendable goals. In her analysis of U.S. welfare reform, sociologist Sharon Hays makes a similar argument, suggesting that distortions in how reform was actually implemented transformed its meaning and ended up debasing some valuable principles. In Hays's case, those principles included economic autonomy and independence. In the context of the Visions program, they included introspection, reflection, and even "recovery." Given the years of hard time these women have served in the penal system, many of them could use some serious introspection and reflection. Many of them could also use some help coming to terms with the unimaginable abuse they suffered in their lives. Yet it is hard to envision any of them seeking such help since it is now inexorably linked to power and punishment. As Rosa put it when I asked if she would consider going to a therapist to deal with the crying spells and panic she endured after her release, "That'd be like going back to prison. . . . Why would I do that?"

Conclusion

The ethnographic story I told in this book centered on a series of "how" questions: How were women governed in the two penal institutions, Alliance and Visions, at two moments in time? How did those in charge of these facilities create narratives to relay their interpretation of inmates' problems? How did these narratives set boundaries around the areas of women's lives in need of regulation? How did these narratives transform into concrete institutional practices and relationships? In addressing these questions, I tried to keep my own narrative as close as possible to the lived experiences of the women in these institutions. I put their words and actions at the forefront of the account, describing the rituals, negotiations, and struggles that comprised life in these "alternative" penal facilities. Like other ethnographers, I journeyed into a world that few people would otherwise have access to in order to chronicle its inner

207

workings and everyday practices. In my case, this meant uncovering the complex layers of control and contestation, and relations of power and dominance, that characterized this arm of the penal system—as well as the different ways the inmates of Alliance and Visions made sense of those relations.

Underlying this descriptive "how" story was an analysis of why these institutional narratives took the forms they did. At key moments in the ethnographic story, I broke from the empirical account to move beyond the experiences of Alliance and Visions and reveal how they reflected general shifts in the structure of the contemporary state. In doing so, I attempted to broaden my study of the penal system by connecting it to larger patterns of state power and governance. On the one hand, this meant using a wide-angle lens to situate these penal institutions in time and place and to expose the forces impinging on them. With this lens, the larger processes of state hybridity and government from a distance came into view. I also exposed the external and internal dilemmas that such hybridity posed for these state satellites—from financial insecurity to regulatory uncertainty to interagency competition to staff and client diversity. All of these factors helped to explain why Alliance ended up fixating on the "dependency" of their girls while Visions was preoccupied with their charges' "dangerous desires." An early form of state hybrid, Alliance was caught between two large institutions, which presented its staff with a variety of challenges that a discourse of need allowed them to grapple with. Ten years later, Visions emerged out of a state of advanced hybridity, with a dizzying array of diversity, which led its staff to a discourse of desire that seemed to address the institutional instability and bridge the programmatic divisions. In this way, by extending outside the life at Alliance and Visions, this ethnographic story took on broader meaning: it offered a glimpse into the structural underpinnings of different penal discourses and the institutional roots of different strategies of governance.

There is a second way this story has relevance beyond the confines of these specific penal facilities, one that remained largely in the background of the empirical case studies. As I recounted these institutions' many trials and tribulations, I noted that these programs were very consequential for the women caught up in them. These consequences become even clearer when the facilities' battles are seen as symptomatic of general shifts in the content of state politics, particularly those targeting poor women. Although the penal system encompasses only a small percentage of all poor women, its approach to them ends up replicating a broader politics of disentitlement. Since the 1990s, the governance of poor women has involved a process of disentitlement, from social policy reforms that restrict their access to public assistance to state institutions that undermine their claims to social support. Of course, these state projects rarely admit to such intentions—instead, they often claim to be empowerment projects, designed to teach independence or enhance self-reliance. But, in reality, they end up teaching women the depth and parameters of their new disentitlement. This book uncovered two ways that states of disentitlement can operate: one, through the narrowing of women's needs; and another through the regulation of women's desires. Tracing the similarities and differences between these modes of disentitlement provides yet another way to locate the penal system in broader discussions of state governance—and to draw out critical lessons about the gender politics of power, punishment, and desire.

POWER, PUNISHMENT, AND THE DENIAL OF THE SOCIAL

If we step back and look at Alliance and Visions from a distance, their similarities are perhaps most striking. They emerged from similar processes of state devolution, decentralization, and diversification. They thus occupied similar positions in the criminal-justice system, forming part of its alternative apparatus established as a corrective to traditional corrections. They both took their alternative mandates quite seriously and located their programs in the "community" as a way to fight against the isolation of incarceration and to empower their female charges. For both facilities, this empowerment ideal meant addressing the "real" issues plaguing female offenders. As both grappled with women's problems, the facilities had to negotiate with much larger institutions that had more money, power, and influence. Both Alliance and Visions were sandwiched between big, centralized state bodies, like the California Youth Authority and the California Department of Corrections, and large NGOs, like the Fellowship for Change and the Recovery Project. Both penal facilities had to contend with the competing commands and directives of these other bodies. Their institutional livelihood and longevity depended largely on just how well they negotiated with these influential entities.

Indeed, much of what was said and done in these two facilities on a daily basis was shaped by their locations in the penal system. However tempting it may be to attribute their institutional practices to some abstract "culture" effect, I repeatedly argued against this. Clearly, the facilities' programmatic narratives were culturally recognizable. Their staffs' discourses drew on familiar cultural symbols, from Queen Latifah and Ronald Reagan to Oprah and Dr. Phil. The arguments each facility mobilized to bolster these narratives were similarly resonant: Alliance advanced the myth of the welfare queen and panic over her dependency, while Visions marshaled the myth of the overindulgent ghetto girl and panic over her many addictions. The same was true of the actual emphases of their programs: from Alliance's Brennan Bucks program and self-sufficiency training to Visions's yoga, focus seats, and spa days, the imprint of popular culture was obvious.

Yet there was a vast repertoire of cultural scripts these facilities could have drawn on and an array of cultural icons their staffs could have mobilized. They chose these particular signs and symbols because they helped resolve particular institutional dilemmas. Alliance's discourse of dependency and Visions's discourse of desire were ways to address the internal and external challenges these programs confronted as state satellites—from Alliance's dependence on other state bodies to Visions's need to form a distinctive line about itself. Herein lies the first convergence between them: both institutions' structural positions created organizational challenges, which then led to governance strategies that drew on surrounding cultures, communities, and contexts. Put more simply, these facilities' discourses and practices served the needs of those institutionalizing them.

These institutional narratives served yet another need. Those in charge of both penal facilities were women. Although they worked nearly a decade apart, these women were instrumental in carving out a feminized arm of the penal system—a space in the system where women governed other women. But this created dilemmas for the staff. They had to negotiate among contradictory mandates: they wanted to empower their charges, but they also felt it necessary to control and constrain them; they wanted to help other women, but they also believed they could resocialize and reeducate them. As they grappled with these tensions, the staffs at both facilities did a whole lot of projecting and imposed their concerns onto their charges. At Alliance, this involved the staff projecting their own need to differentiate themselves from other penal facilities and their own issues with dependency onto the girls; it was no coincidence that the staff's fear of being reliant on CYA and the Fellowship for Change paralleled their concern with their girls' dependency on the state. Similarly, at Visions it was not by chance that a discourse of recovery was used to unite and unify the staff just as it became the central way to interpret the inmates' problems. In both cases, the staffs gravitated toward cultural scripts that captured their imaginations and interests—and that seemed to provide a way to bridge the divisions between them and the women they oversaw.

In the process, the women working in this alternative arm of the penal system lost their social imaginations. Their discourses and practices led them to deny the social origins of their charges' problems. They were not alone in this regard: one feature common to many "gender-specific" or "gender-responsive" treatment programs is their emphasis on personal, individual trauma as opposed to social, structural inequality. Here, too, the staffs' causal theories for why their charges had gone astray ended up deflecting from the very real social marginalization and material inequities that every one of the inmates faced. Instead, at both Alliance and Visions social marginalization surfaced as the outcome of the inmates' problems and not as a factor contributing to them. So the Alliance girls' dependency led to their social marginalization—not vice versa. And their bad choices and irresponsible actions were what caused the dependency in the first place. This denial of the social was even clearer at Visions.

With counselor Lesley's mantra that the "system is in your head" came a series of causal connections through which women's addictions led to their poverty and dislocation. The sources of these addictions paralleled those of the Alliance girls' dependency: they were rooted in the women's distorted selves, dangerous impulses, and misguided behavior.

After years of working in these penal facilities, I remain perplexed by the staff members' consistent and persistent denial of the social. On the one hand, I understand the many needs the institutional narratives served for these women—that is, how the narratives allowed the Alliance and Visions staffs to deal with the tensions inherent in their programs in culturally resonant ways. Nevertheless, I have a harder time understanding why these women refused to infuse their narratives with some social content; and why they used these narratives instead to drain their charges' experiences of all social significance. Perhaps the staffs truly did not see the social basis of these women's problems? Perhaps they censored these aspects of their charges' lives because they felt unable to deal with them? Or perhaps this denial was another form of projection, a way for the staffs to conflate their struggles with the inmates' struggles? Whatever the particular motivation, it is clear that by leaving no space for a social analysis, the staff of both facilities acted in ways that were symptomatic of, and not alternative to, the contemporary politics of disentitlement.

It is also clear that the denial of the social underlay many of the battles the staffs then faced on a daily basis. The specific conflicts they confronted were certainly different, from Alliance's fights over Aid to Families with Dependent Children checks, baby food, and Brennan Bucks to Visions's battles over smoking, shopping, and snack food. But in both cases the disputes followed a similar pattern of control and contestation: the staffs insisted on the individual basis of the female inmates' problems, only to be confronted by fierce resistance. In effect, the denial of the social became a form of control, an expression of staff members' power and ability to punish. It also became a motivation for the inmates' contestation, forming the foundation of their critique of the staffs' discourses and practices. When the Alliance girls accused the staff of being "out of touch," they were differentiating between the staff's fantasies and their own social realities; when they formed their Welfare Club and mobilized Men in Suits, they were defending the forms of power they had access to. When the Visions inmates rejected Luna Bars and fought for Top Ramen, they were differentiating between the staff's fantasies and their own economic realities; when they refused to drop their masks and insisted on retaining internal lives of their own, they were defending survival strategies that worked for them given their social histories.

In this way, one of the main lessons to be drawn from my case studies of Alliance and Visions is that power and punishment do not simply evaporate when women are in charge of other women in community-based institutions. The power relations in such facilities may be disguised or denied, but they certainly do not disappear. This may seem like an obvious point—it is certainly an argument others have made about the gender politics of punishment in different historical and national contexts.[1] But it is one that bears repeating given the prominent role of the "community" in contemporary calls for progressive penal reform. Over and over again, scholars and activists assume that decarceration through community-based corrections will necessarily be more responsive to inmates' needs.[2] This is true despite critical reminders of the opposite: as early as the mid-1980s, sociologist Stanley Cohen showed how systems of social control actually expand as they become more decentralized and diffuse.[3] His insight is all the more relevant decades later, as state power operates increasingly from a distance and as everything from workfare workshops to drug courts try to alter the psyches and souls of those they target. Such projects do not simply extend the tentacles of social control; they also deepen the intervention. It is no longer enough to engineer female inmates' behavior—the goal is now to get inside their heads and change their ideas about what is socially acceptable and pleasurable. Most of all, the goal is to teach them they are no longer in need of, or entitled to, social support.

From this lesson emerges another: as we contemplate alternatives to the carceral state, perhaps we should begin focusing less on an institution's level of "stateness" and more on what it says and does with its charges. From scholarly accounts to policy recommendations, it seems like the only imaginable alternative to mass incarceration is to get men and women out of the formal penal system by moving them as far from the state arena as possible—that is, to deinstitutionalize through the community and nonprofit organizations. If only it were so simple. As the examples of Alliance and Visions remind us, the content of corrections is just as important as its context—if not more so. These cases warn against the temptation to see what happens outside of official state boundaries as necessarily more empowering than what occurs within them. They prompt us to begin to imagine more creative and inventive ways to reform the content of penal programs so they might work against the politics of disentitlement—and not become symptoms of it. And these cases suggest that we take a serious look at both the intended and unintended consequences of penal programs for those they target.

This is precisely why the comparison between Alliance and Visions is so important. Despite the similarities in their institutional form, organizational tensions, and staff-inmate conflicts, their programs were dramatically different. While they both governed through the denial of the social and set out to teach women about individual ir/responsibility, they did so in divergent ways. The responses they provoked in the inmates were therefore quite different—a difference that is suggestive of the broad, long-lasting effects of these institutions.

NEEDS, DESIRES, AND PATHS TO DISENTITLEMENT

If the similarities between Alliance and Visions are highlighted through a wide-angle analytical lens, the differences between them are most pronounced when we zoom in on everyday life in these facilities. Throughout this book, as I recounted the facilities' daily struggles and conflicts, I focused on the differences between each staff's institutional narrative and their charges' responses to them. Of all the differences that surfaced, perhaps the most significant was related to the content of the two programs. These two penal facilities' interpretations of women's problems varied; their actual strategies of governance contrasted. As a result, the particular routes they took to the denial of the social diverged. The facilities disentitled their charges in quite different ways: Alliance through a program of dependency that emphasized its girls' insatiable, unacceptable needs; Visions through a program of recovery that stressed its inmates' insatiable, unacceptable desires.

Framing the central difference between these penal facilities as connected to their modes of disentitlement leads back to a question I posed at the beginning of the book: As strategies of governance, is the regulation of desire related to the regulation of need? Has the former surfaced as an alternative to the latter, as a way to counteract even the recognition of women's needs? Indeed, these forms of state regulation do appear to be related and responsive to each other. And, indeed, the focus on desire does seem to be a way to deflect from women's needs—or, as Visions counselor Evelyn put it, it teaches women that what they thought they needed they really just desired. But instead of conceptualizing desire talk as a replacement for needs talk, it may make more sense to view these discourses as coexisting and codependent. While they can both work to weaken broad statements about women's entitlements, a discourse of desire achieves this by bypassing even the idea of socially recognized needs or necessities. While both discourses can serve to undermine calls for more equitable resource redistribution, a discourse of desire may offer a more direct route to blaming women's problems on their emotional and psychological composition. So while both discourses move the focus away from women's social rights and entitlements, the discourse of desire may do so in a more effective way.

Of course, to suggest that a focus on desire has become a way of dislodging the recognition of need does not imply some grand historical shift in state governance. Nor does it mean that one mode of regulation has overtaken or replaced the other. Over the many years I conducted this ethnographic research, I went back and forth on this point: Was I witnessing a general change in how female inmates were governed? Did these institutions evidence a shift to the control of women's desires as the new mode of state punishment? For much of the time I worked at Visions, I insisted that the facility did exemplify a new world of punishment. Perhaps it did. But arguing this puts me on shaky methodological ground. On the one hand, such an argument goes far beyond the empirical scope of this historical ethnography—a study that is, after all, based on two case studies that are limited in time and space. Moreover, to sustain an argument about a generalized shift in governance I would have to ignore the abundance of evidence of the persistence of needs talk as a strategy of control. From the welfare system to the penal system, needs talk is still deployed with great regularity to cut off women's claims to social assistance and public support.[4]

So instead of claiming that one mode has replaced the other, I have come to view the regulation of need and the regulation of desire as constituting different paths to disentitlement. One path travels through women's social relationships in order to cure them of their dependent ways, while the other journeys into women's heads in order to fix their emotional and psychological flaws. But both paths end in a similar place: in a state where social marginalization and inequality are wished away. In this way, it is possible to think of these modes of regulation as two techniques that state institutions use to deny the realities of social injustice; they are two movements away from the recognition of social rights and protections. The first movement marks a shift from rights to needs, whereby what could be defined as inalienable rights get framed as needs—and thus become subject to negotiation. This was the Alliance project. The second movement marks a shift from need to desire, whereby what could be understood as socially recognized needs get interpreted as desires—and thus become subject to therapeutic cleansing. This was the Visions project. Again, to say that these projects constituted two paths to disentitlement is not to imply a historical shift from one to the other. But it is also not to deny that, at least in hybrid state institutions, the second movement is currently in full swing, as more and more satellite institutions begin to focus on regulating their charges' impulses and psyches through therapeutic intervention.

Further complicating the picture are the ways these paths to disentitlement can cross, coexist, and overlap. In some state arenas, the regulation of need intersects with the regulation of desire. This is one way to read the relationship between Alliance and Visions: as two parts of an overlapping process through which women moved further from a state of entitlement. The first part of the process involved Alliance's imperative that women learn to correct their wayward ways and break their dependencies on the state. Then, later down the line, those who failed to learn these lessons encountered another attempt to teach them to self-regulate—this time through a combination of self-help and state therapeutics. In the process, these women's problems deepened and intensified. Their problems were first interpreted as dependency on the state, a disorder to be remedied with some self-esteem training, Brennan Bucks, and lectures on personal responsibility. A decade later, their dependency had evolved into a full-fledged addiction; it had been transformed into a pathological reliance on everything from money to men to drugs to tobacco. So by the time Visions entered the picture, women were thought to have far more serious ailments of the mind, body, and soul. These ailments then required far more serious intervention, from focus seats to public exposure to confessionals. For some, their pathologies even necessitated medication to reign in their impulses and take control of the pleasure centers of their brains.

Although these paths to disentitlement often end up in similar places, it is not irrelevant which path an institution takes. In fact, one of my main findings in this book is that it is enormously consequential whether state institutions govern women through need or desire. The path chosen matters because of the different possibilities inherent in these modes of regulation for those they target. In this way, while scholars like R. W. Connell raised the specter of the state's regulation of cathexis, I have tried to extend the insight by analyzing how such regulation emerged from concrete institutional narratives and how those narratives were received by women themselves.[5] In each institutional case study, I assessed the extent to which female inmates could extract something productive from these narratives. Here I uncovered a critical divergence: unlike the Alliance girls, who undermined the staff's dependency discourse as they contested it, the Visions women could not transform the staff's desire training into a productive narrative. Given the other similarities between the women of the two facilities, this difference is telling. It reveals something significant about the effects of these institutional discourses and the particular ways they disentitle. It does so for three reasons.

First, as a strategy of governance, the discourse of desire was more individualizing than the discourse of need. This becomes clear when we look at the struggle each discourse gave rise to in these institutions. At Alliance, a collective struggle unified the girls and coordinated their actions. This was a struggle the girls engaged in as a group—their resistances were orchestrated and enacted with striking consistency. In one sense, the collective nature of the girls' contestation was somewhat surprising: after all, these were otherwise competitive teenage girls, known to be petty and back-biting in other environments. But when they came to Alliance, this changed. Instead of turning on each other, they joined forces to launch into an "us versus them" struggle with the staff. Together, the girls rapped about the benefits of welfare, formed secret clubs to commiserate and converse, took Men in Suits on tours of the home, and turned to their babies when their sense of worth was challenged. They used Alliance's common construction of them as hopelessly dependent teen mothers to find common cause. There was little dissent from the ranks, little individualizing of the struggle.

Fast-forward ten years to the vastly different world of Visions. While these inmates also engaged in a prolonged struggle with the staff, there was almost nothing collective about it. Except for a few rare moments of unity, these women contested Visions's desire training in their own, individual ways, using their own, individual survival strategies. What is more, their survival strategies led them to personalize the fight and regulate each other—by turning the most mundane daily conflicts into all-out wars, competing over the confessional, and finding pleasure in others' pain. This was not because they were more competitive or nastier than the Alliance girls. Rather, it was an artifact of how Visions staff positioned these women vis-à-vis themselves and one another. The staff's discourse of desire required that they see the inmates' impulses as dangerous—and their desires as rooted in what criminologist Mariana Valverde aptly calls "diseases of the will."[6] The Visions women had malformed, addictive selves and lacked a sense of their personal "triggers." Yet they could not rely on others to help them recover. Their "sisters" were not support systems but were mirrors to reflect their own faults and failings—and thus to be hidden from in bathrooms. Theirs was an internal struggle, involving others only as an audience for their confessionals and exposure. In short, the construction of women's problems at Visions was profoundly individualizing and internalizing.

It was also deeply depoliticizing. This leads to the second divergence between these paths to disentitlement: the route through desire made it close to impossible for women to find a way back to common issues around which political struggle could form. This is not to say it was easy for the Alliance girls to extend dependency discourse beyond its original scope and intention. As Nancy Fraser has cautioned, needs talk can quickly devolve into a depoliticized discourse disconnected from the practice of social rights.[7] But, as the Alliance girls demonstrated, it is also possible to use needs talk to revive rights talk. It was possible for the girls to take this discursive path in a different direction—to detour back to issues of social justice and fairness. Over and over again, the Alliance girls expanded the staff's focus on needs to question what it would really take for them to meet those needs. What would they really need to become independent upon release? What kind of education and work would they need to live free of state assistance? What would it mean for them to engage in carework on their own terms? These were, of course, profoundly political questions. Thus, the debate over them took on social significance and meaning. It was also a debate in which the girls found themselves on the same side, which only further politicized their institutional struggle.

Things worked quite differently when the fight was over desire. At Visions, the women seemed to have no way to politicize the fight or to move the struggle to a social terrain. This was not because they were less inventive, intelligent, or rhetorically skilled. If anything, these women's ages and life experiences made them a bit wiser and savvier than their Alliance counterparts. Once again, the problem was rooted in the discourse they confronted. Visions's focus on desire narrowed the terms of the debate, making it close to impossible to raise questions of social justice and fairness. In fact, it is not even clear what such questions would have looked like—or what kind of connection between desire and social rights the women could have drawn. Could the inmates have argued for their "right" to find joy, fulfillment, and physical pleasure wherever they wanted? Could they have demanded a "right" to an unexposed internal life? Could they have turned the injustice of their constant emotional exposure into a political issue? Could they even have found a language to politicize the things that Visions governed? Moreover, on those rare occasions when they did find such a language, the staff's discourse of desire was an amazingly effective way to silence them. It undermined inmate demands for equitable and meaningful social relationships—often by accusing the women of letting the "system" rule their "heads." In effect, desire became a way to derail political discussion and debate, only further depoliticizing the inmates' institutional struggle.

This leads to the third way the politics of need differs from the politics of desire: the latter is far more disempowering for those it targets. I use *disempowering* intentionally, since both state institutions promised to empower their charges. Alliance and Visions sold themselves as empowerment projects; their staffs held this out as the ultimate goal for their charges. When it came to institutional reality, however, neither fulfilled the promise. But their failures ended up in different places. At Alliance, it ended with a group of girls emboldened by their ability to fight the power and to rap their way to a powerful social critique. It ended with girls who were convinced of their entitlement to good jobs, good education, good housing, and good childcare. It ended with girls who were savvier about how to work the politics of need to their own advantage. It ended with girls who had allied and found common cause with each other.

By most definitions, these would all be key aspects of female empowerment—young women who were emboldened, astute, and unified. Granted, this was not the kind of empowerment that the staff wanted their girls to experience. Nor was it the kind that many feminist scholars might want for these women in the abstract—after all, their empowerment was often achieved by appealing to unreliable Men in Suits. In this way, it was not even the kind of empowerment that would pay off for them in the long run: eventually, those Men in Suits did abandon them by closing down Alliance instead of reforming or restructuring it. But my point here is that the politics of need may not always work as intended—in certain contexts, it can actually enable women to protect themselves, if only for a short while.

The jury is still out on where the politics of desire will end up. In large part, this is because we know far less about how desire operates as a strategy of governance and as an institutional path to disentitlement. But if what occurred at Visions is any indication, the potential verdict does not look good. It would be very difficult to see what occurred at Visions as empowering—even for a short while. Instead, its discourse of desire lent itself to a version of state therapeutics that trapped and disarmed those it targeted. State institutions do many things well, but therapeutics is not one of them—especially when those therapeutic practices are coercive and tied to punishment. This is not to say that Visions's therapeutics taught the inmates nothing. Of course it did: the inmates left Visions prepared to take down other women in focus seats and to find pleasure in a sister's pain. They could get up in front of a large group of strangers to reveal traumatic experiences in the language of Dr. Phil and Oprah. They could participate in the competitive confessional and show why their lives had been the hardest, most "off the hook." And they could advance elaborate arguments about why some department stores, snack foods, and skin creams were superior.

Yet there were other things that Visions's discourse of desire left the inmates unprepared for. When their sentences ended, these women were not any less likely to feel ashamed by their limited formal education and lack of work experience. They did not feel any sense of entitlement to the public-assistance benefits or voting rights that had been rescinded while they were incarcerated. Most of all, if they failed to "recover" or experienced setbacks upon release, they were unprepared to explain why they may not be the only ones to blame—and how the social world changed in ways that often worked against their recovery. In short, they were left without an effective way to counter the broader politics of disentitlement; they had no framework to challenge the metamorphosis of societal problems into problems of individual will, vice, and desire. It is hard to imagine anything more disempowering than that.

So what would have been empowering for these women? How could these penal institutions have been structured to fulfill their promises of empowerment? In the many years I worked at Alliance and Visions, I have been asked these questions many times by many people. In fact, I came to expect them: rarely have I discussed this research without such questions being raised. In anticipation of them, I began to develop a list of all the things I would change about these facilities to make them more "women friendly." Over time, the list got longer and longer: it began with very general things like disentangling therapy from punishment and finding ways to connect women to existing community-support systems and networks. Eventually, it evolved to include specific reforms, like banning focus seats, establishing partnerships with local high schools and GED programs, creating clear promotional paths and benefit structures for staff, and drawing in Head Start programs to help address the children's many educational needs.

Then, as I was running down this long list of reforms at the end of one lecture, it occurred to me that I was doing exactly what I had found fault with at Alliance and Visions: I was interpreting these women's problems for them. In doing so, I was also making the same mistake that others had made for centuries: from nineteenth-century maternalist "do-gooders" who helped construct Progressive Era welfare policies to twentieth-century prisoner reformers who created "women-friendly" facilities for "their girls," the assumption has been that others know what is best for poor women, and that they can figure this out without listening to poor women themselves. Sometimes there are good reasons for failing to listen. The environment surrounding on-the-ground state actors can work against it; their work lives can be unimaginably challenging and thankless. Particularly in the new world of hybrid states, frontline workers are often forced to listen instead to those on whom their funding depends. With institutional survival tied to the ever-changing directives of funders, program staffs often stop listening to women themselves. Also, the way women transmit their messages can be confusing: some do it through rap, others through direct resistance, still others through emotional withdrawal. Their messages can therefore be hard to decipher and even harder to interpret.

Yet if we fail to do this interpretive work, we end up missing critical insights into these women's life experiences and possible ways to improve them. In fact, most of the ideas on my long list of penal reforms came from the women of Alliance and Visions themselves—if not directly from their words, then from their actions and contestation. This leads back to a point made long ago by Marxist standpoint theorists: those subjected to power often have particularly astute analyses of it because their livelihoods rest on their ability to navigate power relations.[8] This is not to imply that the marginalized are all-knowing or all-seeing. Nor is it to suggest that they are undamaged by their experiences of injustice and inequality. As I argued in chapter 6, the behavior of Visions inmates was often quite damaging. But even in their most disturbing moments, as when the inmates took advantage of other women's weaknesses or found pleasure in their pain, their diagnoses of what occurred around them were usually quite suggestive.

In the end, their assessments suggest a few chief insights for progressive penal form and change. First, they warn us that there is no one-size-fits-all approach to female inmates' problems. The women in my case studies did not struggle with the same issues: there was incredible diversity in their needs and incredible variation in their desires. Many insisted that what they needed most was help securing decent housing, education, work experience, and that everything else would fall into place once these needs were met. Others claimed that their sense of loneliness, isolation, and anxiety were most pressing and that their other troubles would end once those feelings were addressed. Still others declared that their familial and intimate relationships were fractured and that these would stop acting as "triggers" once repaired. Given such diversity, it would be a mistake to lump all these women together or to reduce all their problems to one source, whether it be dependency, addiction, or low self-esteem.

What is more, these women's problems intersected in complex ways: there was not one causal sequence running through their lives to explain why they ended up in prison. For some, the sequence did appear to go from a reliance on drugs or alcohol to illegal activities and destructive behavior. But for many others, there was no such link; their actions seemed motivated by all kinds of factors, working in all kinds of directions, and were thus not reducible to one explanatory variable. Recognizing this diversity then leaves us with the real challenge of inventing new ways to approach and address these intersections. It pushes us to find ways to disentangle the many factors shaping women's lives and to make sense of the different causal roles these factors play for different women. It encourages us not to let one explanatory framework subsume all others or to force one interpretation of women's needs onto all others.

Clearly, it is exceedingly difficult to run an institution in this way. As I revealed throughout this book, institutional narratives can be necessary and useful parts of state programs; their scripts can unite staff members and facilitate their work. This is especially true in an era of hybrid states, when organizational competition, instability, and diversity threaten to make state institutions unmanageable. But precisely because these narratives must now accomplish so much, they cannot be homogenizing or reductionist. Nor can they capture only the interests and imaginations of those in charge of state institutions. If they do, these narratives are doomed to fail—and to cause the perpetual struggle and strife that characterized everyday life at Alliance and Visions.

The inmates at Alliance and Visions also provide a clue as to how we might arrive at more encompassing, inclusive narratives. While their experiences caution against reductionist institutional narratives, they also warn of the dangers of ignoring the points where their problems do converge. Put another way, we must not confuse the diversity of women's needs and desires with their individualization and internalization. One way to avoid this is to reinsert a social analysis into these institutional narratives. As I argued throughout this book, there are very real dangers to bracketing the social from these women's lives—not only does it psychologize their troubles and distort their lives, but it denies them a potential source of alliance. Despite these women's many differences, most of their problems had social roots: the women all faced poverty and restricted access to public support; they all came from neighborhoods decimated by abandonment and neglect; and they all struggled to keep their familial bonds intact despite histories of absence and abuse. It took an enormous amount out of these women to survive—materially, physically, and emotionally—in the communities they came from and would soon return to. Whether they were teen mothers in 1994 or middle-aged mothers in 2004, they insisted that any narrative about them must acknowledge the social realities of their lives.

Of the many offenses recounted in this book—from the criminal offenses of the inmates to the institutional offenses of the staff members—the failure to recognize these social realities seemed most consequential. Without an analysis of injustice and inequality, any claim to empowerment made by these penal facilities will continue to be a farce. Without a sense of the material realities of the inmates' lives, these institutions will continue to bear the imprint of the worst, most troubling aspects of the culture surrounding them. Without an understanding of societal relations of power and dominance, their staffs will continue to act out this culture as opposed to acting against it. But if we can find ways to refocus institutional narratives on the social, these programs might begin to challenge the therapeutics of neoliberalism. Their narratives might then give rise to institutional practices that address inmates' experiences of social vulnerability and insecurity. All of this might then enable these institutions to counteract the contemporary politics of disentitlement and to live up to their promise as real alternatives to incarceration.

Notes

INTRODUCTION

1. U.S. Department of Justice, *Prisoners in 2006.*
2. These numbers are even more stunning when compared to those of western European countries—the U.S. incarceration rate is up to ten times higher than European rates. While Britain and the Netherlands have also experienced sharp increases in incarceration, their rates do not rival those of the United States. For instance while the prison population in the Netherlands quadrupled since the 1980s, its rates remain just below the European average. Most other European countries, including France and Germany, have kept their incarceration rates fairly steady. Most Scandinavian countries continue to keep their imprisonment rates very low, with countries like Finland actually reducing its incarceration levels in the last decade. For more on these international trends, see Downes, "*Macho* Penal

Economy"; and Sutton, "Imprisonment and Social Classification in Five Common-Law Democracies" and "Imprisonment in Affluent Western Democracies."

3. The literature on the carceral revolution is voluminous. For some of the best descriptive accounts of it, see Garland, *Culture of Control* and "Introduction: The Meaning of Mass Imprisonment"; Simon, *Governing through Crime;* and Beckett, *Making Crime Pay.* For debates about why incarceration rates have risen so quickly, see Garland, *Mass Imprisonment;* Davis, *Are Prisons Obsolete?;* Gilmore, *Golden Gulag;* Beckett and Western, "Governing Social Marginality"; Pettit and Western, "Mass Imprisonment and the Life Course"; Zimring, "Imprisonment Rates and the New Politics of Criminal Punishment"; and Wacquant, "Deadly Symbiosis."

4. Put another way, there are now close to 200,000 female inmates in the United States.

5. According to most studies, roughly 25 percent of the children of incarcerated mothers end up in the foster-care system—while another 60 percent stay with grandparents and relatives. Yet there seems to be racial variation here, with African American inmates relying more heavily on kin and community networks to care for their children while white inmates use the foster-care system. For more on these trends, see Enos, *Mothering from the Inside;* Snell, *Women in Prison: Survey of State Prison Inmates;* Bloom and Steinhart, *Why Punish the Children?;* and D. Johnson, "Care and Placement of Prisoners' Children." For more on the social and psychological effects of imprisonment for the children of the incarcerated, see Seymour and Hairston, *Children with Parents in Prison;* Johnson and Gabel, *Children of Incarcerated Parents;* and Boswell and Wedge, *Imprisoned Fathers and their Children.*

6. More specifically, numerous studies have examined what happens to women once incarcerated. This work has exposed how prisons operate according to a gendered division of labor that reflects larger forms of stratification and inequality. For these analyses, see Britton, *At Work in the Iron Cage;* Owen, *In the Mix;* and Watterson, *Women in Prison: Inside the Concrete Womb.* This literature also reveals how female prisoners grapple with their roles as mothers—and how they confront legal and practical constraints on their parenting at the same time as prison officials require them to demonstrate "maternal fitness" as part of their recovery. For more on mothering in prison, see Bosworth, *Engendering Resistance;* Enos, *Mothering from the Inside;* and Ferraro and Moe, "Mothering, Crime, and Incarceration." And for a particularly insightful account of women's lives as the partners of male inmates, see Comfort, *Doing Time Together.*

7. Unfortunately, this rarely happens. On the one hand, most analyses of gender and punishment tend not to situate prison amid larger patterns of state governance. On the other hand, feminist scholars who do theorize the state more broadly tend to conceptualize it as the welfare state. That is, they take welfare

states, both past and present, as the point of departure from which they analyze broad patterns of redistribution, recognition, and de/commodification. One of the main goals of my analysis in this book is to connect these approaches—to take feminist theorizations of the state beyond a particular arena and unpack the institutional channels through which states govern gender relations.

8.   This conceptualization of governance is drawn from the work of Nikolas Rose, particularly his analysis in *Powers of Freedom* and *Governing the Soul*.

9.   That is, many scholars draw on conceptions of governance to highlight the management of conduct in nonstate institutions like families, schools, community groups, and so on. They have also used conceptions of governance to accentuate the more informal dynamics through which social behavior is constrained and enabled. While I appreciate the impulse to draw out these forms of control, this should not blind us to the ways that states regulate their citizens' conduct and the formal techniques that state institutions deploy to manage the behavior of their charges.

10.   For an example of how the concept of governance can be used to expose the linkages between the contemporary welfare and penal systems, see L. Haney, "Gender, Welfare, and States of Punishment."

11.   The literature here is enormous. For work on the gendered agendas of welfare reform in general, see Hays, *Flat Broke with Children*; Mink, *Welfare's End* and *Whose Welfare?*; and Reese, *Backlash against Welfare Mothers*. For research on how state policies structure marital relations, see Abramovitz, *Regulating the Lives of Women*; Curran and Abrams, "Making Men into Dads"; and Willrich "Home Slackers." For discussions of how state policies shape labor markets in gendered ways see Riemer, *Working at the Margins*; Bashevkin, *Welfare Hot Buttons*; and Blank and Schmidt, "Work, Wages, and Welfare."

12.   For a particularly comprehensive overview of feminist work on the "governance of gender" and the "gender of governance," see Brush, *Gender and Governance*.

13.   Much of this work on women's rights to social protection and resources has been done by feminist legal scholars. In particular, see Weisberg, *Feminist Legal Theory*; Eisenstein, *Female Body and the Law*; Rhode, *Justice and Gender*; MacKinnon, *Toward a Feminist Theory of the State*; West, "Jurisprudence and Gender"; and Schneider, "Dialectic of Rights and Politics."

14.   See Orloff, "Gender and the Social Rights of Citizenship" and "Gender and the Welfare State"; Sainsbury, *Gender, Equality and Welfare States* and *Gendering Welfare States*; and Lewis, "Gender and the Development of Welfare Regimes."

15.   See Harrington, *Care and Equality*; Harrington-Meyer, *Carework*; Neysmith, *Restructuring Caring Labour*; Oliker, "Examining Carework at Welfare's End"; and Kittay, "Welfare, Dependency, and a Public Ethic of Care."

16. For example, see Ginsburg and Rapp, *Conceiving the New World Order;* Solinger, *Pregnancy and Power;* O'Connor et al., *States, Markets, Families;* and Brush, "Changing the Subject."

17. For general conceptualizations of how states engage in need interpretation, see Fraser, *Unruly Practices.* For concrete empirical examples of the institutionalization of these interpretations, see L. Haney, *Inventing the Needy;* Little, "Independent Workers, Dependent Mothers"; and Korteweg, "Welfare Reform and the Subject of the Working Mother."

18. For analyses of the two-tiered welfare state, see Fraser, *Unruly Practices;* Gordon, *Pitied but Not Entitled;* and Nelson, "Origins of the Two-Channel Welfare State."

19. See Gordon, *Pitied but Not Entitled;* Adams and Padamsee, "Signs and Regimes"; and Brush, *Gender and Governance.*

20. See L. Haney, *Inventing the Needy.*

21. See Manza and Uggen, *Locked Out* and "Democratic Contraction?"

22. In fact, it was their denial of the facility's power relations that largely influenced my decision to use many "prison" terms throughout this book. One of the most common ways the staffs at both Alliance and Visions exerted power over their charges was by denying that they had any power—by promising to empower the women, the staffs obscured the profound control they wielded. The women were quite aware of this and often insisted on calling themselves and other women "inmates" and "prisoners"—as a way of bringing the institutional power relations back into view. In recognition of this, I also use the terms *inmate* and *prisoner* when referring to the women of Alliance and Visions. Of course, by doing this, I am fully aware that I may seem to be adopting the language of the "system." And since the politics of language is particularly fraught in the penal system, my use of these terms may prompt some concern and run the risk offending some readers. Yet I hope the content of my analysis is responsive and sensitive enough to ease such concerns and lessen the risks.

23. When questions of desire surface in feminist state theory, they tend to be confined to sexuality and/or reproduction. In their early articulations of the "patriarchal state," feminist scholars often asserted that it was somehow in the state's interest to control women's bodies and to police their sexual practices. More recently, state restructuring in the post–Aid to Families with Dependent Children era has been interpreted as a new way for the state to regulate women's reproductive choices and options. For more on how welfare reform intervenes into women's sexual and reproductive lives, see Mink, *Welfare's End* and *Whose Welfare?;* Thomas, "Exchanging Welfare Checks for Wedding Rings"; and Scott et al., "Dangerous Dependencies."

24. See Connell, *Gender and Power,* 111–16.

25.   Clearly, as Foucault reminds us in *The History of Sexuality*, this is not always the way the regulation of desire has worked across time and place—the connection between the "self" and "desire" is a relatively modern invention. For more on historical and cultural variations in social assessments and patterns of desire, see Valverde, *Age of Light, Soap, and Water* and *Diseases of the Will*.

26.   Connell himself provides one of the best, most insightful discussions of the dynamics of prohibition and enticement. See Connell, *Gender and Power*, 112–16.

27.   For more on the therapeutic dimensions of welfare programs, see Polsky, *Rise of the Therapeutic State*; Nolan, *Therapeutic State*; Cruikshank, *Will to Empower*; Fraser, *Unruly Practices*; and Little, "Independent Workers, Dependent Mothers." For the emergence of therapeutic corrections, see Rose, *Governing the Soul*; Furedi, *Therapy Culture*; Garland, *Culture of Control*; and Nolan, *Therapeutic State*.

28.   Fraser, *Unruly Practices*.

29.   U.S. Department of Justice, *Prisoners in 2006*.

30.   More specifically, in 2006, there were just over 2 million Americans incarcerated in state and federal prisons and jails, 4.2 million on probation, and 800,000 on parole. See U.S. Department of Justice, *Correctional Population in the U.S.*

31.   For a discussion of sociologists' unsuccessful attempts to break into the contemporary penal system, see Wacquant, "Curious Eclipse of Prison Ethnography in the Age of Mass Incarceration."

32.   Rose, *Powers of Freedom*.

33.   The literature on state devolution is vast and varied. For analyses that center on the discursive and spatial dimensions of devolution, see Peck, *Workfare States*; Schram, *After Welfare*; Brenner et al., *State/Space*; and Brenner, *New State Spaces*. For analyses that focus on the organizational and structural shifts of state devolution, see Conlan, *From New Federalism to Devolution*; Salamon, *Partners in Public Service*; Seidenstat, *Contracting Out Government Services*; Smith and Lipsky, *Nonprofits for Hire*; and Marwell, "Privatizing the Welfare State."

34.   For more on the politics of state decentralization from a historical perspective, see Katz, *In the Shadow of the Poorhouse*; Schram and Beer, *Welfare Reform*; Reese, *Backlash against Welfare Mothers*; and Soule and Zylan, "Runaway Train?"

35.   As with the work on state devolution and decentralization, much of the scholarship on state privatization deals exclusively with the welfare system. For examples of this theorizing, see Marwell, "Privatizing the Welfare State"; Meyers et al., "More, Less, or More of the Same?"; and Peck, *Workfare States*. For analyses of the privatization of the penal system, see Gilmore, *Golden Gulag*; Garland, *Culture of Control*; Davis, *Are Prisons Obsolete?*; and Wacquant, "Deadly Symbiosis."

36. In fact, according to some estimates, up to 58 percent of service providers in the job retraining, education, and workfare arena are nonprofit or hybrid organizations. The percentage is even higher if you consider those working in public childcare centers and abstinence-only and marriage promotion programs. For more on these estimates, see Boris, "Introduction—Nonprofit Organizations in a Democracy"; and Marwell "Privatizing the Welfare State."

37. For a discussion of this bifurcation, see L. Haney, "Homeboys, Babies, Men in Suits."

38. For example, see McCorkel, "Criminally Dependent?."

39. I say "no longer" because there does seem to be a time when national-level forces had a more direct influence on state institutions and programs. For example, many analyses of the Progressive and New Deal eras make the case for the importance of such national-level political actors and alliances. See Gordon, *Pitied but Not Entitled*; Muncy, *Creating a Female Dominion in American Reform, 1890–1935*; Koven and Michel, *Mothers of a New World*; and Goodwin, *Gender and the Politics of Welfare*.

40. When these conspiratorial arguments surface, they tend to be framed in race and class terms. For instance, the punitive penal policies that underlie mass incarceration are usually interpreted as a way to regulate race and class relations—that is, as part of a new prison-industrial complex that acts as a modern form of slavery and surplus-labor control. For more on these arguments, see Davis, *Are Prisons Obsolete?*; and Wacquant, "Deadly Symbiosis."

41. There are, of course, exceptions. For examples of those who expose the actual practices of state hybridity, and analyze them as such, see Eliasoph, *Plug-in Volunteers and Empowerment*; Minkoff, "Emergence of Hybrid Organizational Forms"; Marwell, "Privatizing the Welfare State"; and Smith and Lipsky, *Nonprofits for Hire*.

42. Other scholars have also theorized the emergent linkages between the welfare and penal systems. But instead of looking at concrete institutional overlaps, they have examined convergences in the form and function of these state structures. For more on these systemic and structural overlaps, see Beckett and Western, "Governing Social Marginality"; Pettit and Western, "Mass Imprisonment and the Life Course"; Sutton, "Imprisonment in Affluent Western Democracies"; Wacquant, "Deadly Symbiosis"; and L. Haney, "Gender, Welfare, and States of Punishment." One exception to this is Jill McCorkel, whose work explores how bridge agencies set out to reorganize case processing, retrain staff, and revise rules in these two systems. See McCorkel, "Criminally Dependent?"

43. While dependency discourse has long been a central fixture of the U.S. welfare system, it has begun to resound throughout the penal system—partic-

ularly in its feminine arm. In the process, dependency discourse has effectively dislodged long-standing notions of female offenders as weak and in need of paternalistic treatment—and replaced them with images of "criminally dependent" women in need of tougher treatment. For a concrete empirical account of this discursive shift and its implications for penal practices, see McCorkel, "Criminally Dependent?"

44. For the most comprehensive history of U.S. drug courts, see Nolan, *Reinventing Justice*. For accounts of how these courts operate in the contemporary period, and their use of therapeutic models and practices, see Peele, *Diseasing of America;* Nolan, *Therapeutic State;* and Furedi, *Therapy Culture.*

45. For more on the practices of therapeutic communities in prisons, see McCorkel, "Going to the Crackhouse" and "Embodied Surveillance and the Gendering of Punishment"; Fox, "Changing Violent Minds" and "Reproducing Criminal Types."

46. For historical accounts of the development of dependency discourse, see Fraser and Gordon, "Dependency Demystified"; and Misra et al., "Envisioning Dependency."

47. Sennett, "Work and Social Inclusion."

48. Here it seems important that commercials for Prozac and other antidepressants were permitted beginning in 1997—inundating the airwaves thereafter. The so-called addiction drug, which received enormous media attention in 2007, is set to be released and marketed in the next few years.

49. See Steinem, *Revolution from Within.*

50. Scott, *Seeing Like a State.*

51. Adams and Padamsee, "Signs and Regimes."

52. When I carried out this ethnographic work, I was actually working on another study that compared the institutional relations at Alliance with those of the county probation department. While I decided not to include the latter analysis in this study, many of the insights I gained from it shaped my understanding of Alliance's institutional practices and perspective. For more on this other comparative study, see L. Haney, "Homeboys, Babies, Men in Suits."

CHAPTER ONE

1. There is a large literature on contemporary welfare reform and the programs it gave rise to—and much of it is ethnographic. For examples, see Peck, *Workfare States;* Hays, *Flat Broke With Children;* Kingfisher, *Women in the American Welfare Trap;* Korteweg, "Welfare Reform and the Subject of the Working Mother"; and Little, "Independent Workers, Dependent Mothers."

2. For a more elaborate version of this argument, see L. Haney, "Home-boys, Babies, Men in Suits." In fact, many of the ideas discussed in this chapter were first presented and developed in that article.

3. For just a few examples, see Abramovitz, *Regulating the Lives of Women;* MacKinnon, *Toward a Feminist Theory of the State;* Boris and Peter, "Transformation of Patriarchy"; and Brown, "Finding the Man in the State."

4. Or that dependency discourse would have such a deep and long-lasting effect on so many aspects of U.S. culture. For more on its general cultural influence, see Fraser and Gordon, "Dependency Demystified"; Misra et al., "Envisioning Dependency"; Sennett, "Work and Social Inclusion"; and Haney and Rogers-Dillon, "Beyond Dependency."

5. Here I should thank Julia Adams and Tasleem Padamsee for pointing out the connection between Alliance's dependency discourse and the broader cultural panic. In their critique of the article this chapter is based on, Adams and Padamsee argue against my claim of the state's multiple and conflicting institutional "gender regimes" by pointing to the larger cultural messages inherent in Alliance's practices. At the time of the research, in the early 1990s, these parallels were not as clear—but they became more so almost a decade later, when Adams and Padamsee made their critique. See Adams and Padamsee, "Signs and Regimes."

6. For another account of how the dependency discourse became dominant in the penal system, see McCorkel, "Criminally Dependent? Gender, Punishment, and the Rhetoric of Welfare Reform."

7. CYA was the statewide youth prison. At the time of my research, the main facility was located in Southern California.

8. That is, some social-scientific accounts simply show welfare workers articulating the party line, without an explanation for why they are doing it. Others argue that welfare workers are forced to adhere to this line—either through explicit threats, surveillance techniques, or limitations on their resources. For the most part, these causal arguments often remain hidden parts of the analysis. See Mink, *Welfare's End;* Morgen, "Agency of Welfare Workers"; Little, "Independent Workers, Dependent Mothers"; Peck, *Workfare States;* and Hays, *Flat Broke with Children.*

9. Despite my best attempts, I could never get the Alliance staff to reveal to me exactly how much CYA gave them. Their budget breakdowns were part of the facility's big funding secret. And it was a secret that the girls also did their best to gain knowledge about—always to no avail.

10. The Fellowship for Change was created in the 1950s by a local pastor who wanted to give his congregation a channel to pursue social change. When it started, the fellowship had strong religious overtones—most of its activities were geared toward helping the poor. Yet with the politicization of 1960s, the religious components were toned down. Many members also developed ties to the

Black Panthers, which helped to move the fellowship further from the church. It was also around this time that the fellowship began doing charity work with ex-prisoners. So by the time I began working with the group in the 1990s, its religious content was minimal—instead, it was the community organization known for working for alternatives to the prison system. But the leadership decided to retain its name for the sake of continuity.

11.   This was also true for adult mothers—in the early 1990s, there were no facilities devoted to serving incarcerated adult mothers. There were only a few halfway houses and reentry programs that allowed women with children as residents. See chapter 3 for more on the history of California penal facilities for mothers.

12.   That is, while it was never clear to me what a particular staff member's background was, it was obvious that the staff's racial differences intersected with other social divisions. For instance, the Anglo staff members seemed to have more formal education and thus to be in positions of authority in the home—from Rachel the schoolteacher to Marlene the house director, the majority of white staffers had advanced degrees. The African American and Latina staffers tended to be counselors and house coordinators, which required them to have less formal education. So most of them were high-school graduates; some had a bit of university experience and/or degrees from local community colleges. And, not surprisingly, all of this overlapped with socioeconomic class: the Anglo staffers tended to be from middle-class, suburban backgrounds, while everyone else came from the surrounding lower-middle-class community.

13.   This formula was laid out quite clearly in the Fellowship's promotional materials for its men's programs—fliers and informational packets on the nature of male addiction and its relationship to criminality and imprisonment. Interestingly, the Fellowship did not include Alliance in any of these materials. When I asked about this, I was told it was because the Fellowship did not have to fundraise for Alliance—its funds came from CYA and this did not require additional fund-raising.

14.   While Alliance's representation of the dangers confronting its girls did differ from the Fellowship's portrayal of its men, Alliance's plans for change were not all that different. Once these groups were removed from the system, the plan was to make them "independent"—and that independence included heavy doses of wage labor and self-sufficiency. This overlap then allowed Alliance and the Fellowship to work together a bit—and for the former to use the latter's resources, like its job-referral services and employment training.

15.   This dependence on CYA also made Alliance different from other group homes. Most group homes recruit their residents and clients from various sources—from the court system to probation offices to the foster-care system to

Child Protective Services. But Alliance got all of its inmates from one place—the juvenile-justice system. It also got all its girls from one of two institutions within this system—they either came from CYA or from juvie as they awaited transfer to CYA.

16. For more on nineteenth-century child savers, see Platt, *Childsavers*. For accounts of female prison reformers, see Freedman, *Their Sisters' Keepers*; and Rafter, *Partial Justice*.

17. Rumor had it that girls in CYA had to perform sexual acts with the guards in order to get cigarettes and other forbidden things.

18. The fact that this "us vs. them" division also intersected with gender only deepened its power. It turned what could have been a simple programmatic difference into a gender struggle—with the Alliance women fighting against CYA men. The gender divide was also what made the us versus them perspective so clear and seemingly easy to draw boundaries around.

19. This was the Alliance staff's language—they all called the inmates "their girls," which was a way both of staking a claim to them and of pointing out just how young they were. The "girls," for their part, never liked this label very much and often questioned the staff's intentions in using it.

20. For young offenders, CYA was very much the end of the line. Thus, most of the Alliance girls had already made their way through the system—going from probation to stints in juvenile hall to long-term sentences in CYA. Only a few of them had committed crimes so serious that they bypassed the other parts of the system and were sent straight to CYA.

21. For an example of how other state actors conflate criminality and state dependence, see McCorkel, "Criminally Dependent?"

22. Hays, *Flat Broke with Children*.

23. Alliance claimed that this was because their inmates were minors and official wards of the state of California, both of which required higher levels of control and surveillance than in community-based facilities for adults. They also insisted that CYA mandated such control. Since Alliance was the only facility of its kind operating at that time in the state, it is hard to know how accurate this representation was.

24. The Alliance curriculum was set through complex negotiations with a nearby public school. Because the girls were officially attending this local school, its administrators wanted some say over the curriculum. But, according to Rachel, school administrators were out of touch with what the girls needed to learn as well as the most effective methods for teaching them. So she spent much of her time fighting and negotiating with these administrators over what she should be teaching. Similarly, school officials also required that the girls come to their facility at least once a week for face-to-face meetings, to turn in their atten-

dance records, and to update officials on their progress. Rachel hated this rule as well, claiming that it subjected her to unnecessary surveillance and disrupted the girls' schedules. So, to the dismay of these administrators, Rachel often went to the school on her own to take care of this bureaucratic business.

25.   Restricting the girls' access to their children was usually only done for a short amount of time—a few hours at the most. In these instances, the staff would take the kids to other rooms or give them to other staff members as a reprimand and as a way to force the girls to change their behavior.

CHAPTER TWO

1.   For studies of how mass incarceration affects the social organization of caretaking, see Bernstein, *All Alone in the World;* Seymour and Hairston, *Children with Parents in Prison;* and Enos, *Mothering from the Inside.*

2.   Although this may not seem entirely surprising, the girls' resistance was unexpected for the staff articulating this needs talk. Of course, the Alliance staff realized the road to independence would be rocky. But the staff also insisted that it was in the girls' best interest and that they would ultimately realize this. After all, Alliance formed its approach in opposition to a justice system that had little investment in helping girls. The staff even insisted that one way this system discriminated against girls was by denying them autonomy and selfhood. Given this, the staff's emphasis on independence could have seemed radical—and they really believed it was, despite all the pushback they encountered from the girls.

3.   In part, young women's unawareness of their options comes from their relative "newness" to the system itself. Many adult women in the criminal-justice system spend decades in and out of the system. And through their experiences, they accumulate knowledge about the programs available to female offenders. They are also quite likely to share this information with one another—many of the adult women in Visions claimed to have learned of the program from cell mates and other prison acquaintances. By contrast, teen offenders have far less knowledge about how to work the system or what kinds of options they have within it. Given their ages, they frequently know much less about their legal and social rights—making them far more "dependent" on justice officials and judges for such information. There is also some evidence that young female offenders do less information sharing than their adult counterparts—and that they are a bit more cliquish and standoffish with one another while incarcerated. For more on girls' experience in the juvenile-justice system, see Schaffner, *Girls in Trouble with the Law;* Chesney-Lind, *Female Offender;* and Chesney-Lind and Sheldon, *Girls, Delinquency and Juvenile Justice.*

4. Because CYA was in Southern California and Alliance in Northern California, prison officials often used geographical distance to deter pregnant girls from requesting a transfer to Alliance. Apparently, this often worked: the Alliance staff told stories of girls who were discouraged from moving to Alliance by CYA officials who convinced them that such transfers could jeopardize their pregnancies—or that they would be doing their time alone since their family and friends would never visit them up north.

5. This argument echoed one of the most common scholarly claims about the juvenile-justice system: that it punishes girls less for breaking the law and more for breaking the norms of acceptable female behavior. For various articulations of this argument, see Schaffner, *Girls in Trouble with the Law;* and Chesney-Lind, *Female Offender.*

6. While the girls' numbers changed, there always seemed to be equal percentages of these three ethnic/racial groups. During my time at Alliance, I met only one Native American and one Asian inmate.

7. The girls' bedrooms were decorated in a style completely different from the rest of the house. Most of them looked like they were for much younger girls—consisting of white furniture, pink and yellow bedding, and flowered wallpaper. The staff insisted that the rooms' overly feminine style was not intentional. They claimed that all the bedroom furniture had be donated and they could not afford to replace it.

8. Because the Alliance girls were minors, they had to have their legal guardians sign off on all overnight stays outside the facility. Since many of them had strained (or nonexistent) relationships with their guardians, they were frequently forced to remain at Alliance even when eligible for home passes or visits.

9. These incidents took their toll of everyone involved. In this particular instance, I recall Rachel returning to the back office, herself crying. She then closed the office door and sat alone for over an hour. When she reemerged, she was still clearly upset and shaken by the exchange with Janice. The following day, she did not come into work, claiming that she needed a "personal day" to get her head together.

10. For example, counselor Colorado often told the girls stories about when she was on AFDC. Her story was the Alliance equivalent of the Horatio Alger myth: After her husband left her and her three kids, she turned to assistance, "thinking I had no other choice." But she soon felt even worse "getting money for doing nothing" and sank into a deep depression, which she often called the "dependency depression." Then, one afternoon, she decided she had had enough and set out to change her life, pulling herself up through a series of service-sector jobs before returning to school to get her associate's degree and landing a position at Alliance. Colorado told this story to each new girl upon her arrival—

frequently to the rolling eyes and exasperated sighs of those girls who had heard it many times before.

11.   This was particularly true in the 1990s, when a kind of scholarly "fixation" with resistance prevailed. Perhaps it was a sign of the time—after decades of studying large-scale social movements, many social scientists shifted their lenses to illuminate those acts of resistance that were far less spectacular and far more ordinary. For example, see Scott, *Weapons of the Weak* and *Domination and the Arts of Resistanc;* Ong, *Spirits of Resistance and Capitalist Discipline;* and Abu-Lughod, "Romance of Resistance."

12.   For examples of misdirected acts of resistance in the context of the welfare system, past and present, see Goodwin, *Gender and the Politics of Welfare Reform;* Gordon: *Pitied but Not Entitled;* Rains, *Becoming an Unwed Mother;* Reese, *Backlash against Welfare Mothers;* Block et al., *Mean Season;* Hays, *Flat Broke with Children;* Little, "Independent Workers, Dependent Mothers"; and Fraser, *Unruly Practices.*

13.   While there is very little discussion of inmates turning on one another in the context of women's prisons, many accounts of the dynamics of power and resistance in men's prisons do highlight this phenomenon. For some particularly poignant examples, see Rhodes, *Total Confinement;* Sabo et al., "Gender and the Politics of Punishment"; Messerschmidt, "Masculinities, Crime, and Prison"; Holmberg, "Culture of Transgression"; Kupers, "Rape and the Prison Code"; and Paczensky, "Wall of Silence."

14.   When I say that the "state" was present at Alliance, I am referring to the fact that the Alliance staff had full custodial authority over the girls, who were official wards of the state of California, and that the girls were recipients of AFDC benefits.

15.   The girls communicated by way of their altered rap songs especially when outside the facility. On our walks around the neighborhood and afternoon outings, the girls often spoke so fast and in rhyme that few staff members could understand what they were saying. This was, of course, the point: rap became the girls' secret language, a way to communicate with one another without staff intervention.

16.   According to both the staff and the girls, everyone who escaped was eventually caught. After all, these were young women with few social and familial ties—so it was not very hard to figure out where they went after leaving the facility. And because they had small children with them, their movements were even more constrained. While Alliance did not keep statistics on escapes, the staff claimed that most escapees were found within a few weeks.

17.   See chapter 1 for a discussion of Maria's superstar status—and all the ways she seemed to practice independence perfectly, right up until her escape from Alliance.

18. Or, at least to my knowledge, she was never found. I kept up with Maria's case for over a year—partly because what happened to her seemed like such a grave injustice and partly because she had been the shining star of the program. Within that year, there was no sign of her and no evidence of her being reincarcerated. Some of the Alliance girls told me in secret that Maria had been "hooking up" with an older man who lived in an apartment building on the same block as Alliance—apparently she had been sneaking out at night to visit him (which was another reason why she had gone on the birth-control pill while still at Alliance). The girls believed that he had helped her escape to Mexico, where she had family. The fact that she lived undetected for at least a year after her escape indicates that the girls might have been correct.

19. Fraser, *Unruly Practices.*

20. For other analyses of the shift to a discourse of need and its potential for disentitlement, see Bashevkin, *Welfare Hot Buttons;* Fraser and Gordon, "Dependency Demystified"; Little, "Independent Workers, Dependent Mothers"; Hays, *Flat Broke with Children;* and Reese, *Backlash against Welfare Mothers.*

CHAPTER THREE

1. For some of the most provocative discussions of this spatial shift, see the work of Neil Brenner, particularly *New State Spaces;* and see Ferguson and Gupta, "Spatializing States."

2. For an excellent overview of emergent patterns of state malleability, both transnational and national, see Sharma and Gupta, "Rethinking Theories of the State in an Age of Globalization."

3. The most interesting of these discussions have occurred surrounding the linkages forming between states and civil societies or NGOs. For a few examples of the vast literature, see Smith and Lipsky, *Nonprofits for Hire;* Marwell, "Privatizing the Welfare State"; Mitchell, "Society, Economy, and the State Effect;" Paley, "Toward an Anthropology of Democracy;" and Gupta, "Blurred Boundaries."

4. For instance, see Saskia Sassen's work on the "unbundling" of sovereignty in *Globalization and Its Discontents,* as well as Bob Jessop's "remapping" of state regulation across spheres of power and authority in "Narrating the Future of the National Economy and the National State."

5. Rose, *Powers of Freedom.*

6. U.S. Department of Justice, *Prisoners in 2006.*

7. Here I should emphasize what we *thought* we knew about traditional state institutions has proven to be inaccurate and incomplete. As organizational scholars have consistently shown, "old-fashioned" bureaucracies rarely worked

as they claimed to. They were not as sealed and bound by bureaucratic procedure as was often assumed. In fact, much network and institutional analysis has shifted to study organizational heterogeneity and contradiction—or, as Elizabeth Clemens and James Cook put it, analyses have redirected attention to analyze the "disruption of reliable reproduction." For an overview of these shifts, see Clemens and Cook, "Politics and Institutionalism"; DiMaggio and Powell, *New Institutionalism in Organizational Analysis;* and Lipsky, *Street Level Bureaucracy.* I thank Nina Eliasoph for this important insight about traditional bureaucracies.

8. These terms come from Brenner, *New State Spaces.* Other scholars have begun to use similar terminology, claiming that states are now "polycentric" and "rescaled" instead of decentralized, or "nonisomorphic" and "rebordered" instead of devolved and privatized.

9. Similarly, it is impossible to see like a state, which is of course why the title of James Scott's book *Seeing Like a State* is so intriguing and provocative.

10. See Ferguson and Gupta, "Spatializing States."

11. Much of the scholarship on state devolution focuses on the welfare state. For instance, see Peck, *Workfare States;* Schram, *After Welfare;* and Smith and Lipsky, *Nonprofits for Hire.* For more general accounts of the organizational shifts involved in state devolution, see Conlan, *From New Federalism to Devolution;* and Seidenstat, *Contracting Out Government Services.*

12. See Marwell, "Privatizing the Welfare State."

13. See Rogers-Dillon, *Welfare Experiments.* Rogers-Dillon's account includes an enormous amount of original data on the causes of this shift. Among them are interviews with David Ellwood and Mary Jo Bane, arguably the two architects of U.S. welfare reform, in which they claim that Bill Clinton's experiences as a governor were critical to his decision to allow so much control over welfare policy be shifted to the states.

14. Ibid., afterword.

15. Peck, *Workfare States.*

16. For more on the historical variation of services and eligibility across locales, see Reese, *Backlash against Welfare Mothers;* Katz, *In the Shadow of the Poorhouse;* and Soule and Zylan, "Runaway Train?"

17. Reese, *Backlash against Welfare Mothers.*

18. Peck, *Workfare States.*

19. For a general discussion of the different ways that government can work through "community," see Rose, *Powers of Freedom,* chapter 5. And for one of the most insightful overviews of the effects of this shift in emphasis on the terrain of government, see Smith and Lipsky, *Nonprofits for Hire.*

20. See Marwell, "Privatizing the Welfare State."

21.   In large part, this religious revival is attributable to the Personal Responsibility and Work Opportunity Reconciliation Act of 1996, which introduced charitable-choice legislation and carved out more powerful roles for faith-based providers in the delivery of social services. President George W. Bush's Office of Faith-Based and Community Initiatives contributed to this revival, since it not only got rid of many of the restrictions against government funding for religious groups but also set out to encourage these groups to apply for competitive federal grants. See Bartkowski and Regis, *Charitable Choices.*

22.   For more on the religious influence in abstinence-only programs and education, see Irvine, *Talk about Sex;* and Cahill, "Welfare Moms and the Two Grooms."

23.   Hess, "Keeping the Faith?"

24.   For one of the most comprehensive and powerful examples of these critical accounts, see Harvey, *Brief History of Neoliberalism.*

25.   More specifically, this restriction of services occurred with the 1998 reauthorization of the 1965 Higher Education Act. While the constraint was only supposed to apply to students receiving federal aid at the time they were convicted of a drug offense, the ban ended up getting applied more broadly. Ultimately, the provision was even used against students whose drug convictions predated their college attendance. And the actual punishments were quite harsh: for the first offense, students remained ineligible for aid for one to two years; and they were permanently deemed ineligible after their second or third offense. These penalties were enacted despite data that show definitively that education is one of the most important factors leading to a decline in recidivism rates. See Center for Law and Social Policy, *Every Door Closed;* and McGlaze, "Making the Most of California's Correctional Educational Reform."

26.   For more on the ideology and reality of sentencing reform, see Christie, *Crime Control as Industry;* Tonry, *Sentencing Matters;* and Garland, *Culture of Control.*

27.   These risk classifications are central to most discussions of the new penal regime in the United States, and particularly of descriptions of the "new penology." See Feeley and Simon, "New Penology."

28.   For an ethnographic account of these risk classifications and their physical embodiments, see Wacquant, "Curious Eclipse of Prison Ethnography in the Age of Mass Incarceration."

29.   There are countless examples of cases when penal officers refuse to use a specific program, causing it to become defunct. As I describe in the next section, the California state legislature actually created the legal basis for community-based programs for incarcerated mothers in the 1970s. But it took a series of lawsuits

and a statewide media blitz in the 1990s before any facilities opened up—largely because penal officials and correctional officers resisted these programs and thus refused to allow inmates to apply to be transferred to them.

30.   For some of the best work on the causes and effects of prison over-crowding and warehousing, see Gilmore, *Golden Gulag;* Elsner, *Gates of Injustice;* C. Haney, *Reforming Punishment;* and Irwin, *Warehouse Prison.*

31.   Garland, *Culture of Control,* 18. Garland has presented a particularly com-prehensive picture of these public-private partnerships in the penal system. See also Johnston, *Rebirth of Private Policing.*

32.   For an account of the historical shift back to prison labor, see Davis, *Are Prisons Obsolete?* For more on the contemporary politics of prison labor, see Lafer, "Captive Labor"; Lipez, "Return to the 'World of Work'"; and Domanick, *Cruel Justice.*

33.   Initially, most faith-based prisons were for male inmates—touted as ways to teach discipline and responsibility. The first such facility, the Lawtey Correction Institution, opened in 2004 in Florida with a capacity of 788 inmates. The first female facility, the Hillsborough Correction Institution, also opened in Florida but had a capacity half that of Lawtey's. In 2005, the largest faith-based prison opened in Wakulla, Florida, with a capacity of 1,205. Since then, many other states have followed the trend and have turned over entire penal facilities to faith-based groups to run.

34.   Garland, *Culture of Control.*

35.   Ibid., 123. See also Karp, *Community Justice.*

36.   Little Hoover Commission, *Solving California's Corrections Crisis.* This 2007 report was especially insistent on using ATI programs for female offend-ers. Since the commission saw women as especially "community worthy," one of its most comprehensive proposals was to move 4,500 female offenders to ATI programs immediately. See p. 8 for more on this proposal.

37.   Another big area of change was probation and parole. For more on changes in the California probation system and its increased use of residential treatment programs, see Lynch, "Rehabilitation as Rhetoric."

38.   For a more detailed discussion of this bifurcation, see L. Haney, "Home-boys, Babies, Men in Suits."

39.   At the other extreme, there are many accounts of the institutional ten-sions and conflicts of contemporary state programs that fail to link these strug-gles back to their structural underpinnings—or to relate them to the broader dynamics of state hybridity. For examples of this in the welfare arena, see Hays, *Flat Broke with Children;* Kingfisher, *Women in the American Welfare Trap;* and Mor-gen, "Agency of Welfare Workers."

40. For more on the tension between formal organization and day-to-day activities in bureaucratic organizations, see Meyers and Rowan, "Institutionalized Organizations"; and Lipsky, *Street Level Bureaucracy.*

41. As I discussed earlier, one way that state satellites are governed is through centrally defined rules and regulations. Many of these rules set eligibility and entitlement requirements for entire social groups; they also mandate how such groups will be treated. So, in the penal system, there are rigid sentencing guidelines, like three-strikes laws, which fix the sentences of certain categories of felons. California's Prop. 36, for instance, includes pages and pages of who is eligible and how their eligibility is determined. All of these rules create their own dilemmas—while they may help to undermine the kind of discretion and nepotism that state institutions are often known for, they also present new administrative challenges because these institutions themselves are governed increasingly from a distance.

42. Feeley and Simon, "New Penology."

43. Ibid., 456.

44. See Drug Policy Alliance, "Governor's Drug Treatment Funding Proposal Short by $109 Million"; and Garvey and Leonard, "Drug Use Re-arrests Up after Prop. 36."

45. That diversifying into new program areas increases funding options is often a misguided assumption. In fact, by expanding their size and extending their scope, satellites can create more problems for themselves. As I explain in the next chapter, they can end up diversifying their programs and staffs to unmanageable levels, thus making any sort of institutional coherence a real challenge. On the other hand, for a case study in how hybrid organizations can indeed utilize their diversity to expand their resource base and anchor their viability under otherwise uncertain conditions, see Minkoff, "Emergence of Hybrid Organizational Forms."

46. Another factor in funding success is almost the exact opposite: many satellites survive by creating nepotistic relations with local governments and public agencies. For more on these relations, see Marwell, "Privatizing the Welfare State."

47. While conducting my fieldwork at Visions, on several occasions the prison asked me to attend these grant-training sessions on its behalf. Since these were seminars aimed at all kinds of state satellites, I became quite familiar with how such agencies were being trained and the messages transmitted to them about the new world of state-NGO funding.

48. Peck, *Workfare States,* 361–62.

49. This kind of recruitment work can create real tensions among facilities—particularly when agencies recruit clients who are being treated in other facili-

ties. Not only can this competition undermine the clients' treatment, but it can offer them a bargaining tool—creating a situation where facilities negotiate with clients to strike better "deals" with them. For instance, I saw several clients come to Visions from other facilities after being offered shorter stays (or sentences) at Visions. Similarly, I also saw several of these clients then face a rude awakening when their recruitment deals and promises were not met after they transferred institutions. For a concrete example of this, see chapter 5.

50. Working in a very different empirical context, sociologist Debra Minkoff has made a similar point about hybrid organizations—warning that organizations with mixed mandates, traditions, and forms risk falling prey to institutional contradictions and uncertainty as well as serious boundary issues. See Minkoff, "Emergence of Hybrid Organizational Forms." For other examples of the tensions embedded in hybrid organizations that combine disparate elements, see Bordt, *Structure of Women's Non-Profit Organizations;* Smith and Lipsky, *Nonprofits for Hire;* and Marwell, "Privatizing the Welfare State."

51. For examples of how cultural influences seeped into penal institutions of the past, see Freedman, *Their Sisters' Keepers;* Rafter, *Partial Justice;* Hannah-Moffat, *Punishment in Disguise;* and Britton, *At Work in the Iron Cage.*

52. In fact, most of the existing work on the role of cultural scripts and ideas in state development operates at the national level. There is a burgeoning literature on how ideas matter in moments of state policy change—that is, in how cultural categories can shape the perceptions of policy makers, the ways policies get framed, the responses of the public to these policies, and social definitions of what policies can and should address. For more on the role of ideas in policy development and change, see Steensland, "Cultural Categories and the American Welfare State"; Beland, "Ideas and Social Policy"; and Campbell, "Ideas, Politics and Public Policy."

53. See Eliasoph, *Plug-in Volunteers and Empowerment.*

54. Perhaps the best example of this is Eliasoph's account of the "van for needy youth." One afternoon, the program Eliasoph researched won an award for community service—and the staff decided to take a group of its kids to the ceremony. What the staff failed to recognize was how their framing of the group's needs would be used by their funders. The kids arrived at the ceremony to read about themselves in the award listing: "Community House: Van to transport needy youth." Clearly, a case of a message that was tailored for one audience (of funders) falling on the wrong ears (the kids'). See Eliasoph, *Plug-in Volunteers and Empowerment.*

55. For a short history of the development of this penal program written by one of its main proponents, see Barry, "Pregnant Prisoners."

56. Center for Law and Social Policy, *Every Door Closed,* 1.

57.   Specifically, the statute was Section 3411 of the 1979 California penal code passed by an unusually progressive state legislature. Still, when it was passed, the section carried with it so many requirements that it was nearly impossible for inmates to learn about it or to gain admittance into a community-based facility. These requirements were loosened somewhat and made somewhat less restrictive in 1981, although the number of female inmates with access to the program remained minimal.

58.   The big case here was the 1985 *Rios v. McCarthy*, which reaffirmed the right of incarcerated mothers to apply to serve out their sentences with their children in community-based facilities. The Rios case then received a considerable amount of media attention. See *San Francisco Chronicle*, "Court Ruling on Law on Mothers in Prison"; *Los Angeles Times*, "Prison Doors Unlocked for Motherhood"; and *San Jose Record*, "Pregnant Inmates Win Injunction, Childcare."

59.   More specifically, the LSPC won a final settlement of the Rios case, which had been held up in appeals and legal battles since the mid-1980s. With the settlement, the CDC could no longer avoid Section 3411 of the penal code and thus had to begin accepting applications for MIP facilities.

60.   The stress on the foster-care system created by increases in female incarceration is rarely discussed in the academic literature but was of grave concern to policy makers from the child-welfare system. For more on these concerns, see Center for Law and Social Policy, *Every Door Closed*, 7; and Seymour and Hairston, *Children with Parents in Prison*.

61.   In order to protect their confidentiality, I cannot use the actual names of these facilities. This is unfortunate since their names were reflective of their approach and perspective. However, in coming up with pseudonyms, I did try to capture the gist of their real names.

62.   Although the CDC did not have any official rules against women working, most CPMP organizations decided on their own that employment could interfere with the inmates' "recovery" and thus forbade them from working. I discuss the implications of this at length in chapters 4 and 5.

63.   Then, in 2005, toward the end of my fieldwork, a new one opened. My point here is that the uncertainties of state hybridity were clearly felt in this arena—with facilities opening, closing, and merging at unusually rapid rates.

CHAPTER FOUR

1.   The literature on the rise of drug courts in the United States is voluminous. For insightful overviews of this movement and research on court prac-

tices, see Nolan, *Therapeutic State;* Burns and Peyrot, "Tough Love"; and Peyrot, "Coerced Volunteerism."

2. Many social scientists and cultural critics have explored the rise of U.S. therapy culture. For some of the more interesting and provocative work, see Polsky, *Rise of the Therapeutic State;* Furedi, *Therapy Culture;* Moskowitz, *In Therapy We Trust;* and Nolan, *Therapeutic State.*

3. More specifically, the actual numbers of prisoners in treatment rose from 1,544 in 1974 to 56,193 in 1984 to 218,534 in 1990. Put another way, the percentage of prisoners engaged in some sort of therapy increased from 1.3 percent in 1974 to 14 percent in 1984 to 32 percent in 1990. As a result, from 1990 to 1995, there were large increases in the staffing and programs devoted to counseling and therapy in prison. For more on these trends, see Nolan, *Therapeutic State,* 114–15; and Garland, *Culture of Control,* 268n7.

4. See Foucault, *History of Sexuality,* vol. 1.

5. The historical work on state control of various "uncivilized" behaviors is broad. For constructions of sole mothers as deviant, see Kunzel, *Fallen Women, Problem Girls;* and Gordon, *Pitied but Not Entitled.* For work on the regulation of alcohol and alcoholics, see Valverde, "Slavery from Within" and *Diseases of the Will.* And for work on addiction and mental health, see Weinberg, *Of Others Inside;* R. Smith, *Inhibition;* and Rose, *Psychological Complex.*

6. Rose, *Powers of Freedom,* 46.

7. These personalities, associations, and identifications run the gamut: from women who love too much to people who eat too much to kids who play video games too much to workers who do not sleep enough.

8. Nolan, *Therapeutic State.*

9. Cruikshank, *Will to Empower.*

10. This avoidance can be a problem with much Foucault-inspired work, which is often exceptional at describing cultural dynamics but far weaker when it comes to explaining them. For example, Frank Furedi, one of the most prolific and prominent scholars of therapy culture, attributes the rise of therapeutics to a slew of factors but never disentangles the relative influence of the social and economic processes that therapeutic interventions are linked to. This is only exacerbated by such scholars' tendency to rely on cultural vignettes and media imagery as their main documentation—which makes it hard to decipher the larger significance of these trends as well as the factors shaping them. In this way, historical research on nineteenth-century therapeutic movements tends to be far more nuanced, detailed, and revealing than its contemporary counterpart.

11. For more on the emergence of the CPMP network, as well as a short history of the development of these prisons, see chapter 3.

12.   For instance, in my initial interviews with CDC officials, I was often encouraged to work in one of these two facilities. Officials always sang their praises, explaining how they were "cutting edge" and "innovative." Such encouragement continued when I had to get research approval from these officials—initially, I decided to research another CPMP facility, which the CDC folks did not like. Over and over again, they told me that facility was "ghetto" and pushed me to work in one of their flagships. After the other facility closed and I had to move my work to Visions, CDC officials could not have been more supportive. Clearly, these were model programs that they wanted to be studied, analyzed, and even publicized.

13.   For more on who these women were and how they reached Visions, see chapter 5. Because the women at Visions were so diverse, I use different terms when discussing different groups of them. When referring to all the women at Visions, I use the term *inmates;* when discussing those brought to Visions from a California Department of Corrections prison, I use the term *CDC inmates;* and when describing those from alternative-to-incarceration programs, I use the term *clients.* These distinctions become particularly important in chapters 5 and 6, where I analyze how different groups of women reacted to Visions's program of recovery.

14.   The salaries at Visions were nowhere near those of CDC employees. For instance, those staff members who maintained and administered Visions on a day-to-day basis rarely made more than $25,000—many of them actually made far less. Even the clinical staff was poorly paid—clinical counselors made $28,000–$40,000 a year, depending on their education, experience, and seniority. Rumor had it that the clinical director, Jane, kept her salary at a low $40,000 as a way of capping the salaries of all staff members. Since she had worked for years on the counseling staff of a local hospital, her Visions salary was only a supplement to her hospital pension.

15.   This county funding constituted roughly 40 percent of Visions's overall funding—and the bulk of it was Prop. 36 funding. While Visions does not make such information public, I had access to it as their grant writer. Although I had not intended to do this for the facility, when the director heard I was a sociology professor, with my own funding to research Visions, she requested that I use my skills to help the prison. This turned out to be a very time-consuming job, as I ended up preparing and writing many grants for the facility. It also carried several perks for my research. The most important of these was that Visions administrators gave me information I would have never thought to ask for. Their budgetary breakdown was one such piece of information—while I knew the facility relied on several funding sources, I had no idea how diverse its funding structure was until I saw its actual budget while writing a state grant for them.

16.   Despite my best attempts, I never got any official data on the staff turn-over rate. I was told repeatedly that Visions did not keep such data. Yet during my three-year stay at Visions, I would estimate that over half of the staff turned over. This included the entire clinical staff, two house managers, and the facility director. When I returned to the field two years after I completed this research, only a handful of staff members I had worked with were still there.

17.   For another account of self-esteem movement, see Cruikshank, *Will to Empower.*

18.   See chapter 3 for a more detailed account of the history of Prop. 36 and its effects on the ATI arena.

19.   These gaps in the program were not simply funding issues. Given that the inmates had such different educational backgrounds, it would have been hard for Visions to hire a teacher to cover their diverse needs. But the staff could have allowed the women to take advantage of local educational resources—by attending county GED classes, taking classes at a nearby community college, or finishing up their high-school degrees at a neighboring school. Actually, this was exactly what the staff did with Alcoholics Anonymous and Narcotics Anony-mous meetings—they let the women go off-site for them. Yet they insisted on denying women such access when it came to all other education. This was even true when the women put time and energy into planning it on their own: Kar-rina, for instance, spent months getting the curriculum of a local community college and applying for funding to take classes and buy books. Once everything was worked out, the Visions director denied her request to leave the facility twice a week for the classes, arguing it was a "security risk."

20.   This lack of job counseling and placement was in contrast to the South-ern California CPMP facility, which did allow its inmates to work. The Visions women knew about this, so whenever the staff blamed the CDC for the no-work rule, the arguments would start. In fact, one inmate even had herself transferred to the Southern California program so she could gain some work experience prior to her release: Vonda had spent much of her teen years in CYA and most of her adult life in CDC prison. Thus, two years before her release date, she began to demand that the Visions's staff allow her to work so she would have a way to support her six-year-old daughter. After the staff rejected her request several times, she appealed to the CDC and got transferred to the Southern California facility. Once there, she got a job at a nearby fast-food restaurant, where she con-tinued to work after her release.

21.   In fact, a nonprofit legal-services organization had a very difficult time getting into Visions for even a one-day visit with the inmates. In an interview, one of their lawyers explained to me that it was far easier for them to get into Valley State Prison than Visions: in the former, there were rules guiding who

could visit when, while at Visions there seemed to be no clear regulations about this.

22.   This restriction against convicted felons receiving social assistance was part of the Personal Responsibility and Work Opportunity Reconciliation Act passed in 1996, which was after some Visions inmates had been incarcerated.

23.   The "Miss" moniker gave the facility a bizarre, Southern-like feeling. With groups of African American women calling white counselors "Miss," it often felt like Visions was a Southern plantation—which was completely counter to the overall ethos of this part of California.

24.   The newer women often struggled with their Visions autobiographies because they had not already created similar texts they could draw on. Those with experience in Alcoholics Anonymous and other penal facilities had usually produced such scripts many times; some had crafted and honed them to the point of perfection. I discuss the women's relationships to these scripts in more detail in chapter 6.

25.   In fact, because of these translations, the staff considered the mantras to be "poetry." The staff were exceptionally proud of the texts and often had the inmates recite them publicly. One counselor even suggested that some inmates submit their safe-to-speaks in poetry contests—but the women never followed up on this.

26.   This led to an interesting outcome: very little was known about what the women were in for. It often felt like their crimes remained a secret, something they only talking about with a select few. Because I had such a good relationship with Margaret, the CDC officer, I could always find out a particular inmate's crime. Without Margaret, that information would have been difficult to get. For instance, I recall one afternoon when we were taking a delegation from Russia on a tour of the facility. The Russian visitors were very direct and felt comfortable asking all kinds of sensitive questions. When they met their first inmate, they immediately asked her what she had done. The inmate froze, while the staff nervously changed the topic. When the Russians did the same with the next inmate, the staff had to educate them—explaining that, at Visions, such things were not discussed openly.

27.   This explanation seemed like a smokescreen, since there does not seem to be anything unhygienic about wearing one's hair down. A CDC official also told me once that it was a security issue; it was harder to identify female inmates when their hair was down. Thus, it always seemed to me like this CDC rule was more about defeminizing inmates than safeguarding their hygiene or security.

28.   These counts were visible reminders that Visions women were in fact prisoners. The counts were mandated by the CDC, and at count time all CDC inmates had to line up in front of the "cell" or bedroom doors and be counted.

The staff member doing the count then had only a few minutes to report the number to the central CDC office and to Margaret. Because of this, Visions took counts very seriously and required that all inmates be on-site at all count times.

29. For more on the cultural movement of "magical thinking," see its handbook, Rhonda Byrne's *The Secret* (www.thesecrettv.com). In fact, this movement has become so pervasive that Oprah Winfrey even devoted a show to it in 2007.

30. This substitution of one compulsive behavior for another is one of the most pervasive criticisms of Alcoholics Anonymous programs. While I would not support a blanket critique of AA—as it has clearly helped millions of people around the world—it does seem like the intense preoccupation with banishing one substance from people's lives can blind them to other compulsions. Or it can obscure the ways a compulsion for alcohol simply gets replaced with other compulsions—many of which are equally dangerous. Again, it is not my objective to critique 12-step programs, but rather to point to how obsession with drugs and alcohol can morph into other obsessions. Despite this, the Visions staff refused to consider any other approach to addiction—such as teaching moderation or questioning the cycle of repetition/compulsion more generally.

31. For more on the conflict and ambivalence that many incarcerated mothers feel, see Enos, *Mothering on the Inside;* and Bosworth, *Engendering Resistance.*

32. What is more, something similar occurred at Alliance a decade earlier. As I argued at the end of chapter 2, there was a clear divergence between intentions and effects at Alliance: while the staff intended to teach the Alliance girls the virtues of independence, the staff ended up showing them how they could use dependence for their own ends. Moreover, what seemed like a controlling agenda by the staff ended up enabling the girls' resistance and prompting them to move beyond a needs discourse to speak of their collective rights.

CHAPTER FIVE

1. As the number of U.S. prisoners has soared, so have popular media accounts of "living behind bars." These accounts are often compelling and accomplish what many social-scientific analyses fail to deliver: intimate, personal portrayals of the human toll of mass incarceration. Most of this work is also critical of hyperincarceration and thus usually ends by proposing alternatives to it—usually by turning to community-based, alternative-to-incarceration programs as the solutions. The best of these accounts include Bernstein, *All Alone in the World;* Gonnerman, *Life on the Outside;* Rierden, *Farm;* Elsner, *Gates of Injustice;* and Domanick, *Cruel Justice.*

2. This assumption underlies most feminist research on female inmates. For example, see Bosworth, *Engendering Resistance;* Chesney-Lind, *Female Offender;* Enos, *Mothering from the Inside;* Ferraro, *Neither Angels nor Demons;* O'Brien, *Making it in the "Free World";* Owen, *In the Mix;* and Watterson, *Women in Prison: Inside the Concrete Womb.*

3. In fact, this argument has become the rallying call for the contemporary prison-abolitionist movement, which challenges the prison-industrial complex by calling for reform to decarcerate through community-based policies and programs. See Davis, *Are Prisons Obsolete?*

4. Rose, *Powers of Freedom,* 89.

5. The critique that the U.S. penal system ignores rehabilitation is so ubiquitous that it is impossible to cite everyone who has made it. Trends toward and away from rehabilitation are reflected in the CDC itself, as it continually removes and adds *rehabilitation* to its name—in the 1970s it officially relinquished its commitment to rehabilitation, only to reinstate it some thirty years later. For some of the best social-scientific analyses of this overall punitive turn, see Garland, *Culture of Control;* Simon, *Governing through Crime;* Kruttschnitt and Gartner, *Marking Time in the Golden State;* Zimring et al., *Punishment and Democracy.*

6. For more on the connection between female crime and victimization, see Ferraro, *Neither Angels nor Demons;* Bosworth, *Engendering Resistance;* and Watterson, *Women in Prison: Inside the Concrete Womb.*

7. See Enos, *Mothering from the Inside;* Chesney-Lind, *Female Offender;* and O'Brien, *Making It in the "Free World."*

8. See Boudin, "Lessons from a Mother's Program in Prison"; Covington, "Women in Prison: Approaches to the Treatment of Our Most Invisible Population"; Merriam, "To Find a Voice"; and Tuesday, "Girls in Jail."

9. There is something quite naïve about the belief that the "community" is in the position to take on such lofty responsibilities. This is particularly true given the many forces working to disenfranchise and marginalize inner-city communities. Yet no one seems to be asking critical questions here: How can the community be so empowering when it is itself so disempowered? Isn't it idealistic to ask the community to solve the carceral problem as well as so much else? Isn't this too much to ask of any "community"?

10. In fact, the empirical findings on the effects of community-based therapeutics would be very disappointing to many alternative-to-incarceration proponents. In the last few years, a handful of comprehensive studies have revealed that clients of ATI programs frequently do far "worse" than those who serve time in prison. This is particularly true of Prop 36. programs, which have actually been linked to an increase in rates of recidivism and reincarceration. Of course, there is enormous debate over how these evaluation studies measure success

and recidivism. In this chapter, I do not hold Visions up to these kinds of performance measurements or outcomes. Rather, I assess the program on its own terms—Visions promised to empower female inmates, so did it? But, for more on these evaluation studies, see Knight, *Treating Addicted Offenders*.

11.   O'Malley, "Risk and Responsibility." *Responsibilization* has become the term used to describe the many techniques used to shift accountability to the governed—that is, to hold them responsible for their own rehabilitation and treatment as well as to blame them for all faults and failings. For other examples of the use of the term, see Lynch, "Rehabilitation as Rhetoric"; and Garland, *Culture of Control.*

12.   CPMP facilities varied in this regard: most had only CDC inmates, while a few housed both CDC inmates and perinatal/ATI clients. Yet, unlike Visions, the other CPMP facilities with mixed inmate pools separated them in different housing units and programs. Hence, Visions was the only CPMP facility to integrate fully these two populations.

13.   I never saw the CPMP recruitment techniques, but CDC inmates from a variety of programs told me they never heard any mention of drug/alcohol treatment until they actually reached the facility. This was corroborated by legal representatives from Legal Services for Prisoners with Children—they spent a lot of time with inmates in Valley State, a CDC prison, and confirmed that none of them knew of the CPMP focus on "recovery."

14.   According to official CDC rules, CPMP applicants were assessed according to a long list of factors, including offense time, length of sentence, criminal background, health history, county of residence, marital status, number of children, and ages of children. Supposedly, each applicant was ranked based on these criteria—and those with a sufficient number of points were given CPMP clearance. Yet, informally, everyone knew that such decisions were open to considerable manipulation and pressure, both from the inmates themselves and from the staff of CPMP facilities. For more on the official list of factors shaping CPMP placement, see California Department of Corrections, *California Code of Regulations Title 15*, 38–40.

15.   Because some CPMP facilities also had non-CDC clients, space for the CDC inmates was limited. Even so, I never saw Visions fill their CDC contract to capacity. That is, while they were contracted for twenty-five CDC inmates, they usually took in about twenty at any given time. Visions actually had no incentive to take in any more—it received the same amount of support from the CDC whether it had five or twenty-five inmates in residence.

16.   Almost without exception, inmates in my writing class said they were devastated when they arrived at Visions. They felt duped, disappointed, and manipulated when they saw where they would be living. Having no other channel for their disappointment, they often funneled it into their writing. For

instance, this was how Towanda described arriving at Visions, from the perspective of her five-year-old daughter:

> We finally pulled up to the place where I would be living with my mommy and I wasn't sure that I really wanted to stay. It was an ugly looking place. It did not look like a place where anyone should live, especially a little girl. There was no grass or pretty flowers outside. There was no playground, at least none that I could see. Instead of looking like a house, it looked more like the hospital for old people where my grandma works at. But I knew my mommy was somewhere in that place and suddenly that place didn't look so bad at all. In fact it was kind of beautiful.

17.   This institutional preference for perinatal clients reigned even though all the Visions staff agreed that these clients were more difficult to deal with. If the staff had their way, Visions would have had far fewer of these women. But they were the bread and butter of the facility—on a per client basis, Visions received roughly 25 percent more for perinatal clients than for CDC inmates. There were also special grants and resources Visions had access to because it "served" this population—like National Institutes of Health grants for mentally ill clients and state/county funds to treat "dual diagnosis" cases. It is also important to recall that the CDC budget was fixed, so there was no way for Visions to increase resources for CDC inmates.

18.   Because CDC applicants received "points" for being married and having relatively limited criminal backgrounds, the vetting system ended up favoring white women. See note 14 for more on the formal criteria used by the CDC to assess applicants.

19.   That is, CDC officials reasoned that it would be more difficult for a woman to escape during transport if clothed in short, checkered nightgowns—it would be harder for them to fit in on the street and easier for guards to spot them. Never mind that these women were also shackled, which one would think acted as enough of a deterrent to escape.

20.   Safe-to-speaks were shortened forms of the inmates' autobiographies that they had to recite for a designated amount of time whenever they encountered a staff member. For more on how they were constructed and how they were used in the facility, see chapter 4.

21.   For a classic account of the perils of tightrope walking in other total institutions, see Goffman, *Asylums*.

22.   When women complained about these shifts, which they did on an ongoing basis, they were told that change is "constant" and a "normal" part of life. Thus, part of their recovery was to learn to deal with inconsistency—to be unafraid of change and able to respond to it in a healthy way.

23.   Such deals between Prop. 36ers and Visions were not unusual. It often seemed like Visions actively courted and recruited these clients. And, indeed, it

frequently did—Visions competed with other ATI programs for clients and tried to make the deal as sweet as possible for those considering coming to Visions. Promising to take time off of sentences was a common way of sweetening the pot. This became clear to me about midway into my fieldwork when I was given my own desk in the room adjoining Mildred's, who was Visions's head administrator, intake officer, and "heart" of the program. Mildred had worked for decades in banking and, after retirement, came to Visions so she could "make a difference" and supplement her pension. Her background in the private sector certainly showed: whenever potential clients or criminal-justice officials called to inquire about the program, they would be transferred to Mildred, who would begin her sell. She was incredibly skilled at pitching the program—she could convince almost anyone that Visions was right for them. She tended to lay it on particularly thick when the program was low on clients—she would break out all kinds of deals and promises to attract inmates. My guess is that this was what happened to Keisha.

24.   Some of these rule violations were actually quite consequential for the women. Tiffany had actually broken a major house rule, since inmates were not allowed to socialize with nonfamily members in the facility; so she was put on house probation and dephased. Marika's counselor wrote up the account of her hitting her child, which was probably used against Marika in her pending CPS case. Nicole's late-night snacking was also written up and put in her file and thus could have come into play when CDC was considering releasing her. Finally, Brenda's tendency to "hook up" with new inmates eventually got her kicked out of Visions because sexual contact between inmates was prohibited.

25.   For an excellent account of these relations in more "traditional" women's prisons, see Kruttschnitt and Gartner, *Marking Time in the Golden State.*

26.   In particular, see Bosworth, *Engendering Resistance;* and Enos, *Mothering from the Inside.*

27.   Rosa and Samantha were very open about these yearnings and spoke about their desire for privacy all the time. In a sense, they used my writing class for this: they never missed a class, no matter what was going on in the facility. And they often told me how much they appreciated the class because it allowed them to sit quietly and reflect while they wrote—almost like a retreat, even though they were surrounded by others.

28.   That the inmates rooms were not private was actually intentional on the staff's part. Even when the facility was not filled to capacity and there were empty rooms, Visions had the inmates doubling or even tripling up. This enraged the women, especially those with small babies who had a hard time getting them to sleep in rooms with several other kids. Although the staff never admitted it to the women, they often told me that there had to be at least two women to a room so they could watch each other.

29. Sociologist Jill McCorkel puts this best in her study of an experimental treatment program operating inside an East Coast women's prison—she argues that the program forced women to make the "internal" more "external." See McCorkel, "Unruly Subjects."

30. McCorkel, "Going to the Crackhouse."

31. For some of the most comprehensive and engaging discussions of this shift away from rehabilitation and the factors underlying it, see Garland, *Culture of Control* and "Introduction: The Meaning of Mass Imprisonment"; Feeley and Simon, "New Penology"; and Kruttschnitt and Gartner, *Marking Time in the Golden State.*

32. This was especially true of early female reformatories, which often insisted that female inmates were in need of rehabilitative treatment. Of course, this approach was always racialized, with women of color subjected to treatment that was far more punitive and far less rehabilitative than their white counterparts. For more on this approach and the birth of female prisons, see Freedman, *Their Sisters' Keepers;* and Rafter, *Partial Justice.* For a discussion of how its contemporary manifestation acts as a form of "penal paternalism," see McCorkel, "Criminally Dependent?"

33. For more on the general discrediting of social explanations for crime and deviance, see Wacquant, "Deadly Symbiosis."

34. The most notorious of these criticisms is Alan Dershowitz's "abuse excuse," which he claims is the tendency to use social factors as cop-outs and ways of evading personal responsibility. See Dershowitz, *Abuse Excuse.*

35. For many Visions staff members, the distinction between rehabilitation and recovery signaled how they differed from traditional prisons. Rehabilitation was what they tried in prisons—it was more social and often less than successful in altering inmates' behavior. The Visions staff considered recovery to be a more internal change—and thus potentially more transformative.

36. As I described in chapter 4, some inmates spent an inordinate amount of time making arrangements to attend nearby community colleges and schools, only to have their plans nixed by the Visions staff. One inmate, Vonda, even went so far to get herself transferred to the Southern California CPMP facility just so she could gain some work experience before being released.

37. In fact, many women like Jacinta did end up having a great deal of work experience—they just did not see it as such. So part of my work was to get them to see the experience they had and to find a way of putting it on their résumés. For instance, many Visions inmates had worked for years as childcare providers for friends and family. Others had worked informally doing the hair and nails of acquaintances. Still others had spent years doing all kinds of "marketable" work assignments in prison. So in our résumé-writing workshops, we simply found ways of describing all these experiences.

38.   Karrina's idea to head to Sacramento came from real experience. The year before I began working at Visions, there was some talk in the state Senate of closing all CPMP facilities. So the Visions director rented a bus and took a group of Visions kids to testify to a Senate subcommittee in Sacramento. Apparently, the kids made such a good impression that the proposal to close the program was abandoned.

39.   Never mind that there was no gym or exercise equipment at Visions; or that the inmates regularly complained about this failing, noting that they had ample opportunity to work out in other prison environments. Instead, a few Vision staff members brought in old exercise videos to be used in the TV room. But the inmates never used them—as Rosa once noted, "I ain't gonna make a fool out of myself for all to see."

40.   To my knowledge, the women never got their Top Ramen.

41.   The staff in charge claimed that, by law, they had to remove Mary's children immediately after learning she was using again. Since the children's father still had legal parental rights, the staff also claimed that they had to send the kids to him. Mary contested this—to no avail.

42.   This is not to suggest that the poor and marginalized are necessarily psychologically troubled. Rather, it is to respect and acknowledge the emotional life of power—or the emotional costs of being disempowered and the very real wounds this can leave. For more on these wounds in the context of Visions, see chapter 6.

CHAPTER SIX

1.   At times, it even seemed like these daily crises at Visions were created to deflect attention from the program's more debilitating aspects. To use a diagnosis the staff frequently offered up to explain inmate behavior, there appeared to be a lot of "displacement" acted out at Visions, with small skirmishes between the inmates and staff taking the place of larger, more significant conflicts. To use another one of the staff's diagnoses, it often felt like the staff-inmate crises were propelled by experiences of trauma—the intense reactions both groups had to the daily infighting indicated that this exchanges may have touched off something deeper in the staff and inmates.

2.   In fact, by the end of my fieldwork at Visions, the staff had become so exhausted that most of them stopped coming to the weekly community meetings; they claimed it was a waste of time to listen to the inmates recycle the same complaints over and over again. Yet the staff's withdrawal from these meetings only made the gatherings devolve into more of a complaint fest—with the

inmates protesting not only about how the house functioned but also about how the staff were no longer present to hear their grievances.

3. There was a curious parallel between the inmates "us versus us war" and the way the Visions staff grappled with their own vulnerability to other state institutions—the staff also ended up turning on themselves. This is yet another way the facility's control and inmates' struggles mimicked each other. For more on the staff's "us versus us" war, see chapter 4.

4. See Wacquant, "Scrutinizing the Street."

5. On the other hand, ethnographers' sensitivity to our subjects has often enabled us to produce important work debunking the demonization of stigmatized groups. For one of the most powerful and effective examples of such ethnographic work, see Duneier, *Sidewalk*.

6. Goffman, *Asylums*.

7. Sharon Hays makes a similar point in her ethnographic study of contemporary welfare reform in the United States. She also does an excellent job describing the downside of welfare while remaining sensitive to the realities recipients confront. See Hays, *Flat Broke with Children*.

8. See Havel, *Power of the Powerless*; and Scott, *Weapons of the Weak*.

9. This terminology is drawn from Lila Abu-Lughod's classic essay, "Romance of Resistance."

10. For just a few examples, see Bosworth, *Engendering Resistance*; Owen, *In the Mix*; and Raphael, *Freeing Tammy*.

11. Interestingly, this victimizer/victim divide is less true of studies of men in prison. Many of these accounts emphasize prison rape and the violence male inmates inflict on each other and thus construct male prisoners as both actors and subjects, as victimizers and victims. For an excellent example of this construction, see Sabo et al., *Prison Masculinities*.

12. More specifically, women are often portrayed as struggling to maintain their identities, senses of self, and abilities to resist prison life—but they are not shown as themselves acting in painful ways to themselves and others. For example, see Faith, *Unruly Women*; Diaz-Cotto, *Gender, Ethnicity, and the State*; and Bosworth, *Engendering Resistance*. For exceptions to this tendency, see Kruttschnitt and Gartner, *Marking Time in the Golden State*; and Eaton, *Women after Prison*.

13. In particular, Kruttschnitt and Gartner reveal that some women take an "adaptive" approach by managing the contradictions and conflict of prison life. Others adhere to a "convict" style by looking out for themselves and their friends while distancing themselves from correctional authorities. And others still take on an "isolated" style by keeping to themselves and maintaining distance from both other inmates and the staff. For more on these modes of doing time, see Kruttschnitt and Gartner, *Marking Time in the Golden State*, especially chapter 6.

14.   This was true at Visions as well—some women did develop networks of support, particularly for their childrearing. Some even formed connections they would define as friendships. But such positive experiences seemed to be the exception rather than the rule—for all the reasons I discuss in this chapter.

15.   There are also political consequences to this empirical gap. By not telling the full story of how women react to incarceration, we end up doing a disservice and an injustice to these inmates, implicitly deeming their experiences serving time as deviant, problematic, or anomalous. There are real dangers to putting our subjects on a pedestal. For more on this, see Wacquant, "Scrutinizing the Street."

16.   For a similar analysis of how penal institutions end up exacerbating what they are designed to control, see Rhodes, *Total Confinement*. And for another articulation of this argument in a very different kind of setting, see Gremillian, *Feeding Anorexia*.

17.   For more on these two groups of inmates, and their different positions in the penal system, see chapters 4 and 5.

18.   This was how the other CPMP flagship, located in Southern California, did it—it had both CDC inmates and perinatal clients but housed them in different areas of the facility and offered them different services and programs. Of course, this created its own problems. For instance, this CPMP facility had a swimming pool on site, which the CDC women were forbidden to use. Not surprisingly, this created enormous animosity among the women, especially on hot days when the perinatal clients could use the pool as the CDC inmates watched from a distance.

19.   *Dosing* was the term used to describe the behavior of women after their methadone treatments, which seemed to mimic the highs of heroin. So for a few hours after a treatment, these women could seem quite out of it, with slurred speech, unstable movements, and heavy eyes.

20.   The hair divide broke down into another: those who shook their heads and hair and those who did not. Some perinatal clients insisted on shaking their long, flowing hair right in front of the CDC women. They also styled it in elaborate and fancy ways. Quite often, this seemed intentional, a way to provoke envy in CDC inmates who were forced to wear their hair back and off their faces.

21.   This "big kids" group was on shaky ground since—according to CDC rules—children were supposed to leave the facility once they turned five. But this was one of those rules that Visions broke all the time—although it varied, I would estimate that 30 percent of Visions kids were over the cut-off age. So when this group of mothers mobilized, they had to be careful not to call too much attention to how the presence of older kids was itself a major rule violation. In fact, this was one reason the staff gave for why there were not more activities organized for these children.

22.   See chapter 4 for a discussion of how motherhood and consumption were transformed into acceptable desires.

23.   For other accounts of female prisoners' practices of self-mutilation, see Liebling, *Suicides in Prison;* and Eaton, *Women after Prison.*

24.   I never got Claire's story.

25.   I found this interaction impossible to watch. In fact, although there were very few times when I had to remove myself from the field physically, this was one of them. Toward the end of the debriefing, I had to walk out of the room, as the dynamics were just too much for me. I simply could not watch as a group of relatively privileged women thanked the inmates for demonstrating their courage and for helping put their problems in perspective. What is more, my inability to watch and participate in the evaluations actually had effects I did not foresee. After the event, many staff members asked me why I didn't offer my assessment of the performance. In fact, a few seemed angered by my silence, using it to question my commitment to the women's "recovery." And, indeed, a few inmates also seemed taken aback by my behavior. In response, I did my best to explain my discomfort without making the inmates and staff feel bad about the event. Such are the difficulties of working in environments like Visions.

26.   The actual process of distributing medication created quite a scene. Since nearly all perinatal women were on meds, a long line would form at med-call time. Then fights frequently broke out as the women anxiously awaited their pills and argued about who should get theirs first. At times, the med-call lines did begin to seem like a group of desperate addicts waiting for a fix.

27.   This is not to suggest that these women did not need these drugs—or that they did not experience real relief from them. In fact, many of these women had been on medications for most of their lives and thus probably would have had a hard time living without them. Rather, my point here is related to how medications were used at Visions—how they became a way for the staff to placate some women as well as a route of withdrawal for some women.

28.   Informally, the staff frequently discussed their own experiences with medications—from the side effects of different antidepressants to their histories abusing prescription drugs to their dependencies on sleeping pills. I knew of very few Visions staff members who were not on some kind of medication.

29.   Before gaining approval to be transferred to Visions, CDC inmates had to complete long and detailed medical forms. They had to establish that they did not have any underlying medical condition that could become serious once outside the centralized CDC prison system. Here the CDC was not merely concerned with liability but also was worried about affordability—since securing medical care for inmates on the outside was far more expensive than ministering to the sick on the inside. Among other things, this restriction ended up discriminating against

many CDC applicants. It also prompted some CDC inmates to go off their medications while in prison in the hopes of increasing their chances of being transferred to CPMP facilities. Of course, this was a recipe for disaster since many of the inmates had a hard time functioning off their meds. For more on the issue of healthcare in CPMP facilities and a lawsuit filed on behalf on CPMP children, see Moore, "California Investigates a Mother-and-Child Prison Program."

30.   It was actually never clear to me if CDC inmates were completely prohibited from using antidepressants or antipsychotic medications. The Visions staff insisted that they were; they often told me how unfortunate it was that they could not use meds to "treat" the CDC women. But I knew a few CDC inmates who claimed to be on antidepressants—and who did line up with the others during med calls. My guess is that Visions received special permission from the CDC to give these women medication. But I never confirmed this for fear of drawing attention to a potential rule violation.

31.   See Knight, *Treating Addicted Offenders*. For summaries of this study, see Garvey and Leonard, "Drug Use Re-arrests Up after Prop. 36."

32.   Recidivism rates seem a bit lower for CPMP facilities like Visions. In 2007, as part of Governor Schwarzenegger's overhaul of the state prison system, the CDC did a one-year study of existing CPMP institutions. It found that one year after being released from a CPMP facility, 22 percent of women were back in prison. However, had the time frame been longer—like the thirty months used in the larger Prop. 36 study—it is possible that CPMP facilities would have recidivism rates similar to other ATI programs. For more on this CPMP study, see California Department of Corrections and Rehabilitation, *Community Correctional Facilities for Women*.

CONCLUSION

1.   Most notably, see Estelle Freedman's *Their Sisters' Keepers* for an example of this argument applied to the nineteenth-century penal reformers, as well as Kelly Hannah-Moffat's *Punishment in Disguise* for a more contemporary example.

2.   For a recent example of how progressives assume that community corrections will necessarily serve inmates' needs better, see *New York Times*, "Juvenile Detention Trap."

3.   Cohen, *Visions of Social Control*.

4.   For empirical examples of the use of needs talk in the welfare system, see Hays, *Flat Broke with Children*; Little, "Independent Workers, Dependent Mothers"; and Korteweg, "Welfare Reform and the Subject of the Working Mother."

For discussions of how needs talk is used to disentitle in the penal system, see McCorkel, "Criminally Dependent?"; and L. Haney, "Gender, Welfare, and States of Punishment."

5. Connell, *Gender and Power.*

6. See Valverde, *Diseases of the Will.*

7. See Fraser, *Unruly Practices.*

8. For different articulations of Marxian-inspired standpoint theory, see D. Smith, *Everyday World as Problematic;* Collins, *Black Feminist Thought;* and Hartsock, "Feminist Standpoint."

Bibliography

Abramovitz, Mimi. *Regulating the Lives of Women: Social Welfare Policy from Colonial Times to the Present.* Boston: South End Press, 1988.

Abu-Lughod, Lila. "The Romance of Resistance: Tracing Transformations of Power through Bedouin Women." *American Ethnologist* 17 (1990): 41–55.

Adams, Julia, and Tasleem Padamsee. "Signs and Regimes: Reading Feminist Research on Welfare States." *Social Politics* 8 (2002): 1–23.

Allard, Patricia. *Life Sentences: Denying Welfare Benefits to Women Convicted of Drug Offenses.* Washington, DC: The Sentencing Project, February 2002.

Atkinson, Rob, and Knut Rostad. "Can Inmates Become an Integral Part of the U.S. Workforce?" Paper presented at the Urban Institute Reentry Roundtable, New York University, May 19–20, 2003.

Barry, Ellen. "Pregnant Prisoners." *Harvard Women's Law Journal* 12 (1989): 189–203.

Bartkowski, John, and Helen Regis. *Charitable Choices: Religion, Race, and Poverty in the Post-Welfare Era.* New York: NYU Press, 2003.

Bashevkin, Sylvia. *Welfare Hot Buttons: Women, Work, and Social Policy Reform.* Toronto: University of Toronto Press, 2002.

Beckett, Katherine. *Making Crime Pay.* New York: Oxford University Press, 1997.

Beckett, Katherine, and Bruce Western. "Governing Social Marginality: Welfare, Incarceration, and the Transformation of State Policy." In *Mass Imprisonment: Social Causes and Consequences,* edited by Garland.

Beland, Daniel. "Ideas and Social Policy: An Institutionalist Perspective." *Social Policy and Administration* 39 (2005): 1–18.

Bernstein, Nell. *All Alone in the World: Children of the Incarcerated.* New York: New Press, 2005.

Blank, Rebecca, and Lucie Schmidt. "Work, Wages, and Welfare." In *The New World of Welfare,* edited by Rebecca Blank and Ron Haskins. Washington, DC: Brookings Institution, 2001.

Block, Fred, Barbara Ehrenreich, Frances Fox Piven, and Richard Cloward, eds. *The Mean Season: The Attack on the Welfare State.* New York: Random House, 1987.

Bloom, Barbara, and David Steinhart. *Why Punish the Children? A Reappraisal of the Children of Incarcerated Mothers in America.* San Francisco: National Council on Crime and Delinquency, 1993.

Bordt, Rebecca. *The Structure of Women's Non-Profit Organizations.* Bloomington: Indiana University Press, 1997.

Boris, Elizabeth. "Introduction—Nonprofit Organizations in a Democracy: Varied Roles and Responsibilities." In *Nonprofits and Government: Collaboration and Conflict,* edited by Elizabeth Boris and C. Eugene Steuerle. Washington, DC: Urban Institute Press, 1999.

Boris, Eileen, and Peter Bardaglio. "The Transformation of Patriarchy: The Historic Role of the State." In *Families, Politics, and Public Policy,* edited by Irene Diamond. New York: Longman, 1983.

Boswell, Gwyneth, and Peter Wedge. *Imprisoned Fathers and their Children.* London: Jessica Kingsley Publications, 2002.

Bosworth, Mary. *Engendering Resistance: Agency and Power in Women's Prisons.* Aldershot, U.K.: Ashgate, 1999.

Boudin, Kathy. "Lessons from a Mother's Program in Prison: A Psychosocial Approach Supports Women and their Children." *Women and Therapy* 21 (1998): 103–25.

Brenner, Neil. *New State Spaces: Urban Governance and the Rescaling of Statehood.* New York: Oxford University Press, 2004.

Brenner, Neil, Bob Jessop, Martin Jones, and Gordon MacLeod, eds. *State/Space: A Reader.* Boston: Blackwell, 2003.

Brenner, Neil, and Nik Theodore. "Cities and the Geographies of 'Actually Existing Neoliberalism.'" *Antipode* 34 (2002): 349–79.

Britton, Dana. *At Work in the Iron Cage: The Prison as a Gendered Organization.* New York: New York University Press, 2003.

Brown, Wendy. "Finding the Man in the State." *Feminist Studies* 18 (1992): 7–34.

Brush, Lisa. "Changing the Subject: Gender and Welfare Regime States." *Social Politics* 9 (2002): 161–86.

———. *Gender and Governance.* New York: Rowman and Littlefield, 2003.

Burns, Stacy Lee, and Mark Peyrot. "Tough Love: Nurturing and Coercing Responsibility and Recovery in California Drug Courts." *Social Problems* 50 (2003): 416–38.

Byrne, Rhonda. *The Secret.* New York: Atria Books, 2006. www.thesecrettv.com.

Cahill, Sean. "Welfare Moms and the Two Grooms: The Concurrent Promotion and Restriction of Marriage in U.S. Public Policy." *Sexualities* 8 (2005): 169–87.

California Department of Alcohol and Drug Programs. *Evaluation of the Substance Abuse and Crime Prevention Act.* Sacramento, 2005.

California Department of Corrections (CDC). "Joint Venture Employers." *Joint Venture Program.* Sacramento, June 1994.

———. *California Code of Regulations Title 15: Crime Prevention and Corrections.* Sacramento, 2001.

———. *Programs from Inmate Mothers.* Sacramento, 2002.

California Department of Corrections and Rehabilitation (CDCR). *Community Correctional Facilities for Women.* Sacramento, 2006.

Campbell, John. "Ideas, Politics, and Public Policy." *Annual Review of Sociology* 28 (2002): 21–38.

Center for Law and Social Policy. *Every Door Closed: Facts about Parents with Criminal Records.* Washington, DC: Community Legal Services, 2005.

Chesney-Lind, Meda. "Rethinking Women's Imprisonment." In *The Criminal Justice System and Women,* edited by Barbara Price and Natalie Skoloff. New York: McGraw-Hill, 1995.

———. *The Female Offender: Girls, Women, and Crime.* Thousand Oaks, CA: Sage, 2004.

Chesney-Lind, Meda, and Randall Sheldon. *Girls, Delinquency and Juvenile Justice.* Belmont, CA: Wadsworth, 2004.

Christie, Nils. *Crime Control as Industry: Towards Gulags, Western Style?* London: Routledge, 1993.

Clemens, Elizabeth, and James Cook. "Politics and Institutionalism: Explaining Durability and Change." *Annual Review of Sociology* 25 (1999): 441–66.

Cohen, Stanley. *Visions of Social Control.* Cambridge: Polity Press, 1985.

Collins, Patricia Hill. *Black Feminist Thought.* New York: Routledge, 2000.

Comfort, Megan. *Doing Time Together: Love and Family in the Shadow of the Prison.* Chicago: University of Chicago Press, 2008.

Conlan, Timothy. *From New Federalism to Devolution: Twenty-Five Years of Inter-governmental Reform.* Washington, DC: Brookings Institution, 1998.

Connell, Robert. *Gender and Power.* Palo Alto, CA: Stanford University Press, 1987.

Covington, Stephanie. "Women in Prison: Approaches to the Treatment of Our Most Invisible Population. *Women and Therapy* 21 (1998): 141–55.

Cruikshank, Barbara. *The Will to Empower: Democratic Citizens and Other Subjects.* Ithaca, NY: Cornell University Press, 1999.

Curran, Laura, and Laura Abrams. "Making Men into Dads: Fatherhood, the State, and Welfare Reform." *Gender and Society* 14 (2000): 662–78.

Daly, Kathleen. *Gender, Crime, and Punishment.* New Haven, CT: Yale University Press, 1994.

Daly, Kathleen, and Lisa Maher. "Crossroads and Intersections: Building from Feminist Critique." In *Criminology at the Crossroads: Feminist Readings in Crime and Justice.* New York: Oxford University Press, 1998.

Davis, Angela. *Are Prisons Obsolete?* New York: Seven Stories Press, 2003.

Dean, Mitchell. *Governmentality: Power and Rule in Modern Society.* London: Sage, 1999.

Dershowitz, Alan. *The Abuse Excuse.* Boston: Little, Brown and Co., 1994.

Diaz-Cotto, Juanita. *Gender, Ethnicity, and the State: Latina and Latino Prison Politics.* Albany: SUNY Press, 1996.

DiMaggio, Paul, and Walter Powell. "Introduction." In *New Institutionalism in Organizational Analysis,* edited by Powell and DiMaggio.

———, eds. *The New Institutionalism in Organizational Analysis.* Chicago: University of Chicago Press, 1991.

Domanick, Joe. *Cruel Justice: Three Strikes and the Politics of Crime in America's Golden State.* Berkeley: University of California Press, 2004.

Downes, David. "The *Macho* Penal Economy: Mass Incarceration in the United States—A European Perspective." In *Mass Imprisonment,* edited by Garland.

Drug Policy Alliance. "Governor's Drug Treatment Funding Proposal Short by $109 Million." April 13, 2007. www.drugpolicy.org/news/pr041307.cfm.

Duneier, Mitchell. *Sidewalk.* New York: Farrar, Strauss and Giroux, 2000.

Eaton, Mary. *Women after Prison.* New York: McGraw-Hill, 1993.

Eisenstein, Zillah. *The Female Body and the Law.* Berkeley: University of California Press, 1988.

Eliasoph, Nina. *Plug-in Volunteers and Empowerment: The Case of American Youth Civic Education Programs.* Princeton: Princeton University Press, forthcoming.

Elsner, Alan. *Gates of Injustice: The Crisis in America's Prisons.* New York: Prentice Hall, 2006.

Enos, Sandra. *Mothering from the Inside: Parenting in a Women's Prison.* Albany: SUNY Press, 2001.

Faith, Karlene. *Unruly Women: The Politics of Confinement and Resistance.* Vancouver, BC: Gang Publishers, 1993.

Feeley, Malcolm, and Jonathan Simon. "The New Penology: Notes on the Emerging Strategy of Corrections and Its Implications." *Criminology* 30 (1992): 449–79.

Ferguson, James, and Akhil Gupta. "Spatializing States: Toward an Ethnography of Neoliberal Governance." *American Ethnologist* 29 (2002): 981–1002.

Ferraro, Kathleen. *Neither Angels nor Demons: Women, Crime, and Victimization.* Lebanon, NH: Northeastern University Press, 2006.

Ferraro, Kathleen, and Angela Moe. "Mothering, Crime, and Incarceration." *Journal of Contemporary Ethnography* 32 (2003): 9–40.

Fox, Katherine. "Changing Violent Minds: Discursive Correction and Resistance in the Cognitive Treatment of Violent Offenders in Prison." *Social Problems* 46 (1999): 88–103.

———. "Reproducing Criminal Types: Cognitive Treatment for Violent Offenders in Prison." *The Sociological Quarterly* 40 (1999): 435–53.

Foucault, Michel. *The History of Sexuality.* 3 vols. New York: Random House, 1978–86.

Fraser, Nancy. *Unruly Practices.* Minneapolis: University of Minnesota Press, 1989.

———. *Justice Interruptus.* New York: Verso, 1997.

Fraser, Nancy, and Linda Gordon. "Dependency Demystified: Inscriptions of Power in a Keyword of the Welfare State." *Social Politics* 1 (1994): 4–31.

Fraser, Nancy, and Axel Honneth. *Redistribution or Recognition? A Political Philosophical Debate.* New York: Verso, 2003.

Freedman, Estelle. *Their Sisters' Keeps: Women's Prison Reform in America, 1830–1930.* Ann Arbor: University of Michigan Press, 1981.

Furedi, Frank. *Therapy Culture: Cultivating Vulnerability in an Uncertain Age.* London: Routledge, 2004.

Garland, David. "Punishment and Society Today." *Punishment and Society* 1 (1999): 5–10.

———. *The Culture of Control: Crime and Social Order in Contemporary Society.* Chicago: University of Chicago Press, 2001.

———. "Introduction: The Meaning of Mass Imprisonment." In *Mass Imprisonment*, edited by Garland.

———, ed. *Mass Imprisonment: Social Causes and Consequences.* London: Sage, 2001.

Gartner, Rosemary, and Candace Kruttschnitt. "A Brief History of Doing Time: The California Institution for Women in the 1960s and the 1990s." *Law and Society Review* 38 (2004): 267–303.

Garvey, Megan, and Jack Leonard. "Drug Use Re-arrests Up after Prop. 36."
    Los Angeles Times, April 14, 2007.
Gilmore, Ruth. *Golden Gulag: Prisons, Surplus, Crisis, and Opposition in Globaliz-
    ing California.* Berkeley: University of California Press, 2007.
Ginsburg, Faye, and Rayna Rapp eds. *Conceiving the New World Order: The
    Global Politics of Reproduction.* Berkeley: University of California Press, 1995.
Goffman, Erving. *Asylums: Essays on the Social Situation of Mental Patients and
    Other Inmates.* New York: Penguin, 1961.
Gonnerman, Jennifer. *Life on the Outside: The Prison Odyssey of Elaine Bartlett.*
    New York: Farrar, Straus and Giroux, 2004.
Goodwin, Joanne. *Gender and the Politics of Welfare.* Chicago: University of Chi-
    cago Press, 1997.
Gordon, Linda. *Pitied but Not Entitled: Single Mothers and the History of Welfare.*
    Cambridge, MA: Harvard University Press, 1994.
Gremillian, Helen. *Feeding Anorexia: Gender and Power at a Treatment Center.* Dur-
    ham, NC: Duke University Press, 2003.
Gupta, Akhil. "Blurred Boundaries: The Discourse of Corruption, the Culture
    of Politics, and the Imagined State." *American Ethnologist* 22 (1995):
    375–402.
Hamilton, Gayle. *Moving People from Welfare to Work: Lessons from the National
    Evaluation of Welfare-to-Work Strategies.* Washington, DC: MDRC, 2002.
Haney, Craig. *Reforming Punishment: Psychological Limits to the Pains of Imprison-
    ment.* Washington, DC: American Psychological Association, 2006.
Haney, Lynne. "Homeboys, Babies, Men in Suits: The State and the Reproduc-
    tion of Male Dominance." *American Sociological Review* 61 (1996): 779–93.
———. *Inventing the Needy: Gender and the Politics of Welfare in Hungary.* Berke-
    ley: University of California Press, 2002.
———. "Gender, Welfare, and States of Punishment." *Social Politics* 11 (2004):
    333–62.
Haney, Lynne, and Miranda March. "Married Fathers and Caring Daddies:
    Welfare Reform and the Discursive Politics of Paternity." *Social Problems* 50
    (2003): 461–81.
Haney, Lynne, and Robin Rogers-Dillon. "Beyond Dependency: Welfare States
    and the Reconfiguration of Social Assistance." *Qualitative Sociology* 28 (2005):
    235–54.
Hannah-Moffat, Kelly. *Punishment in Disguise: Penal Governance and Federal
    Imprisonment of Women in Canada.* Toronto: University of Toronto Press, 2001.
Harrington, Mona. *Care and Equality.* New York: Routledge, 2000.
Harrington-Meyer, Madonna. *Carework: Gender, Labor and the Welfare State.* New
    York: Routledge, 2000.

Hartsock, Nancy. "The Feminist Standpoint: Developing the Grounds for a Specifically Feminist Historical Materialism." In *Feminism and Methodology*, edited by Sandra Harding. Bloomington: University of Indiana Press, 1987.

Harvey, David. *A Brief History of Neoliberalism*. New York: Oxford University Press, 2005.

Hasenfeld, Yeheskel. "Organizational Forms as Moral Practices: The Case of Welfare Departments." *Social Service Review* (September 2000): 329–51.

Havel, Vaclav. *The Power of the Powerless*. Armonk, NY: M. E. Sharpe, 1985.

Hays, Sharon. *Flat Broke with Children: Women in the Age of Welfare Reform*. New York: Oxford University Press, 2003.

Hess, Amie. "Keeping the Faith? Examining FBOs as Quasi-State Agents." Unpublished paper.

Holmberg, Carl Bryan. "The Culture of Transgression: Initiations into the Homosociality of a Midwestern State Prison." In *Prison Masculinities*, edited by Sabo et al.

Irvine, Janice. *Talk about Sex: The Battle over Sex Education in the United States*. Berkeley: University of California Press, 2000.

Irwin, John. *The Warehouse Prison: Disposal of the New Dangerous Class*. Los Angeles: Roxbury, 2005.

Jessop, Bob. "Narrating the Future of the National Economy and the Nation State: Remarks on Remapping Regulation and Reinventing Governance." In *State/Culture: State Formation after the Cultural Turn*, edited by George Steinmetz. Ithaca, NY: Cornell University Press, 1999.

Johnson, Denise. "The Care and Placement of Prisoners' Children." In *Children of Incarcerated Parents*, edited by Johnson and Gabel.

Johnson, Denise, and Katherine Gabel, eds. *Children of Incarcerated Parents*. New York: Lexington Books, 1995.

Johnson, Paula. *Inner Lives: Voices of African American Women in Prison*. New York: NYU Press, 2003.

Johnston, Les. *The Rebirth of Private Policing*. London: Routledge, 1992.

Karp, David. *Community Justice: An Emerging Field*. Lanham, MD: Rowman and Littlefield, 1998.

Katz, Michael. *In the Shadow of the Poorhouse: A Social History of Welfare in America*. New York: Basic Books, 1996.

Kingfisher, Catherine. *Women in the American Welfare Trap*. Philadelphia: University of Pennsylvania Press, 1996.

Kittay, Eva Feder. "Human Dependency and Rawlsian Equality." In *Feminists Rethink the Self*, edited by Diana Tietjens Meyers. Boulder, CO: Westview Press, 1997.

———. "Welfare, Dependency, and a Public Ethic of Care." In *Whose Welfare?*, edited by Gwendolyn Mink. Ithaca, NY: Cornell University Press, 1999.

Klingemann, Harald, Jukka-Pekka Takala, and Geoffrey Hunt, eds. *Cure, Care, or Control: Alcoholism Treatment in Sixteen Countries.* Albany: SUNY Press, 1992.

Knight, Kevin, ed. *Treating Addicted Offenders: A Continuum of Effective Practices.* Kingston, NJ: Civic Research Institute, 2004.

Korteweg, Anna. "Welfare Reform and the Subject of the Working Mother: 'Get a Job, a Better Job, Then a Career.'" *Theory and Society* 32 (2003): 445–80.

Koven, Seth, and Sonya Michel, eds. *Mothers of a New World: Maternalist Politics and the Origins of Welfare States.* New York: Routledge, 1993.

Kruttschnitt, Candace, and Rosemary Gartner. *Marking Time in the Golden State: Women's Imprisonment in California.* New York: Cambridge University Press, 2005.

Kunzel, Regina. *Fallen Women, Problem Girls: Unmarried Mothers and the Professionalization of Social Work, 1890–1945.* New Haven, CT: Yale University Press, 1993.

Kupers, Terry. "Rape and the Prison Code." In *Prison Masculinities,* edited by Sabo et al.

Lafer, Gordon. "Captive Labor: America's Prisoners as Corporate Workforce." *The American Prospect,* November 30, 2002.

Lewis, Jane. "Gender and the Development of Welfare Regimes." *Journal of European Social Policy* 2 (1992): 159–73.

Liebling, Allison. *Suicides in Prison.* London: Routledge, 1992.

Lipez, Julia. "A Return to the World of Work: An Analysis of California's Prison Job Training Programs and Statutory Barriers to Ex-Offender Employment." Social Science Research Network working paper, January 27, 2006. http://ssrn.com/abstract=977255.

Lipsky, Michael. *Street Level Bureaucracy.* New York: Russell Sage Foundation, 1983.

Lister, Ruth. *Citizenship: Feminist Perspectives.* New York: NYU Press, 1997.

Little, Deborah. "Independent Workers, Dependent Mothers: Discourse, Resistance, and AFDC Workfare Programs." *Social Politics* 6 (1999): 161–202.

Little Hoover Commission. *Solving California's Corrections Crisis: Time is Running Out.* Sacramento, 2007.

Lorprest, Pamela. *Families Who Left Welfare: Who Are They and How Are They Doing? Assessing the New Federalism.* Discussion Paper Number 2. Washington, DC: Urban Institute Press, 1999.

Los Angeles Times. "Prison Doors Unlocked for Motherhood." June 6, 1985.

Lynch, Mona. "Rehabilitation as Rhetoric: The Ideal of Reformation in Contemporary Parole Discourse and Practices." *Punishment and Society* 2 (2000): 40–65.

MacKinnon, Catherine. *Toward a Feminist Theory of the State.* Cambridge, MA: Harvard University Press, 1989.

Mann, Coramae Richey. *When Women Kill.* Albany: SUNY Press, 1996.

———. *Locked Out: Felon Disenfranchisement and American Democracy.* New York: Oxford University Press, 2006.

Marcus-Mendoza, Susan, Jody Klein-Saffran, and Faith Lutze. "A Feminist Examination of Boot Camp Prison Programs for Women." *Women and Therapy* 21 (1998): 173–85.

Marwell, Nicole. "Privatizing the Welfare State: Nonprofit Community-based Organizations as Political Actors." *American Sociological Review* 69 (2004): 265–91.

McCorkel, Jill. "Going to the Crackhouse: Critical Space in Total Institutions and Everyday Life." *Symbolic Interaction* 21 (1998): 227–52.

———. "Embodied Surveillance and the Gendering of Punishment." *Journal of Contemporary Ethnography* 32 (2003): 41–76.

———. "Criminally Dependent? Gender, Punishment and the Rhetoric of Welfare Reform." *Social Politics* 11 (2004): 386–410.

———. "Unruly Subjects: Gender, Punishment, and the Self." Unpublished manuscript.

McGlaze, Aidan. "Making the Most of California's Correctional Educational Reform." Social Science Research Network working paper, April 10, 2006. http://ssrn.com/abstract=977001.

Mecca, Andrew, Nel Smelser, and John Vasconcellos, eds. *The Social Importance of Self-Esteem.* Berkeley: University of California Press, 1989.

Merriam, Beth. "To Find a Voice: Art Therapy in a Women's Prison." *Women and Therapy* 21 (1998): 157–71.

Messerschmidt, James. "Masculinities, Crime, and Prison." In *Prison Masculinities,* edited by Sabo et al.

Meyers, John, and Bryan Rowan. "Institutionalized Organizations: Formal Structure as Myth and Ceremony." In *New Institutionalism in Organizational Analysis,* edited by Powell and DiMaggio.

Meyers, Marcia, Janet Gornick, and Laura Peck. "More, Less, or More of the Same? Trends in State Social Welfare policy in the 1990s." *Publius: The Journal of Federalism* (Summer 2002): 91–108.

Miller, Cynthia. *Leavers, Stayers, and Cyclers: An Analysis of Welfare Caseloads.* Washington, DC: MDRC, 2002.

Mink, Gwendolyn. *Welfare's End.* Ithaca, NY: Cornell University Press, 1998.

———. "Introduction." In *Whose Welfare?*, edited by Gwendolyn Mink. Ithaca NY: Cornell University Press, 1999.

Minkoff, Debra. "The Emergence of Hybrid Organizational Forms: Combining Identity-Based Service Provision and Political Action." *Nonprofit and Voluntary Sector Quarterly* 31 (2002): 377–401.

Misra, Joya, Stephanie Moller, and Marina Karides. "Envisioning Dependency: Changing Media Depictions of Welfare in the 20th Century." *Social Problems* 50 (2003): 482–504.

Mitchell, Timothy. "Society, Economy, and the State Effect." In *The Anthropology of the State*, edited by Aradhana Sharma and Akhil Gupta. Oxford: Blackwell, 2006.

Mohanty, Chandra. "Under Western Eyes Revisited: Feminist Scholarship and Anticapitalist Struggles." *Signs* 28 (2002): 499–535.

Moore, Solomon. "California Investigates a Mother-and-Child Prison Program." *New York Times*, July 6, 2007.

Morgen, Sandra. "The Agency of Welfare Workers: Negotiating Devolution, Privatization, and the Meaning of Self-Sufficiency." *American Anthropologist* 103 (2000): 747–65.

Moskowitz, Eva. *In Therapy We Trust: America's Obsession with Self Fulfillment.* Baltimore: Johns Hopkins University Press, 2001.

Muncy, Robin. *Creating a Female Dominion in American Reform, 1890–1935.* New York: Oxford University Press, 1991.

Nelson, Barbara. "The Origins of the Two-Channel Welfare State: Workman's and Mothers' Pensions." In *Women, the State, and Welfare*, edited by Linda Gordon. Madison: University of Wisconsin, 1990.

New York Times. "Juvenile Detention Trap." January 5, 2008.

Neysmith, Sheila. *Restructuring Caring Labour: Discourse, State Practice, and Everyday Life.* Don Mills, ON: Oxford University Press, 2000.

Nolan, James L. *The Therapeutic State: Justifying Government at Century's End.* New York: NYU Press, 1998.

———. *Reinventing Justice: The American Drug Court Movement.* Princeton, NJ: Princeton University Press, 2001.

O'Brien, Patricia. *Making It in the "Free World": Women in Transition from Prison.* Albany: SUNY Press, 2001.

O'Connor, Julia, Ann Orloff, and Sheila Shaver. *States, Markets, Families: Gender, Liberalism, and Social Policy in Australia, Canada, Great Britain, and the United States.* Cambridge: Cambridge University Press, 1999.

O'Malley, Pat. "Risk, Power, and Crime Prevention." *Economy and Society* 21 (1992): 252–75.

———. "Volatile and Contradictory Punishment." *Theoretical Criminology* 3 (1996): 175–96.

———. "Risk and Responsibility." In *Foucault and Political Reason: Liberalism, Neoliberalism, and Rationalities of Government,* edited by Andrew Barry, Thomas Osborne, Nikolas Rose. Chicago: University of Chicago Press, 1999.

Oliker, Stacey. "Examining Carework at Welfare's End." In *Carework: Gender, Labor and the Welfare State,* edited by Madonna Harrington-Meyer. New York: Routledge, 2000.

Ong, Aihwa. *Spirits of Resistance and Capitalist Discipline: Factory Women in Malaysia.* Albany: SUNY Press, 1987.

———. *Buddha Is Hiding: Refugees, Citizenship, and the New America.* Berkeley: University of California Press, 2003.

Orloff, Ann. "Gender and the Social Rights of Citizenship: The Comparative Analysis of Gender Relations and Welfare States." *American Sociological Review* 58 (1993): 303–28.

———. "Gender and the Welfare State." *Annual Review of Sociology* 22 (1996): 51–70.

———. "Ending the Entitlements of Poor Single Mothers: Changing Social Policies, Women's Employment, and Caregiving." In *Women and Welfare: Theory and Practice in the United States and Europe,* edited by Nancy Hirschmann and Ulrike Liebert. New Brunswick, NJ: Rutgers University Press, 2000.

———. "Explaining U.S. Welfare Reform: Power, Gender, Race, and the U.S. Policy Legacy." *Critical Social Policy* 22 (2002): 96–118.

Owen, Barbara. *In the Mix: Struggle and Survival in a Women's Prison.* Albany: SUNY Press, 1998.

Paczensky, Susanne. "The Wall of Silence: Prison Rape and Feminist Politics." In *Prison Masculinities,* edited by Sabo et al.

Paley, Julia. "Toward an Anthropology of Democracy." *Annual Review of Anthropology* 31 (2002): 469–96.

Parenti, Christian. "Rehabilitating Prison Labor: The Uses of Imprisoned Masculinities." In *Prison Masculinities,* edited by Sabo et al.

Peck, Jamie. "Geographies of Governance: TECs and the Neo-liberalisation of 'Local' Interests." *Space and Policy* 2 (1998): 5–31.

———. *Workfare States.* New York: Guilford, 2001.

Peele, Stanton. *Diseasing of America: Addiction Treatment Out of Control.* Lexington, MD: Lexington Books, 1989.

Pettit, Becky, and Bruce Western. "Mass Imprisonment and the Life Course." *American Sociological Review* 69 (2004): 151–69.

Peyrot, Mark. "Coerced Volunteerism: The Micropolitics of Drug Treatment." *Urban Life* 13 (1985): 343–65.

Pierson, Paul. *The New Politics of the Welfare State.* New York: Oxford University Press, 2001.

Platt, Anthony. *The Childsavers: The Invention of Delinquency*. Chicago: University of Chicago Press, 1977.

Polsky, Andrew. *The Rise of the Therapeutic State*. Princeton, NJ: Princeton University Press, 1991.

Rafter, Nicole Hahn. *Partial Justice: Women, Prisons, and Social Control*. New Brunswick, NJ: Transaction, 1990.

Rains, Prudence. *Becoming an Unwed Mother: A Sociological Account*. Chicago: University of Chicago Press, 1971.

Raphael, Jody. *Saving Bernice: Battered Women, Welfare, and Poverty*. Boston: Northeastern University Press, 2000.

———. *Freeing Tammy:* Women, Drugs and Incarceration. Boston: Northeastern University Press 2007.

Reese, Ellen. *Backlash against Welfare Mothers: Past and Present*. Berkeley: University of California Press, 2005.

Reuters News Service. "Sheriff Runs Female Chain Gang." CNN online, October 23, 2003. www.cnn.com/2003/US/Southwest/10/29/chain.gang.reut.

Rhode, Deborah. *Justice and Gender: Sex Discrimination and the Law*. Cambridge, MA: Harvard University Press, 1989.

Rhodes, Lorna. *Total Confinement: Madness and Reason in the Maximum Security Prison*. Berkeley: University of California Press, 2004.

Richie, Beth. *Compelled to Crime: The Gender Entrapment of Battered Black Women*. New York: Routledge, 1996.

Riemer, Frances. *Working at the Margins: Moving Off Welfare in America*. Albany: SUNY Press, 2001.

Rierden, Andi. *The Farm: Life Inside a Women's Prison*. Amherst: University of Massachusetts Press, 1997.

Roberts, Dorothy. *Shattered Bonds: The Color of Child Welfare*. New York: Basic Books, 2002.

Rogers-Dillon, Robin. *The Welfare Experiments: Politics and Policy Evaluation*. Palo Alto, CA: Stanford University Press, 2004.

Rose, Nikolas. *The Psychological Complex: Psychology, Politics, and Society in England, 1869–1939*. London: Routledge, 1985.

———. *Governing the Soul: The Shaping of the Private Self*. London: Free Association Books, 1989.

———. "Governing Risky Individuals: The Role of Psychiatry in New Regimes of Control." *Psychiatry, Psychology and the Law* 5 (1998): 77–195.

———. *Powers of Freedom: Reframing Political Thought*. New York: Cambridge University Press, 1999.

Sabo, Don, Terry Kupers, and Willie London. "Gender and the Politics of Punishment." In *Prison Masculinities*, edited by Sabo et al.

———, eds. *Prison Masculinities.* Philadelphia: Temple University Press, 2001.

Sainsbury, Diane. *Gendering Welfare States.* London: Sage, 1994.

———. *Gender, Equality and Welfare States.* Cambridge: Cambridge University Press, 1997.

Salamon, Lester. *Partners in Public Service: Government-Nonprofit Relations in the Modern Welfare State.* Baltimore: Johns Hopkins University Press, 1995.

San Francisco Chronicle. "Court Ruling on Law on Mothers in Prison." June 6, 1985.

San Jose Record. "Pregnant Inmates Win Injunction, Childcare." June 7, 1985.

Sassen, Saskia. *Globalization and Its Discontents.* New York: New Press, 1998.

Schaffner, Laurie. *Girls in Trouble with the Law.* New Brunswick, NJ: Rutgers University Press, 2006.

Schneider, Elizabeth M. "The Dialectic of Rights and Politics." In *Women, the State, and Welfare,* edited by Linda Gordon. Madison: University of Wisconsin, 1990.

Schram, Sanford. *After Welfare: The Culture of Postindustrial Social Policy.* New York: NYU Press, 2000.

Schram, Sanford, and Samuel Beer, eds. *Welfare Reform: A Race to the Bottom?* Baltimore: Johns Hopkins University Press, 1999.

Scott, Ellen, Andrew London, and Nancy Myers. "Dangerous Dependencies: The Intersection of Welfare Reform and Domestic Violence." *Gender & Society* 16 (2002): 878–897.

Scott, James. *Weapons of the Weak: Everyday Forms of Peasant Resistance.* New Haven, CT: Yale University Press, 1985.

———. *Domination and the Arts of Resistance: The Hidden Transcript of Subordinate Groups.* New Haven, CT: Yale University Press, 1990.

———. *Seeing Like a State.* New Haven, CT: Yale University Press, 1998.

Seidenstat, Paul, ed. *Contracting Out Government Services.* Westport: Praeger, 1999.

Sennett, Richard. "Work and Social Inclusion." In *Social Inclusion: Possibilities and Tensions,* edited by Peter Askonas and Angus Stewart. New York: St. Martin's Press, 2000.

Seymour, Cynthia, and Creasie Finney Hairston. *Children with Parents in Prison: Child Welfare Policy, Program, and Practice Issues.* New Brunswick, NJ: Transaction, 2001.

Shapard, Sarah. "Placement for Children of Incarcerated Mothers: The Proposed North Carolina Prison Mother/Child Program." Policy brief prepared for Senator Ellie Kimaird, 16th District, 2003.

Sharma, Aradhana, and Akhil Gupta. "Rethinking Theories of the State in an Age of Globalization." In *The Anthropology of the State,* edited by Aradhana Sharma and Akhil Gupta. Oxford: Blackwell, 2006.

Simon, Jonathan. "The 'Society of Captives' in the Era of Hyper-Incarceration." *Theoretical Criminology* 4 (2000): 285–308.

———. *Governing through Crime: How the War on Crime Transformed American Democracy and Created a Culture of Fear.* New York: Oxford University Press, 2007.

Simon, Jonathan, and Malcolm Feeley. "The Form and Limits of the New Penology." In *Punishment and Social Control,* edited by Thomas Bloomberg and Stanley Cohen. New York: Adeline de Gruyter, 2003.

Smith, Dorothy. *The Everyday World as Problematic.* Boston: Northeastern University Press, 1987.

Smith, Roger. *Inhibition.* Berkeley: University of California Press, 1992.

Smith, Steven, and Michael Lipsky. *Nonprofits for Hire: The Welfare State in the Age of Contracting.* Cambridge, MA: Harvard University Press, 1993.

Snell, Tracey. *Women in Prison: Survey of State Prison Inmates.* Washington, DC: U.S. Department of Justice, Bureau of Justice Statistics, 1994.

Solinger, Rickie. *Pregnancy and Power.* New York: NYU Press, 2005.

Soule, Sarah, and Yvonne Zylan. "Runaway Train? The Diffusion of State-Level Reform in ADC/AFDC Eligibility Requirements, 1950–1967." *American Journal of Sociology* 103 (1997): 733–62.

Steensland, Brian. "Cultural Categories and the American Welfare State: The Case of Guaranteed Income Policy." *American Journal of Sociology* 111 (2006): 1273–326.

Steinem, Gloria. *The Revolution from Within: A Book of Self-Esteem.* Boston: Little, Brown and Co., 1992.

Stern, Vivien. *A Sin against the Future: Imprisonment in the World.* London: Penguin, 1998.

Sutton, John. "Imprisonment and Social Classification in Five Common-Law Democracies." *American Journal of Sociology* 106 (2000): 350–86.

———. "Imprisonment in Affluent Western Democracies." *American Sociological Review* 69 (2004): 170–89.

Thomas, Susan. "Exchanging Welfare Checks for Wedding Rings: Welfare Reform in New Jersey and Wisconsin." *Afflia* 10 (1995): 120–37.

Tonry, Michael. *Sentencing Matters.* New York: Oxford University Press, 1996.

Tuesday, Verna. "Girls in Jail." *Women and Therapy* 21 (1998): 127–39.

Uggen, Christopher, and Jeff Manza. "Democratic Contraction? Political Consequences of Felon Disenfranchisement in the United States." *American Sociological Review* 67 (2002): 777–803.

U.S. Department of Justice. *Correctional Population in the U.S.* Washington, DC: Bureau of Justice Statistics, 2006. www.ojp.usdoj.gov/bjs/glance/corr2.htm.

———. *Prisoners in 2006*. Washington, DC: Bureau of Justice Statistics, 2007. www.ojp.usdoj.gov/bjs/glance/corr2.htm.

Valverde, Marianna. *The Age of Light, Soap, and Water: Moral Reform in English Canada, 1885–1925*. Toronto: McClelland & Stewart, 1991.

———. "Slavery from Within: The Invention of Alcoholism and the Question of Free Will." *Social History* 22 (1997): 251–68.

———. *Diseases of the Will: Alcohol and the Dilemmas of Freedom*. Cambridge: Cambridge University Press, 1998.

Wacquant, Loic. "How Penal Common Sense Comes to Europeans: Notes on the Transatlantic Diffusion of Neoliberal Doxa." *European Societies* 3 (1999): 319–52.

———. "Deadly Symbiosis: When Ghetto and Prison Meet and Mesh. In *Mass Imprisonment*, edited by Garland.

———. "The Curious Eclipse of Prison Ethnography in the Age of Mass Incarceration." *Ethnography* 3 (2002): 371–97.

———. "Scrutinizing the Street: Poverty, Morality, and the Pitfalls of Urban Ethnography." *American Journal of Sociology* 107 (2002): 1468–1532.

Walby, Sylvia. "The European Union and Gender Equity: Emergent Varieties of Gender Regime." *Social Politics* 11 (2004): 4–29.

Watterson, Kathryn. *Women in Prison: Inside the Concrete Womb*. Boston: Northeastern University Press, 1996.

Weinberg, Darin. *Of Others Inside: Insanity, Addiction, and Belonging in America*. Philadelphia: Temple University Press, 2005.

Weisberg, Denise, ed. *Feminist Legal Theory: Foundations*. Philadelphia: Temple University Press, 1993.

West, Robin. "Jurisprudence and Gender." *University of Chicago Law Review* 55 (1988): 1–72.

Willrich, Michael. "Home Slackers: Men, the State, and Welfare in Modern America." *Journal of American History* 87 (2000): 460–89.

Young, Iris Marion. "Punishment, Treatment, Empowerment: Three Approaches to Policy for Pregnant Addicts." *Feminist Studies* 20 (1994): 33–57.

Zimring, Frank. "Imprisonment Rates and the New Politics of Criminal Punishment." In *Mass Imprisonment*, edited by Garland.

Zimring, Frank, Gordon Hawkins, and Sam Kamin. *Punishment and Democracy: Three Strikes and You're Out in California*. New York: Oxford University Press, 2001.

Index

abortions, 37
abstinence-only programs, 93, 232n36
Abu-Lughod, Lila, 258n9
"abuse excuse," 166, 256n54
Adams, Julia, 21, 234n5
addictions/treatment, 6, 13, 35, 210, 217, 223,
    235n13; drug for, 21, 233n48; and Visions,
    119, 123, 128–32, 134–36, 141, 145–46, 149,
    151, 159, 168, 175–77, 182, 187–88, 190,
    201, 203, 212, 218, 251n30
AFDC (Aid to Families with Dependent
    Children), 19, 23, 91, 108; and Alliance,
    33, 39, 43–46, 48–49, 64, 79, 106, 212,
    230n23, 238–39nn10,14
African American women, 228n5; at Alliance,
    33–34, 61, 156, 235n12; at Visions, 2–3,
    121–22, 126, 134–35, 155, 184, 250n23

age gaps, 3, 124, 130
Alcoholics Anonymous, 20, 98, 110, 117; and
    Visions, 123, 130, 136, 148, 161, 249n19,
    250n24, 251n30
alcoholism/treatment, 13, 35, 122, 235n13;
    and Visions, 128, 139, 141, 155, 165,
    171, 251n30, 253n13. *See also* Alcoholics
    Anonymous
Alliance, 1–5, 29–85, 103, 104–7, 122, 207–25,
    230n22, 233n52, 251n32; Brennan Bucks
    program at, 4–5, 11, 47–48, 51, 53, 55, 70,
    104–5, 210, 212, 217; care versus depen-
    dence at, 63, 66–72; closing of, 85, 106–7,
    111, 220; collective actions at, 60, 72–73,
    77–84, 179, 218, 220, 239nn11–13, 251n32;
    controlled chaos at, 49–55, 64–66, 81–82;
    dependency discourse at, 6, 10, 20,

279

consumer choice/constraint: and Alliance, 42–43, 46, 48, 54, 70–71, 74, 77, 81; and Visions, 157, 183–85, 187, 191, 212, 221

contracts, renewable, 16–17, 19, 88, 94, 96, 101, 108; and Alliance, 33, 36, 68, 81–82, 107; and Visions, 120–21, 123, 155, 253n15

Cook, James, 240–41n7

cost-benefit analyses, 100

counseling, 15, 99, 247n3; and Fellowship for Change, 35; and Visions, 14, 123–24, 127, 129, 146, 158–60, 167, 200, 254n22

courts, 20, 52, 108, 235–36n15, 246nn58,59. *See also* drug courts

CPMP (Community Prisoner Mothers Program), 109–10, 154, 246n62, 253nn12–15, 260–61nn29,32; closing of, 110, 119–20, 125, 131, 248n12, 257n38; Southern California CPMP, 109, 120, 182, 249n20, 256n36. *See also* Visions

CPS (Child Protective Services), 132, 197, 235–36n15, 255n24

crack cocaine, 134, 155, 159–60

criminal-justice system, 3, 23, 87, 94, 96, 120–21, 209, 237n3, 248n12. *See also names of agencies, e.g.,* CDC (California Department of Corrections)

Cruikshank, Barbara, 118, 249n17

cultural scripts, 20–23, 88, 104–6, 110–11, 118–19, 210–11, 245n52; at Alliance, 54–55, 104–5; at Visions, 148, 170

CYA (California Youth Authority), 19, 105, 210; and Alliance, 31, 33–34, 36–38, 40, 44, 54, 57–58, 60–62, 68, 75–76, 81–83, 85, 106–7, 122, 211, 234nn7,9, 235–36nn13,15,17,18,20,23, 238n4; and Visions, 249n20

dangerous desires, 4, 24, 132–43, 171, 208, 218. *See also* desire, regulation of

decentralization, 15–16, 19, 23, 87–88, 92–94, 96–99, 110, 209, 213, 241n8; and Alliance, 54, 85, 107; and Visions, 148

denial, 13, 140, 211–16

dependency discourse, 4, 20–22, 216–17, 223, 232–33n43; at Alliance, 6, 20, 22–23, 30–32, 39–47, 52–55, 59, 61, 83–85, 208, 210–12, 215, 217, 234nn4,5, 251n32; contesting/reinventing of, 23, 57–83, 106–7, 218–19, 237n2, 238–39n10; panic of dependency, 21, 23, 31, 210, 234n5; politics of, 60–72; possibilities/limitations of, 83–85; at Visions, 116, 143. *See also* needs talk

Dershowitz, Alan, 256n54

desire, regulation of, 12–14, 20, 22, 24, 111, 119, 132–43, 148–49, 165, 171–72, 180–81, 187, 208–10, 215–21, 223–24, 230n23, 231n25

devolution. *See* state devolution

discrimination, 9, 167, 177, 183, 185–86, 191

diversification, 15–16, 19, 23, 85, 87–88, 96–99, 120, 209, 244n45, 248n13

diversity, cultural, 88, 99, 103–6, 110, 223–24; and Visions, 119, 130–31, 148–49, 154, 208, 253n12

division of labor, gendered, 7, 9, 228n6

domestic violence, 63, 116, 128, 133, 137, 152, 173–75, 193

dosing, 182, 187–88, 259n19

drama therapy, 124, 136. *See also* public performances

dreams, 202

Dr. Phil, 110, 130, 205, 210, 221

drug convictions, 52, 61, 94, 98, 101, 109, 128, 152, 159, 168, 175, 204–5, 242n25, 257n41. *See also* Proposition 36

drug courts, 20, 109, 116, 213

drug overdoses, 193

drug tests, 15, 100

drug treatment, 20, 98, 101, 110, 117, 204; and addiction drug, 21, 233n48; and Fellowship for Change, 35, 235n13; and Visions, 13, 122–23, 128, 134, 139, 141, 154–55, 159–60, 165, 168, 171, 182, 187–88, 251n30, 253n13, 259n19

"dual diagnosis" clients, 131

education, 3, 11, 16–17, 87, 99–100, 223, 232n36; and Alliance, 2, 4–5, 29–30, 39, 42, 49–51, 53, 59, 64–68, 70, 74–78, 82, 219–20, 235n12, 236–37n24; denial of federal aid to students with drug convictions, 94, 242n25; of staff members, 34, 37, 124–25, 130, 238–39n10, 248n14; and Visions, 14, 116, 132, 167–68, 175, 190–91, 221, 249n19, 256n36

Eliasoph, Nina, 105–6, 245n54

Ellwood, David, 241n13

emotional conduct, 12–14, 116–17, 215–16; and Alliance, 48, 65, 67, 71; and drug courts, 20; and Visions, 25, 116, 129, 133, 135, 139, 144–45, 150, 152–53, 160, 162, 166, 169–70, 173–74, 177, 181, 192–94, 198, 257n42

employment opportunities/skills, 4, 9, 11, 14, 92, 223; and Alliance, 39, 42, 51–52, 54, 59, 69, 219–20; and Visions, 116, 132, 167–68, 175–76, 221, 249n20, 256nn36,37

needs talk, 9–14, 208–9, 216–17, 219–20, 223–24; and Alliance, 6, 10–11, 19–20, 23, 32, 36–38, 48, 52, 55, 83–84, 215; and Alliance, contesting/reinventing of, 59–60, 62, 66–69, 73, 79, 84–85, 237n2; and Visions, 132–33. *See also* dependency discourse
neoliberal governance, 15, 21, 87, 225
nepotism, 244nn41,46
NGOs (nongovernmental organizations), 16–17, 87, 92–93, 109, 210, 244n47; and Alliance, 33–35, 54, 106; and Visions, 120, 122. *See also names of NGOs*
Nolan, James, 118
nonprofit organizations, 16–17, 87, 92, 96, 99, 214, 232n36, 249–50n21; and Alliance, 33, 234–35n10; and Visions, 121
numbness, 181, 191–203

Office of Faith-Based and Community Initiatives, 242n21
O'Malley, Pat, 153, 253n11
Oprah, 21, 110, 170, 205, 210, 221, 251n29
orphans, 196
outsourcing, 16–17, 87, 93, 96
overcrowding, 96, 108

Padamsee, Tasleem, 21, 234n5
panic of dependency, 21, 23, 31, 210, 234n5
parenting. *See* motherhood
parole/parole boards, 7, 15, 76, 95, 103, 205, 231n30, 243n37
pathologization of needs/desires, 12–13, 117, 119, 217; and Alliance, 31, 62; and Visions, 25, 141, 146, 149, 153, 171, 176–77, 183
patriarchy, 12, 18, 30, 230n23
Peck, Jamie, 91–92, 94, 102
Pell Grants, 94, 242n25
penal system, 3, 7, 10, 14–15, 19–20, 24–25, 88, 94–99, 110, 208–16, 221–25; and Alliance, 31, 34, 37, 40, 43–44, 54, 58, 71, 85, 107; ethnographies about, 179–80, 258nn5–13, 259n15; local control, 15–16, 23, 94–95, 97–99, 242–43nn29,36; and rehabilitation, 15, 17, 98, 100, 151, 166, 252n5, 253n11, 256n32; risk classifications, 95, 242–43nn27–29; and therapeutics, 117, 247n3; and Visions, 108, 119, 130, 169, 182, 246n57. *See also names of agencies, e.g.,* CYA (California Youth Authority)
performance measures, 17, 106, 252–53n10
perinatal clients, 155–56, 181–91, 200–201, 204, 253n12, 254n17, 259nn18,20, 259nn18–20, 260nn26,27

phasing/dephasing, 5, 135–36, 138, 188, 192, 255n24
phone calls, 10, 52, 74, 76, 138
pilot programs, 91, 98
pleasures, 4, 6, 12–13, 21, 132–33, 143–49, 165, 171–73, 181, 187, 217–19, 221, 223, 257n40
polycentric states, 88, 241n8
poor/poverty, 3, 7, 49, 55, 100, 117, 184, 209, 212, 222, 224, 234–35n10, 257n42
popular culture, 20–21, 210
pregnancies, 33, 36–37, 58, 60–63, 80–82, 238n4
prenatal care/treatment, 36–37
prison-abolitionist movement, 252n3
"prisoners," 182, 190–91, 230n22
prison-industrial complex, 18, 232n40, 252n3
prison labor, 97, 99, 109, 246n62, 256n37
prison rape, 258n11
privacy, right to, 9–10, 137, 141, 163–65, 185, 255nn27,28, 256n29
private entities, 16, 87–88, 93, 97–99
privatization, 4, 16, 23, 93, 231n35, 241n8
probation/probation officers, 7, 15, 36, 40, 101, 231n30, 233n52, 243n37; and Alliance, 52, 60, 235–36nn15,20
productive lives, 1, 3, 30, 40, 135, 157, 181, 204
program speak, 133–34, 148
Proposition 36 (Substance Abuse and Crime Prevention Act), 98, 101, 103, 204, 244n41; and Visions, 122, 131, 155, 158–59, 248n15, 252–55n23
prostitution, 110, 159, 161–62, 194, 196–97
protections, 8–9, 11, 14, 78, 83, 85, 216
Prozac, 200, 233n48
PRWORA (Personal Responsibility and Work Opportunity Reconciliation Act), 16, 20, 30, 91, 242n21; denial of assistance to drug felons, teen mothers, immigrants, 17, 94, 132, 250n22
pseudonyms, 246n61
psychological pain, 116–18, 124, 129–30, 140, 148, 151, 160, 162–63, 166, 169, 176–77, 180–81, 183, 187–89, 194, 198, 215–16, 221, 223–24, 257n42
psychotherapeutic ethics, 124
public-assistance benefits, 9–10, 16–17, 19, 91, 209, 216, 224, 232n42; and Alliance, 31–33, 39, 43–46, 48–49, 52–53, 56, 83, 219, 230n23, 239n14; and Visions, 132, 167, 177, 191, 221, 250n22. *See also* AFDC; TANF
public-health programs, 122, 131

Text:	10/14 Palatino
Display:	Univers Condensed Light, Bauer Bodoni
Compositor:	BookComp, Inc.
Indexer:	Naomi Linzer
Printer and binder:	Sheridan Books, Inc.